Psychology
and
Anthropology

Psychology and Anthropology

a psychological perspective

GUSTAV JAHODA
Department of Psychology
University of Strathclyde, Glasgow

1982

ACADEMIC PRESS
A Subsidiary of Harcourt Brace Jovanovich, Publishers
London · New York
Paris · San Diego · San Francisco
São Paulo · Sydney · Tokyo · Toronto

Academic Press Inc. (London) Ltd
24/28 Oval Road
London NW1

US Edition published by
Academic Press Inc.
111 Fifth Avenue
New York, New York 10003

British Library Cataloguing in Publication Data

Jahoda, G.
    Psychology and anthropology.
    1. Anthropology—Psychological aspects
    I. Title
    301   GN24

ISBN 0-12-379820-5

LCCCN 82-71239

Photoset by Paston Press, Norwich
Printed and bound in Great Britain by
T. J. Press (Padstow) Ltd, Padstow, Cornwall

For Andrew,
Catherine, Colin,
and Paul

Preface

When this book was first planned several years ago, the intention was that its theme was to be cross-cultural psychology—my main field of research—with an emphasis on connections with anthropology. Progress was slow, partly because I became increasingly absorbed in what had originally been a peripheral aspect, namely, the interface between psychology and anthropology. Moreover, in the meantime a number of good texts on cross-cultural psychology had appeared (Cole and Scribner, 1974; Munroe and Munroe, 1975; Scrpell, 1976; Segall, 1979); and it seemed unnecesary to add yet another, even if it had its own distinctive slant. Thus the specific topic of cross-cultural psychology, which is after all a specialization within psychology, gradually receded into the background until it almost vanished. Accordingly, what was initially marginal has now become central.

The thought has occurred to me that it may be rather presumptuous for someone who has never had any formal training in anthropology to embark on such a venture. There are certainly people better qualified for the task, but they have so far not undertaken it. On the other hand, I can also claim an unbroken connection with anthropology over many years. It began on an unpromising note, at a period when relations between psychology and anthropology in Britain were distinctly cool. As a research student I had read some of Malinowski's work, and when talking to a Cambridge postgraduate in anthropology I mentioned what appeared to me to be exciting possibilities of cooperation between anthropologists and psychologists—I can still recall his horrified rejection of such an idea! Hence, when I took up a post in psychology at the University of Manchester, it was with some trepidation that I knocked at the door of the Department of Anthropology. However, Max Gluckman received me with great warmth and invited me to join his seminar. Thus began an association with anthropologists that has continued ever since, and which I have always felt to be a great privilege.

My enthusiasm for the achievements of anthropology should be evident from these pages, and my chief aim is to communicate something of this to students and teachers of psychology. Yet it will also become apparent that my admiration is not blind, and in the final part of the book dealing with cognition in particular, some fundamental assumptions of much anthropological theory are challenged. At the same time, anthropology is used as a foil for highlighting what I regard as some of the shortcomings of psychology. In fact, I have exposed myself to the risk of becoming unpopular all round! This will not worry me greatly if the book succeeds in contributing towards a more intensive dialogue that can only be beneficial for both disciplines.

The completion of the work was made possible by a fellowship at the Netherlands Institute for Advanced Studies, which I greatly appreciate. I was fortunate in having several psychologists and anthropologists as NIAS colleagues, who patiently discussed various issues with me and read some of the chapters. Among the former are Beatrice de Gelder and Lennart Sjöberg, and among the latter Peter Geschiere and especially David Turner, some of whose own work was particularly relevant.

My greatest debt is to A. L. ('Bill') Epstein, who generously placed his unrivalled anthropological experience at my disposal and took the time to read all the drafts. His constructive criticism was invaluable, and he not merely saved me from some blunders (though he is not responsible for any that remain), but contributed substantially to the final thrust of the argument. Whatever merit there may be in the work is in no small part due to his unstinting help and advice.

I should also like to thank Margaret Ferguson at the University of Strathclyde, who assisted with the preparatory work; Dinny Young the NIAS librarian, who tirelessly tracked down references; and Katherine Murphy, who typed the final manuscript.

Finally, I am grateful to my wife for putting up with an absentee husband for a year without undue complaint!

May 1982   GUSTAV JAHODA

Acknowledgements

Material from published sources listed below is used by kind permission of the copyright holders.

Auden, W. H. (1966). *Collected Shorter Poems, 1927–1957*. Faber, London.

Boas, F. (1910) Psychological problems in anthropology. *American Journal of Psychology* **21**, 371–84.

Bohannan, L. (1976). Shakespeare in the Bush. In *Cultural Anthropology* (J. Friedl, ed.). Harper & Row, New York.

Bolton, R. (1973). Aggression and hypoglycemia among the Quolla: a study in psychological anthropology. *Ethnology* **12**, 227–57.

Chagnon, N. A. (1968). *Yanomamö: The Fierce People*. Holt, Rinehart & Winston, New York.

Cissé, Y. (1973). Signes graphiques, représentations, concepts et tests relatifs à la personne chez les Malinke et les Bambara du Mali. In Colloques Internationaux, *La Notion de Personne en Afrique Noire*. Editions du Centre National de la Recherche Scientifiques, Paris.

Degérando, J.-M. (1800/1969). *The Observation of Savage Peoples*. Translated by F. T. C. Moore. Routledge & Kegan Paul, London.

Dieterlen, G. (1951). *Essai sur la Religion Bambara*. Presses Universitaires de France, Paris.

Fernandez, J. W. (1972). Fang representations under acculturation. In *Africa and the West*. University of Wisconsin Press, Madison.

Firth, R. (1957). *We, the Tikopia*, 2nd ed. Allen & Unwin, London.

Fortes, M. (1977). Custom and conscience in anthropological perspective. *International Review of Psychoanalysis* **4**, 127–54.

Gluckman, M. (1968). Psychological, sociological, and anthropological explanations of witchcraft and gossip: A classification. *Man* **3**, 20–34.

Hanson, F. A. (1975). *Meaning in Culture*. Routledge & Kegan Paul, London.

Irvine, J. T. (1974). Strategies of status manipulation in the Wolof greeting. In *Explorations in the Ethnography of Speaking* (R. Bauman and J. Sherzer, eds). Cambridge University Press, Cambridge.

Malinowski, B. (1926). *Crime and Custom in Savage Society*. Kegan Paul, London. Humanities Press Inc., New York.

Middleton, J. (1970). *The Study of the Lugbara: Expectation and Paradox in Anthropological Research*. Holt, Rinehart & Winston, New York.

Radcliffe-Brown, A. R. (1952). *Structure and Function in Primitive Society*. Cohen & West, London.

Reichel-Dolmatoff, G. (1976). Cosmology as ecological analysis: A view from the rain forest. *Man* **11**, 307–18.

Rogoff, B., Sellers, M. J., Pirrotta, S., Fox, N. and White, S. H. (1975). Age of assignment of roles and responsibilities to children. *Human Development* **18**, 353–69.

Turnbull, C. M. (1972). *The Mountain People*. Simon & Schuster, New York.

Turner, D. H. (1979). Behind the myths. In *Challenging Anthropology* (D. H. Turner and G. A. Smith, eds). McGraw-Hill, Toronto.

Turner, V. W. (1957) *Schism and Continuity in an African Society.* Manchester University Press, Manchester.

Whiting, B. B. and Whiting, J. W. M. (1975). *Children of Six Cultures.* Harvard University Press, Cambridge, Massachusetts.

Zempleni-Rabain, J. (1973). Food and the strategy involved in learning fraternal exchange among Wolof children. In *French Perspectives in African Studies* (P. Alexandre, ed.). Oxford University Press, London.

Acknowledgement is due to Human Relations Area Files, Inc. for providing Fig. 5.3.

Contents

Introduction:
Why Anthropology?

Le grand malheur des sciences de l'homme, si on les compare aux sciences exactes et naturelles, est la pauvreté des relations interdisciplinaires.

Piaget, 1965, p. 10

The form of the question indicates that it is being asked from the standpoint of psychology, but since my aim is to make a modest contribution towards the mutual understanding of the two disciplines, it might equally well be asked, Why psychology?

A simple answer would be that both study man, though from different vantage points; and they are complementary, insofar as their strengths and weaknesses tend to be mirror images of each other. The remainder of this book will be devoted to spelling out this view in some detail in the hope that some readers may be persuaded to share it. Here I shall make only some preliminary remarks, addressed mainly to psychologists.

Some years ago a lively, if somewhat controversial, book about the behaviour of modern man was published by two anthropologists, Tiger and Fox (1974). What is, or at least what should be, disturbing is that they managed to interpret behaviour almost entirely in terms of biology and culture, with scarcely a reference to psychology (which does not even appear in the index). If psychology is indeed the science of behaviour, then how was this possible? The key to the puzzle is that they were writing in the main about the ordinary behaviour of persons in their social setting, on which mainstream psychology has relatively little to say.

1

There are those who would see nothing wrong or strange in this, being content that the object of psychological study should be confined to responses elicited under controlled conditions, or that the person should be regarded as a point in factor-analytic space. Others do worry about it, not least the many students whose expectations that they will learn something about human behaviour in real life are often sadly disappointed. As a reaction, several more or less radical alternatives have been proposed, ranging from mild dissent to a total rejection of academic psychology.[1] One particular sally aimed by Shotter (1975) at psychology at large corresponds well with my own view:

> There is a third term to the relationship between man and nature, *culture*, which is not genetically inherited but communicated to man after birth as a 'second nature'. It is this third term that psychology, in its attempts to be 'scientific', has ignored.
>
> p. 136

Subsequently, Gauld and Shotter (1977) elaborated proposals for an alternative 'hermeneutic' psychology to replace the old mechanistic one. Alas, apart from some occasional lip-service there is precious little about 'culture' in their work—the new hermeneutic dispensation appears to ignore it nearly as much as does the old mechanistic approach. In any case, I personally have little sympathy with proposals, however well intentioned they may be, to make a clean sweep of the past. Wholesale attacks directed at experimental methods seem to me misconceived, as the experiment is undoubtedly the most powerful tool available for the elucidation of causal relationships. It would be foolish to abandon what has been laboriously gained, and remains of great value. We should not abandon such gains, but seek to overcome present limitations by pushing the boundaries outwards while at the same time loosening the methodological shackles.

The suggestion that psychology and anthropology are complementary is itself neither new nor particularly radical. A generation ago, Tolman (1951) wrote that in the case of "society-forming animals such as human beings", one cannot study the behaviour of individuals in abstraction from their social field; that field produces what he called "interfunctional relations",[2] which create two kinds of constraints for psychology. One is that they, as it were, contaminate the independent variables; and even if it were possible to overcome this problem to some extent for particular social fields, the set of relationships would have to be studied anew for a different type of socio-cultural field. Tolman's conclusion was "that an adequate sociology is a precondition for a complete psychology" (p. 188).

It will have been noted that Tolman referred to sociology rather than anthropology, and some reason needs to be given to explain why I am concentrating on anthropology. In the *International Encyclopedia of the Social Sciences*, sociology is defined as "the study of social aggregates and groups in their institutional organization, of institutions and their organization, and of the causes and consequences of changes in institutions and social organization".[3] The emphasis is not merely on institutions, which is shared with anthropology, but on organizations; and this implies a predominant concern with modern technological and bureaucratic societies. Hence, a great deal of sociological research is not directly concerned with individuals, but uses as its raw material secondary sources that are a product of administrative processes. Even when sociologists study individuals, as many certainly do, they are nearly always drawn from the same kinds of populations which supply the bulk of psychological 'subjects'. Thus, while sociology may be complementary to psychology in Tolman's sense, in terms of the range of behaviours displayed it suffers from much the same limitation as psychology. As far as theory is concerned, there is no sharp distinction between sociology and anthropology. Indeed, as will appear later, anthropologists have been greatly influenced by the classical sociological traditions and commonly describe their theories explicitly as 'sociological' ones. Moreover, with the declining opportunities for the study of pre-literate traditional cultures they have increasingly turned to the study of modern societies, though they bring to this task their own methods that are distinct from those of sociology. Their main field of activity, however, remains the study of cultures throughout the globe, thereby providing a unique fund of information about the lives of people in an enormous variety of eco-cultural settings. This is the prime justification for looking towards anthropology rather than sociology for a widening of psychological horizons.

Unfortunately, it must be said that most psychologists are indifferent to anthropology and, consequently, ill-informed about it. Some are actively hostile, critical of what they regard as anthropology's methodological inadequacies. For instance, in his admirable book on ecological factors in human development, Bronfenbrenner (1979) made the following comment:

> There exists a . . . body of scholarly work in which external environmental contexts are described in considerable detail and their impact on the course of development graphically traced. Such investigations are carried out primarily in the field of anthropology. . . . But the descriptive material in these studies is heavily anecdotal and the interpretation of causal influences is highly subjective and inferential.
>
> p. 18

A great deal will be said about anthropological methods in later chapters, so here I shall simply point out that if one is concerned with historical changes, experimentation is excluded and the approach is bound to be inferential. The cavalier dismissal of a vast mass of carefully conducted research by anthropologists is quite indefensible. Such complacent and patronizing stances of superior scientific purity leave out of account the price paid for rigour and precision in terms of narrowness, artificiality, and parochialism.

It is good to be able to record that these dangers are well recognized by some other distinguished psychologists. Cronbach (1975), one of the foremost present-day methodologists, had this to say:

> The two scientific disciplines, experimental control and systematic correlation, answer formal questions stated in advance. Intensive local observation goes beyond discipline to an open-eyed, open-minded appreciation of the surprises nature deposits in the investigative net. This kind of interpretation is historical more than scientific. I suspect that if the psychologist were to read more widely in history, ethnology, and the centuries of humanistic writings on man and society, he would be better prepared for this part of the work.
>
> p. 125

It is likely that Cronbach used the term 'ethnology' (dealing with the description and comparison of cultures) as more or less synonymous with 'anthropology'. In any case, this book has been written in the firm conviction that Cronbach is right.[4]

Notes

1. For an example of a relatively moderate alternative, see Valle and King (1978). Rollo May, in his introduction to the text, was rather less restrained: "Psychology, defending itself against its own anxiety in its state as a quasi-science, acts like a neurotic person in reaction to threat: it crystallizes its dubious method into a rigid principle." (p. viii.)
2. Tolman used this term to describe relationships between independent variables and hypothetical intra-individual 'intervening variables'. They can be of two types: first, intervening variables resulting from independent variables, and second, final dependent variables resulting from intervening variables. For a more complete explication of the scheme, which seeks to link the physiological, psychological, and social levels, Tolman's original chapter should be consulted.
3. The range of variations of definitions of sociology tends to be greater than

that of psychology. Some definitions, like the one cited below, are so wide that they appear to include a good part of both psychology and anthropology: "Sociology is the study of individuals in a social setting that includes groups, organizations, cultures and societies; and of the inter-relationships of individuals, groups, organizations, cultures and societies." (Ritzer *et al.*, 1979, p. 7.)

Systematic comparison of the self-descriptions of the three disciplines would probably reveal a considerable amount of intellectual imperialism!

4. Since this was first written I have come across an article by an anthropologist, Schwartz (1981), which persuasively argues for a rapprochement in the spirit of these pages:

> I am advocating that we put more psychology into psychological anthropology and take responsibility for awareness of developments in academic psychology in order to overcome our own insularity, even if we cannot overcome that of our colleagues in experimental and developmental psychology.
>
> p. 6

It will be evident that Schwartz is not optimistic about the prospects of converting psychologists, but nevertheless advances cogent reasons why they ought to take more interest in the work of anthropologists:

> To many psychologists, culture has always seemed a vague concept with which they cannot come to grips. Anthropological prodding of the "Yes, but the Eskimo . . ." variety is a distracting annoyance. Culture is an obstacle in their quest for universal human nature, to be filtered out where encountered or ignored as content where what is wanted is process or structure. My point is not only that cross-cultural comparison, or the shock of the exotic, is needed to test postulated psychological invariances, but that any study of human behavior or psychological process necessarily deals with the enculturated human being, and that without the incorporated effects of enculturation that behavior or process would either not be possible or would not take the characteristic human form.
>
> p. 8

PART 1

Background

1 | The Common Roots

Now, of all the terms of comparison we can choose, there is none more fascinating, more fruitful in useful trains of thought than that offered by savage peoples. Here we can remove first the variations pertaining to climate, the organism, the habits of physical life, and we shall notice that among nations much less developed by the effect of moral institutions, these natural variations are bound to emerge much more prominently: being less distinguished by secondary circumstances, they must chiefly be so by the first and fundamental circumstances belonging to the very principle of existence. Here we shall be able to find the material needed to construct an exact scale of the various degrees of civilization, and to assign to each its characteristic properties; we shall come to know what needs, what ideas, what habits are produced in each era of human society. Here, since the development of passions and of intellectual faculties is much more limited, it will be much easier for us to penetrate their nature, and determine their fundamental laws. Here, since different generations have exercised only the slightest influence on each other, we shall in a way be taken back to the first periods of our own history; we shall be able to set up secure experiments on the origin and generation of ideas, on the formation and development of language, and on the relations between these two processes.

Degérando: *Considérations sur les méthodes à suivre dans l'observation des Peuples Sauvages* (1800)

Speculation about man and society goes back as far as recorded history, but the eighteenth century marked the beginning of an attempt to trace the origins of ideas and social institutions to mankind and to seek the natural laws that governed their development. This interest was shared by the French encyclopaedists and Scottish moral philosophers, and their writings displayed a concern with the human mind and its relationship to social institutions as these developed from

9

earliest times. They saw the change from 'savagery' via 'barbarism' to 'civilization' as an orderly process, itself subject to an overriding law of inevitable progress. These philosopher-scientists therefore believed that by studying contemporary 'savages' they would be able to reconstruct their own past and the 'laws' that determined the ascent to civilization. The idea of inevitable progress persisted for nearly two centuries, being shattered only by the slaughter of the First World War. Until about the middle of the nineteenth century there was no clear separation between the various disciplines concerned with the study of man, and when in 1799 a society was founded in Paris for this purpose it was called, simply, the Société des Observateurs de l'Homme.

Among the earliest members of the Société were some of the liveliest minds of the time: Cuvier, a zoologist; Pinel, a pioneer of the treatment of mental illness; Jussieu, a naturalist; and Degérando, a philosopher (whose quotation heads this chapter). Degérando was a remarkable person, an 'angry young man' of his period, brilliantly perceptive but somewhat erratic and egotistical. Born in 1772 in Lyons, he had to flee France twice during the nineties owing to his political activities, but was awarded a prize in 1799 by the Institut for his discourse on "Signs". Subsequently he wrote an unsigned letter to a journal praising this work in extravagant fashion. He was known by his contemporaries as a man who had his fingers in every pie, and accordingly was not generally popular. St-Beuve called him "one of those writers who spin out like macaroni, getting longer without ever breaking".

Degérando's essay, which in some respects epitomized the ideas current at the turn of the century and in others was well ahead of them, was addressed to the leaders of two expeditions, to Africa and Australasia, respectively. Their ostensible purpose was exploration, with less publicized military and commercial aims which help to account for the limited scientific success actually achieved. Degérando was intensely concerned with the scientific objectives, since he thought that the study of primitive society would make it possible to discover the 'fundamental laws' of psychological development in a historical sense. Insofar as his theoretical notions were concerned, he was fairly typical of his contemporaries. Where he stood out was in his grasp of the practical problems involved in collecting data. The essay is full of shrewd advice and warnings against methodological pitfalls which have a surprisingly modern ring. Thus he warned against what we would call ethnocentrism in interpreting the customs of 'savages', argued against the collection of isolated facts and emphasized that account must be taken of 'natural connections' and 'order'; in other words, he suggested that facts only acquire meaning when they are treated as part of a system.

Degérando was too far ahead of his time and, as might have been expected, the expeditions were quite unable to live up to the stringent standards he had laid down. Nevertheless, one particular aspect of the work in Australasia is worth mentioning for two reasons: first, it illustrates the kind of 'hypothesis' that was characteristic of contemporary thought; second, it constitutes what was probably the first cross-cultural study employing psychological instrumentation. The hypothesis to be tested was that physical strength varies inversely with degree of civilization—presumably based on the more or less mythical image of the powerful wild man! At any rate, a kind of dynamometer was constructed for this purpose and applied by one of the explorers, Péron, to 85 natives of Timor, Tasmania; there was also a comparison group of French and English subjects. The relationship actually found turned out to be the opposite of that predicted by the hypothesis.[1]

The whole story of the expeditions and their background is a fascinating one, well described by Moore, who translated the essay and set it in its contexts. The kind of empirical approach adopted in some of the work of the expeditions was most unusual for its time. It is true that the Société mooted a number of empirical projects;[2] but these never seem to have got off the ground. The burst of enthusiasm for empirical study petered out, not to be taken up again seriously until almost the end of the nineteenth century. Many of the great ethnologists of the Victorian era were essentially armchair theorists[3] who relied upon reports of travellers and missionaries, but who had themselves no first-hand contact with 'savages'. Thus it is said of Frazer, who is of course best known for his massive work entitled *The Golden Bough* (1890),[4] that when he was asked whether he had ever visited any of the strange peoples about whom he wrote, his answer was "God forbid!" This was not true of the widely travelled German scholar Adolf Bastian (1826–1905), who, together with his contemporary Theodore Waitz, is often credited with having originated the notion of the 'psychic unity of mankind'. In fact, as Harris pointed out, the idea already existed fully blown in the eighteenth century and finds its clearest expression in the writings of Turgot (1744):

> The primitive dispositions are equally active among barbarians and civilized peoples. They are probably the same in every place and time. Genius is spread throughout mankind somewhat like gold in a mine. The more ore you mine, the more metal you extract. The more men you have, the more great ones or ones fitting to become great. The chances of education and circumstances developing them or letting them be is buried in obscurity.[5]

In other words, the key idea is that ability is randomly distributed throughout mankind, irrespective of races, places, or times. Hence such psychological differences as do exist are not hereditary but must, in the main, be a function of environmental influences.

The particular form of this doctrine elaborated by Bastian was that mankind as a whole shares a certain number of *Elementargedanken*, elementary ideas and concepts which account for the similarities in cultural traits that developed independently in widely different parts of the world. Variations are due to the specific environmental, and especially material conditions which determine their particular form. Bastian was also a vocal anti-racist, who poured scorn over the then-prevalent belief that race mixture is deleterious. It is noteworthy that both Bastian and Waitz seem to have been influenced by the pioneer psychologist Herbart (1776–1841), who espoused the view that psychology cannot be confined to the isolated individual, but that man must be looked at as part of society which is itself governed by higher-level psychological laws.

Such laws were also envisaged by John Stuart Mill (1879), who put forward the idea of a new science of the formation of character which he called 'ethology'. It presumes a much greater plasticity of human nature in response to socio-cultural influences than was accepted at the time, as the example below indicates:

> A long list of mental and moral differences are observed, or supposed to exist between men and women: but at some future, and, it may be hoped, not distant period, equal freedom and an equally independent social position comes to be possessed by both, and their differences of character are either removed or totally altered.
>
> p. 456

Ethology, in Mill's sense, would thus be the empirical science based on the elementary laws of psychology which deal with the individual mind; but it would be concerned with another level at which the laws are those governing the relationship between the individual and his social and material environment. In fact, Mill's proposal is a blue-print for a cross-cultural psychology closely linked to sociology and anthropology.[6]

While Mill emphasized psychology in what we would call a socio-cultural context, the latter was most salient for Tylor (1832–1917), who has been described as "the father of modern anthropology". He concentrated on the study of social institutions and examined their functions within particular cultures with a view to embodying his findings into a broader sweep of a developmental scheme. Tylor pioneered the statistical comparative method, looking at the associations between different institutions in a sample of several hundred societies; thereby he founded the modern cross-cultural statistical approach which will in due course be considered. When it came to the explanation of observed phenomena Tylor, who shared Bastian's belief in the 'psychic unity of mankind', turned to psychological concepts which he regarded as fundamental. This is evident from the famous first paragraph of Part I of *Primitive Culture* first published in 1871:

> Culture or Civilization, taken in its wide ethnographic sense, is that complex whole which includes knowledge, belief, art, morals, law, custom, and any other capabilities and habits acquired by man as a member of society. The condition of culture among the various societies of mankind, in so far as it is capable of being investigated on general principles, is a subject apt for the study of laws of human thought and action.
>
> Tylor, 1958, p. 1

The first sentence is Tylor's classical definition of culture, which must be viewed in the context of his wider theoretical stance. Tylor held that man's natural environment is everywhere sufficiently similar to present the same challenges and the same opportunities, and this accounts for the common elements in all world cultures. The problems of survival and social living have evoked responses in terms of the formation of certain institutions like the family, which are universal. But within this very broad framework the solutions to the problems of living have been a function of the particular circumstances in which people found themselves, and therefore differ widely both in content and the level achieved. Like his predecessors, Tylor proposed that each culture undergoes a progressive evolutionary development from savagery to civilization. Underlying his scheme is the assumption that all men have the basic mental capacity to respond adaptively to their situation, though the level of skill and mastery varies according to the stage they have reached. Hence men at each stage are not the same psychologically, especially as far as mental capacity is concerned:

> The trite comparison of savages to 'grown up children' is in the main a sound one, though not to be carried out too strictly. In the uncivilized American or Polynesian, the strength of body or force of character of a grown man are combined with a mental development in many respects not beyond that of a young child of a civilized race.
>
> Tylor, 1865, p. 108

Cultural evolution was thus viewed by Tylor as being accompanied by mental evolution towards more logical thinking, as well as the accumulation of knowledge. People in different cultures vary in their psychological characteristics because they stand on different steps of the evolutionary ladder. These, in essence, are the "laws of human thought and action" to which Tylor referred in his introduction.

The writings of Tylor inspired Frazer (1854–1941) to turn to anthropology. Originally a classical scholar, he was told to read *Primitive Culture* by his friend James Ward, then a noted psychologist, and the experience marked a turning point in his career. Frazer elaborated Tylor's ideas and was, as will be shown later in more detail, particularly interested in the psychological functioning underlying magic and religion—in fact he saw himself as working in the field of 'mental anthropology'. Frazer's monumental work contains his theoretical views but consists mainly of an enormous collection of customs, rites, and folklore to which these were applied. This may sound like a dreary recital, yet the opposite is true; Frazer's was also a literary achievement, and he was able to present his material not as dry 'data', but as drama on a cosmic scale. The moving description of the slaying of the divine king which, as the panorama unfolds comes to be seen as a symbolic ritual of death and rebirth whereby humans not merely re-enacted the cycles of nature but sought to bend them to their purpose. By thus helping to make sense of 'savages' and their ways, Frazer captured the imagination of his contemporaries, educated laymen and scholars alike. His ideas have proved seminal, and their impact has survived many critical onslaughts.

When Freud wrote *Totem and Taboo* (1919), he drew largely upon what was then *the* source of ethnographic material, namely Frazer.[8] In that book Freud dealt with mental evolution in general and individual development in particular. Its subtitle, "Resemblances between the psychic lives of savages and neurotics" indicates that he compared the fantasies, fears, phobias, and obsessions of his patients with what he assumed to be similar tendencies among 'savages' as revealed in their beliefs and customs. The underlying key to these resemblances is the Oedipus complex, which he regarded as common to all humanity and whose source he attributed to the 'primal horde' dominated by a tyrannical father who excluded all his sons from access to the females. Thus Freud sought to account in this work not merely for the vicissitudes of the individual psyche, but nothing less than the origins of human society and culture. Needless to say, this book has been widely attacked as unscientific and implausible, but it does not lack defenders. One of the latest is Badcock (1980), who cited primate evidence in support of the notion of the 'primal horde', and generally attempted to show that Freud's analysis makes evolutionary sense. Since Badcock's provocative thesis bears only marginally on anthropology, it cannot be further considered here; but some of the issues involved, above all the Oedipus complex, will be more fully discussed in later chapters.

Another famous psychologist, Wundt (1832–1920), turned in his later years to what was then known as *Völkerpsychologie* and published over a period of some two decades a massive series of ten volumes bearing that title.[9] Unlike Freud he gathered his own ethnographic data from a variety of sources. Wundt saw the task of folk psychology as that of providing psychological explanations of the thought, belief, and action of 'primitive man' on the basis of facts provided by ethnology. He divided human culture into four main 'ages' or stages: primitive man, the totemic age, the age of heroes and gods, and the development to humanity. However, he postulated no simple parallelism between these stages and the mental endowments of individuals, as some of his contemporaries had done. Thus he clearly understood that even 'primitive' technological skills implied levels of mental ability that are not to be despised, and his general conclusion was that the intelligence of 'primitive man', while restricted to a relatively narrow range of activities, "is not noticeably inferior to that of civilized man" (1916, p. 115) within that sphere.

Wundt marshalled a vast amount of ethnographic material in support of his general thesis; what prompted him to embark upon such a herculean task was his growing conviction that the study of "individual consciousness" in the laboratory has very definite limitations, and 'folk psychology' is necessary to transcend these:

> Its problem relates to those mental products which are created by a community of human life and are, therefore, inexplicable in terms merely of individual consciousness, since they presuppose the reciprocal action of many.
>
> 1916, p. 3

This formulation by Wundt is strikingly similar to the position of the classical French sociologist Durkheim (1858–1917), except for the fact that Durkheim claimed the whole of this sphere for sociology. In his *Rules of Sociological Method* (1895/1947), whose purpose was to carve out a clearly defined territory for sociology, Durkheim discussed the relationship between the two disciplines. For him psychology deals with states of consciousness *internal to the individual,* and the highly restricted way in which he conceived this is apparent from his account of other areas of behaviour to be assigned to sociology:

> The system of signs I use to express my thought, the system of

currency I employ to pay my debts, the practices followed in my
profession, etc., function independently of my own use of them. And
these statements can be repeated for each member of society. Here, then,
are ways of acting, thinking, and feeling that present the noteworthy
property of existing outside the individual consciousness.

These types of conduct or thought are not only external to the
individual but are, moreover, endowed with coercive power, by virtue of
which they impose themselves upon him, independent of his individual
will.

1947, p. 4

Since this may just sound absurd to psychologists unacquainted with
Durkheim's ideas, it should be pointed out that he was a powerful
thinker who developed his thesis in relation to empirical evidence. A
good example would be his famous study of suicide, apparently an
entirely arbitrary act springing from individual consciousness. Yet as
he showed with a wealth of data, suicide rates (and even methods!)
display a remarkable regularity, which can be accounted for by social
factors; hence, suicide may be legitimately regarded as a sociological
phenomenon.

The product of the interaction of individual minds in society, to
which Wundt also referred, constitutes a kind of collective
consciousness; and the ideas and beliefs thus shared are known as
'collective representations'. If one accepts Durkheim's formulation, the
scope of psychology would be radically narrowed, leaving it with little
more than physiological aspects of behaviour and the vagaries of
individual motives. I do not intend to embark upon a critical
examination of Durkheim's position—most psychologists do their work
in blissful ignorance of the fact that Durkheim would have regarded
some of their studies as being sociological. The reason why it is
important in the present context to understand Durkheim is that certain
vital strands in anthropological theory are directly traceable to him; and
as will be seen in the next chapter, Durkheim's views continue to
influence current conceptions by anthropologists about the relationship
of psychology to their own discipline. In particular, they lie at the root
of the assumption that collective representations can provide direct
evidence of cognitive functioning within a culture. The implications of
this assumption, which remains widespread among anthropologists,
will in due course be more fully considered. It should also be mentioned
that Moscovici (1981) has recently introduced into social psychology a
concept derived from Durkheim. Calling it 'social' rather than
'collective' representations in order to indicate the distinctiveness of his
formulation, Moscovici's aim was to preserve some of Durkheim's

valuable insights and use them to counteract some of the more bloodless aspects of social psychology divorced from social reality. Where he departed from Durkheim was in seeking to trace the origins and dynamics of representation rather than simply taking them as 'givens'. Moscovici's attempt to introduce 'representations' into psychological theory and research is certainly interesting and imaginative, but it is perhaps too early to say how far it will be successful.[10] In any case it may be seen as an effort to gain a foothold in territory Durkheim had firmly claimed for sociology.

After this slight anachronistic digression, let me return briefly to Wundt who gave no sign of any awareness of Durkheim's challenge to psychology; and if aware, he chose simply to ignore it. Wundt did, however, refer to the work of the anthropo-geographer Friedrich Ratzel (1844–1904), and the fact that he did so approvingly suggests that Wundt did not fully appreciate the bearing of Ratzel's approach on his own evolutionary thesis. The classical evolutionists, among whom Wundt may be counted, concentrated on what they saw as progressive change over time, whereby cultures passed through a series of stages of increasing complexity until they reached the peak—equated with the level of Western Europe. Similarities in customs and institutions found in various parts of the world were attributed essentially to the underlying similarities of adaptive psychological response everywhere—in other words, the idea of 'psychic unity of mankind'. However, a rival tradition began with Ratzel, who studied the spatial distribution of cultural elements, and in explaining similarities stressed the importance of the natural environment, the role of migration of peoples, and cultural diffusion whereby people borrow customs and institutions from each other. Ratzel's studies led him to a sceptical view regarding the psychological interpretations according to which people in widely different parts of the world independently invented similar institutions, because they all shared the same basic mental characteristics:

> We must beware of thinking even simple inventions necessary . . . It seems far more correct to credit the intellect of 'natural' races with great sterility in all that does not touch the most immediate objects of life.
>
> 1896, p. 79

It should be added that in other parts of his writings Ratzel placed less emphasis on the intellectual differences between races and found himself at least in partial agreement with Bastian. Nevertheless, the fact remains that what came to be known as the 'diffusionist' school repudiated the so-called 'doctrine of the psychic unity of mankind'.

This, together with the rise of biological determinism influenced by Darwin, opened the door to the interpretation of cultural development and change in terms of innate differences between peoples. Accordingly, there followed a shift from psychological unity to diversity, usually though not invariably with the connotation of superiority and inferiority. It is worth noting that parallel radical changes also occurred in psychology during roughly the same period: While the first half of the nineteenth century was dominated by various forms of associationism concerned with mental processes in general, Galton and Cattell heralded a new interest in the systematic study of individual and group *differences*.

The aim of this brief and unavoidably over-simplified sketch has been to demonstrate that strong links existed between anthropology and psychology throughout the nineteenth century. These links have continued in the twentieth century, but their nature has altered and become more complex. One reason has been the increasing professionalization and diversification of both disciplines. Thus, while it had been perfectly possible for a psychologist like Bain or an anthropologist like Frazer to become distinguished in their field without ever conducting any empirical work, armchair theorizing has become increasingly unacceptable.[11] In both anthropology and psychology many specializations, as well as considerable varieties of different approaches, have developed. It would not be profitable for the present purpose to make the attempt to unravel these numerous threads, even if I were competent to do so. Instead, it will be useful to concentrate on a few outstanding figures who manifested the relationship in their own work and had considerable influence on others.

The first to be discussed is Rivers (1864–1922), one of the few names equally well known and respected in psychology and anthropology.[12] Rivers' uncle, James Hunt, had been the founder and first president of the Anthropological Society. Hunt was a controversial figure, who was hissed by his audience at a British Association meeting when he defended slavery on the grounds of the low evolutionary status of Negroes. However, his retiring address from the Anthropological Society contained the following prophetic passage:

> After a time it will be found that the study of physical anthropology will be followed by researches in psychological anthropology.
>
> quoted in Haddon, 1934, p. 60

Hunt presented his nephew with an inscribed copy of a then famous anthropological book—and this when Rivers was three weeks old! This attempt on the uncle's part to stimulate interest in anthropology did not bear fruit until some thirty years later. Rivers was trained in medicine, becoming specially interested in neurology; while working at the National Hospital he came into contact with Henry Head, just back from Germany and full of enthusiasm for Hering's studies on vision. It may well be that this experience sparked off Rivers' later interest in this sphere. After studying some time at Jena he began lecturing on experimental psychology at University College, London, moving on to Cambridge in 1897. At that time A. C. Haddon, an anthropologist who took a broad view of his subject, was organizing an expedition to the Torres Straits. He held the opinion that no investigation of a people was complete that did not embrace a study of their psychology, and therefore persuaded Rivers to take part; the latter in turn enlisted two of his students, C. S. Myers and William McDougall; another member was a young physician, C. G. Seligman.

The most important psychological work done was that of Rivers and, to a lesser extent Seligman, on visual illusions; there were also useful contributions by Myers on hearing, smell, and taste, while McDougall studied cutaneous sensations, muscular sense and reaction times. Rivers' work, often described,[13] has stood up extremely well to the test of time. The investigations served, among other things, to dispose of two false notions then prevalent. The first was that 'primitives', being less intelligent than civilized people, would be more easily taken in by illusions; the second was that 'primitives' possessed quite uncanny sensory acuity compared with people from Western industrialized countries. Generally Rivers' achievement was a landmark, being the first modern empirical cross-cultural psychological study. At the time, however, its impact was limited, and for half a century few followed his example.

For McDougall[14] and Myers the Expedition was merely a transitory episode in their lives, and they went on to become eminent psychologists without much further contact with anthropology; but for Rivers and Seligman it was a turning-point in their careers which led them into anthropology. Seligman became a distinguished anthropologist, who maintained an interest in the relationship between his subject and psychology, especially psychoanalysis.

The development of Rivers' ideas needs to be traced in more detail. While his psychological studies in the Murray Islands were rigorous and carefully controlled, some of the interpretations of findings reveal the persistent influence of classical evolutionism on his early thinking. Thus in his report one of the chains of argument is as follows: hypermetropia (i.e. long-sightedness) is more common among 'savage' races and leads to more extensive use of visual accommodation; this is related to close observation of the minutiae of nature, requiring pre-dominant attention to sense objects; this in turn means that less attention can be paid to the more serious problems of life and therefore constitutes an obstacle to "higher mental development" (Rivers, 1901, p. 44).

Later, on closer acquaintance with 'savages' Rivers acquired considerable respect for their mental abilities. Another consequence of subsequent ethnographic studies in Melanesia was the abandonment of classical evolutionary theory with its somewhat simplistic assumption of 'psychic unity'. He became a prominent diffusionist, but this theoretical conversion did not affect his general stance regarding the importance of psychology for anthropological work:

> One has only to think about the matter for a moment to see that the only way in which the culture of an immigrant people can be carried about the world is in a psychological form, in the form of sentiments, beliefs and ideas.
>
> Rivers, 1926, p. 14

More generally, Rivers adopted a theoretical position regarding the nature of anthropological explanation that has remained a focus of controversy. He took the view that *in principle* all explanations of social behaviour must be in psychological terms (1926, p. 5); and he referred to psychological facts being "interpolated as links in a chain of causation connecting social antecedents with social consequents" (1914, p. 22). On the other hand, it must be understood that he perceived this reduction of sociology and anthropology to psychology as a long-term objective, allowing provisional autonomy to these disciplines. Moreover, in this same book Rivers (1914) himself showed on the basis of his own ethnographic work that the patterns of social relationships in primitive society need not, as Kroeber (1909) had proposed, be explained psychologically; but rather that it could be done entirely with reference to antecedent social conditions. Yet it was always his view that a thorough knowledge of psychology, including training in experimental methods in the laboratory, was the best preparation for the field anthropologist. It was the advice he gave to Frederic Bartlett, who at one time was considering reading anthropology while a student at Cambridge.

Earlier, another student of Rivers had been Radcliffe-Brown (1881–1955), who took psychology for three years and then in 1904 became Rivers' first pupil in anthropology. His initial fieldwork in the Andaman Islands was to a considerable extent psychologically oriented, reflecting Rivers' influence (Radcliffe-Brown, 1922/64). Thus he wrote:

Any attempt to explain or interpret the particular beliefs and customs of a savage people is necessarily based on some general psychological hypothesis as to the real nature of the phenomena to be explained.

p. 232

He also referred to the "psychological methods" that he had applied, and an example is his explanation as to why sick people have their body daubed with red paint. It is the colour of blood and fire, identified with the body and life, and a symbol of mental and physical activity or even energy in general. Radcliffe-Brown suggested that this symbolism might be universal, with a psycho-physial basis. At any rate:

When a person is sick he is in need of vitality, of energy, and so his body is daubed with the red paint that is a symbol of the things that he needs, and by applying the paint to his body he increases his energy and vitality, and so helps himself to get rid of the sickness.

p. 318

Now it should be noted that the interpretation relates to the mental processes of particular individuals as instances of a universal human psychological disposition. Subsequently Radcliffe-Brown came to repudiate such a mode of approach, when he became converted to the ideas of Durkheim. As has already been indicated, for Durkheim the nature of individual psychological processes as such is simply irrelevant to the study of social behaviour, the critical passage being the following:

The determining cause of a social fact should be sought among the social facts preceding it and not among the states of individual consciousness.

1895–1938, p. 110

Comparative sociology being thus concerned with the discovery of sociological laws *sui generis*, Radcliffe-Brown came to regard the business of anthropology as that of explaining customs and beliefs by showing how each one is an example of some general law of human *society* (rather than of the human mind). Society is an ordered arrangement or *structure*, and the components of this structure are human individuals. They are treated not as psychological organisms, but as persons occupying specific positions within the structure to which sets of rights and duties are attached.

The claim that anthropology is a natural science of society studying its 'laws' has not become widely accepted, but some other aspects of Radcliffe-Brown's teaching draw together common elements from a variety of schools, so that they have developed into central tenets of anthropology. One of these is the concept of a *social system*, dating back to Montesquieu, but which has been expressed by Radcliffe-Brown with unsurpassed elegance:

> The idea of a natural or phenomenal system is that of a set of relations amongst events, just as a logical system, such as the geometry of Euclid, is a set of relations amongst propositions, or an ethical system a set of relations amongst ethical judgements. When one speaks of the 'banking system' of Great Britain this refers to the fact that there is a considerable number of actions, interactions and transactions, such, for example, as the payments by means of a signed cheque drawn on a bank, which are so connected that they constitute in their totality a process of which we can make an analytical description which will show how they are interconnected and thus form a system. We are dealing, of course, with a process, a complex part of the total social process of social life in Great Britain.
>
> Radcliffe-Brown, 1952, pp. 5–6

With such theoretical clarity and power he exerted a great influence on British anthropologists, and he was probably largely responsible for the fact that there was a considerable period when many of them were most reluctant to become tainted by any contact with psychology. In this respect they tended to follow the lead of Radcliffe-Brown rather than that of his great contemporary, Malinowski, who was always looking for a psychology that anthropologists could use.

Malinowski (1884–1942) was a very different man, both as a person and professionally. A Pole educated in Cracow, he took a PhD in physics and mathematics. During a period of illness he read Frazer's *Golden Bough*, which fascinated him. He went on to Leipzig where he studied experimental psychology under Wundt, whose 'folk psychology' was an important influence; for in some ways Wundt's views of the close connection of phenomena at the social and psychological levels was closely akin to what was later to become 'functionalism'. This may be characterized as the attempt to describe cultures as integral wholes, all of whose component parts are closely interrelated. Later critics have rightly pointed out that regarding everything as having a function within the cultural system is going too far; thus it avoids the problem concerning the relative weight to be attached to different elements and makes it difficult to account for social change. But Malinowski's emphasis should be viewed in relation to the older approach to fieldwork, which he caricatured cruelly, as follows:

> We can only plead for the speedy and complete disappearance from the records of fieldwork of the piecemeal items of information of

customs, beliefs, and rules of conduct floating in the air, or rather leading a flat existence on paper with the third dimension, that of life, completely lacking. With this the theoretical argument of Anthropology will be able to drop the lengthy litanies of threaded statement, which makes us anthropologists feel silly, and the savage look ridiculous. I mean by this the long enumerations of bald statements such as, for example, "Among the Brobignacians when a man meets his mother-in-law, the two abuse each other and each retires with a black eye" . . . "in old Caledonia when a native accidentally finds a whisky bottle by the road-side he proceeds immediately to look for another" . . .

It is easy, however, to poke fun at the litany-method, but it is the field-worker who is really responsible. There is hardly any record in which the majority of statements are given as they occur in actuality and not as they should or are said to occur. Many of the early accounts were written to startle, to amuse, to be facetious at the expense of the savage, till the tables were turned and it is more easy now to be facetious at the anthropologist's expense. To the old recorders what mattered really was the queerness of the custom, not its reality.

1926, pp. 126-7

This sharp reaction to the older style was a response to Malinowski's own experiences. He went to England in 1910 to become a postgraduate student at the London School of Economics where he worked under Westermarck[15] and came into contact with Seligman, who, as previously stated, had been a member of the Cambridge expedition. Seligman helped him to get support for fieldwork in New Guinea, and he went to work first with the Mailu. During his second trip the First World War had broken out, and this fact contributed to making his fieldwork more extensive than usual. It was more or less accidentally that he ended up in the Trobriands, a small island off New Guinea, where he spent two crucial years. The isolation resulted in a much deeper immersion in the life of the community than anthropologists had experienced before him.[16] From such full participation stemmed the conviction that everything in a culture hangs together and makes sense, which is the essence of functionalism.

While Malinowski was still in the Trobriands, Seligman sent him some literature on psychoanalysis and drew his attention to the opportunity provided by a matrilinear and 'avunculocal' society for testing the cross-cultural validity of Freudian theory. Malinowski (1927) took up the challenge and showed that in the Trobriands it was the mother's brother and not the father who was the main authority figure. Hence, he argued, the nuclear complex as postulated by Freud cannot be universal; and since the Oedipus complex is central to Freudian theory he thereby threatened it, unleashing a controversy which has gone on more or less ever since (Parsons, 1964).

Although Malinowski is probably best known to psychologists in this particular context, his psychological interests extended far more widely. Richards (1957) suggested that he was the first British anthropologist to make use of the concept of 'conditioning', in his discussion of cultural learning (Malinowski, 1931); but if so, it was nevertheless somewhat indirect. What is clear, however, is his insistence that the business of the anthropologist is not confined to the documentation of social structure, the details of behaviour, and descriptions of emotional interactions. He must also collect the people's own views about their actions, their beliefs, and their ideas—in a famous phrase he coined, it is necessary "to grasp the native's point of view". At the same time Malinowski was emphatic that the concern should not be with purely individual experiences and motives, but should concentrate on those characterizing the individual as a member of the community.

This preoccupation with collective aspects of psychological processes is also evident in Malinowski's 'theory of needs', which has been ably discussed by Piddington (1957). His notion of 'needs' differed from such psychological concepts as 'instinct' or 'drive' that were current at the time, but 'needs' also had a biological aspect. A good example of Malinowski's application of this very general notion of 'needs' is his theory of magic. As will be shown in more detail in a subsequent chapter, Tylor and Frazer had interpreted such beliefs as intellectual error, a function of an evolutionarily underdeveloped mentality. Malinowski rejected this on the basis of his own observations of the behaviour of 'savages', which Tylor and Frazer lacked. He argued that for the Trobrianders, both technological and magical procedures constituted reasonable means for achieving given ends. Definite limits are set to the potentiality of technological practices by such extraneous factors as the weather in the growing of crops. There is thus a *psychological need* to attempt such control by magical practices, which spring from "intense desires and strong emotions" (1931, p. 635).

This particular example will also serve to highlight the contrast between Malinowski and Radcliffe-Brown in their positions regarding psychology. While Malinowski explained magical rites in terms of psychological need, Radcliffe-Brown (1952) took a different view:

> I think that for certain rites it would be easy to maintain with equal plausibility an exactly contrary theory, namely, that if it were not for the existence of the rite and the beliefs associated with it the individual would feel no anxiety, and that the psychological effect of the rite is to create in him a sense of insecurity or danger. It seems very unlikely that an Andaman Islander would think it is dangerous to eat dugong or pork or turtle meat if it were not for the existence of a specific body of ritual

the ostensible purpose of which is to protect him from those dangers.
pp. 148–9

The lesson of this clash over the problem of anxiety is that psychologists in particular should be cautious about an explanation in psychological terms which commends itself to them, without considering alternative interpretations giving priority to social structure. Obviously both may be relevant in different types of situations.

So far this survey has dealt in the main with European figures, which reflects their predominance until the end of the nineteenth century. This is not to say that there were no important American scholars; but in the present context, namely, the role of psychological ideas in anthropological theorizing, they can hardly be said to have made an independent contribution. A possible exception is Lewis H. Morgan (1818–81), who pioneered the study of kinship terminology. Like most of his contemporaries, he was a unilinear developmentalist who assumed that the transitions from savagery via barbarism to civilization would be associated with a corresponding mental evolution. Morgan was exceptional insofar as he assigned special weight to the institution of property as a factor in psychological change. The human mind, having created the notion of property, subsequently needed to accommodate itself to the social changes resulting therefrom; and he linked this to the key institution of the family:

> A little reflection must convince anyone of the powerful influence property would now begin to exercise upon the human mind, and of the great awakening of new elements of character it was calculated to produce. Evidence appears, from many sources, that the feeble impulse aroused in the savage mind had now become a tremendous passion in the splendid barbarism of the heroic age . . . The time had now arrived when monogamy, having assured the paternity of children, would assert and maintain their exclusive right to inherit the property of the deceased father.
>
> Morgan, 1877, p. 544

The emphasis on property relationships as a key to the transformation was of course exactly in line with Marxist doctrine; and Engels' work on the origin of the family was very largely based on Morgan's writings. The Marxist approach was thus a special twist within the broad developmental and evolutionary tradition. However, as has been indicated already, a rival and contradictory nineteenth-century synthesis was diffusionism, which involved a non-evolutionary interpretation of human history in terms of successive migrations of early cultures. The man who first tackled these opposing views and attempted to reconcile them was Franz Boas (1858–1942).

Born in Germany, Boas studied physics and geography, the subject of his dissertation being the colour of sea water. In his early career Boas became interested in psychophysics and wrote an article on it in a physiological journal (Lowie, 1937, p. 128). When planning his first expedition to Baffin Island to study the Eskimo, his aim (as quoted in G. Stocking, 1965) was to combine geographical and ''psychophysical'' approaches:

> The general study will be about the knowledge peoples have of the local geography, which will be followed by a psychological study about the causes for the limitation of the spreading of peoples.
>
> p. 56

The first issue concerned the relationship between what we would now call 'cognitive maps' of their environment and their patterns of geographical mobility. As regards the wider problem, one might hazard the view that Boas was trying to establish an empirical basis for the rather vague arguments of the diffusionists, employing psychological methods. While the larger aims were not realized, Boas did obtain a considerable number of drawings from Eskimos and compared these with the maps he himself had to prepare.[17]

Soon after this expedition Boas moved permanently to America, and throughout his career he retained an active interest in psychological aspects of anthropological theory which informed his whole approach. Having been in direct contact with Bastian and Tylor, he adopted their assumption that the common psychological characteristics of humankind cannot be ignored in the analysis of historical development. On the other hand, under the influence of Galton's stress on psychological variations he rejected their notions of psychological uniformity throughout the historical process. The kind of compromise he suggested also owes something to Wundt, whom he brought to the attention of his students. The core of his position was expressed in a lecture given in 1909 (and published in 1910) on ''Psychological problems in anthropology'':

> The science of anthropology deals with the biological and mental manifestations of human life as they appear in different races and in different societies. The phenomena with which we are dealing are therefore, from one point of view, historical. We are endeavoring to elucidate the events which have led to the formation of human types, past and present, and which have determined the course of cultural development of any given group of men. From another point of view the same phenomena are the objects of biological and psychological investigations. We are endeavoring to ascertain what are the laws of hereditary

and environmental variability of the human body . . . We are also trying
to determine the psychological laws which control the mind of man
everywhere, and that may differ in various racial and social groups.
Insofar as our inquiries relate to the last-named subject, their problems
are problems of psychology, though based upon anthropological
material.

p. 371

Subsequently he became somewhat less sanguine about the reductionist possibility of deriving general laws of 'culture growth' on the
basis of an understanding of psychological processes and shifted
towards a greater emphasis on the tracing of historical relationships. It
is only after these have been analysed that one can reach a psychological understanding in terms of the particular forms that psychological processes are taking within a culture shaped by historical and
environmental factors. Such abstract formulations do less than justice
to Boas' work on mythology and art, where he sought to put these
principles into practice. His early work on *The Mind of Primitive Man*
(1911/63) contains some striking anticipations of modern ideas about
culture learning, and he was also interested in the problem of the
relationship between language and thought. Lastly, it should be
mentioned that Boas, while not denying racial differences, played
down their importance and vigorously opposed the then prevalent
naïve biologism.[18]

In sum, Boas was not merely an extremely versatile scholar but also
an outstanding leader who dominated American anthropology and
imparted his interest in psychology to the subsequent generation of
distinguished scholars. Most of them were his students and included
among them were such figures as Kroeber (who first studied psychology
under Cattell), Ruth Benedict and Margaret Mead, whose work will
later be examined in more detail. He may thus be regarded as the
founder of what became known as 'psychological anthropology', which
flourished in America at a time when Radcliffe-Brown's influence in
Britain had led to coolness and scepticism regarding the contribution of
psychology. Closely connected is the fact that American anthropologists were mainly preoccupied with 'culture', while British ones
preferred to analyse their field material within the conceptual framework of 'social structure'. Beattie (1964) suggested a historical reason
for this divergence in perspective. He argued that British anthropologists have always studied peoples whose societies were, even
during the colonial period, essentially intact and functioning; their
system of social relationships was therefore amenable to analysis.
American anthropologists, on the other hand, were for a long time

largely confined to working with American Indians whose societies had effectively disintegrated, though cultural elements such as beliefs, values, and certain skills remained available for scrutiny; perforce, Americans had to concentrate on these cultural features and made a virtue out of necessity. While this may be one relevant factor, it is certainly not the whole story. Writing from a trans-Atlantic perspective, Murphy (1971) saw American anthropology as having far greater breadth and diversity than British anthropology. He attributed this not so much to intellectual influences as to the structure of academic departments in the two countries, the consequences of which he pictured with caustic wit. In America, he said, "the expert on Bongo-Bongo scatological reference terminology becomes a prize because he contributes to academic ecumenism and does not step on anybody else's professional toes" (p. 18); in Britain, "seminars develop the critical faculty to a morbid degree, for mutual criticism, while parading as the forge of discipline, is also a well-known means for maintaining orthodoxy. Its products think well, but they don't think much." (p. 20.)

All such comments capture significant differences between American and not merely British but all European anthropology as well. There is no doubt that the range of interests of American anthropologists is extremely wide, and *pace* Beattie they have long since moved out into the wider world to study the same kinds of 'living' cultures with which British workers have always been concerned. The greater homogeneity of British anthropology has the virtue, according to Murphy (1971, p. 23), that its disputations tend to be "incisive, expert, empirically detailed and finely stated", as contrasted to the more free-wheeling American style. But it should be emphasized that the difference is primarily one of styles and does not imply really disparate approaches dividing 'social' from 'cultural' anthropologists. Social anthropologists cannot study social relationships without also considering the beliefs and values attached to them; conversely, cultural anthropologists do not concern themselves with beliefs and values *in vacuo*, but are bound to look at them within the context of social relationships. Nevertheless, the fact remains that it is impossible to study a 'culture' as a whole, and there has been a greater tendency in America than in Britain for anthropology to split into a series of specialisms, including so-called 'cognitive' as well as 'psychological' anthropology.

Naturally anthropology is far from being an Anglo-American preserve. It has already been mentioned that the ideas of Durkheim have powerfully influenced generations of anthropologists and continue to do so. More recently a massive theoretical jolt has been administered by the French school under the leadership of Lévi-Strauss. This movement has gained adherents in America and Britain and has affected anthropological thinking everywhere, even when it was merely to evoke opposition. Rather confusingly, this school is also called 'structuralist', but in this case the term refers to the structure of ideas rather than to that of society. In order to clarify this distinction Leach (1976) uses the terms 'empiricist' and 'rationalist' to characterize the two approaches. The empiricists are the structuralist–functionalists previously described, who concentrate in the field on the overt behaviour displayed in social relations and regard the participants' own views concerning their social life as necessary but nonetheless secondary data. Rationalists are less concerned with behaviour and more interested in what their informants say: in their notions as to what *ought* to be done in social situations and above all in their mythology and their ideas about the place of man in the universe. Rationalists are always on the look-out for common themes or permutations of such themes as recur in different cultures and are believed ultimately to reflect the fundamental characteristics of the human mind.

All this might give the misleading impression that anthropology is not merely in a state of flux—which is true of any lively discipline—but that it is rent by divisions so sharp that they lack any common ground. This would be quite wrong, as these different theoretical orientations are at least in one respect little more than ripples on a stream. This has been very clearly expressed by Leach (1976):

> The rival theories of anthropologists are themselves parts of a single interacting whole. Both viewpoints accept the central dogma of functionalism that cultural details must always be viewed in context, that everything is meshed with everything else. In this regard the two approaches, the empiricist (functionalist) and the rationalist (structuralist) are complementary rather than contradictory; one is a transformation of the other.
>
> p. 5

Notes

1. The nature of the samples was not made very clear, and Moore (1969) states that Péron's findings are open to doubt since he admitted mistakes in reading the dynamometer scale!
2. These included the observation of deaf mutes from birth, the determination of the influence of different professions on the character of

those pursuing them, and a proposal "to make careful observations, for twelve to fifteen years, of four or six children, an equal number of each sex, remote from any social institution, and left, for the development of ideas and of language, to natural instinct alone" (Moore, 1969, p. 47).

3. This term is intended in a descriptive rather than in a derogatory sense, since many such men must be credited with impressive theoretical achievements based on the analysis of materials from very mixed sources.

4. Originally in three volumes, later expanded to twelve (1925–1930); an abridged edition with a useful introduction by Mary Douglas has recently been published (Frazer, 1978).

5. Quoted in Harris (1968, p. 15).

6. For a more extensive discussion of Mill's ideas, cf. G. Jahoda (1980).

7. Ward wrote the article on 'psychology' in the ninth (1886) and eleventh (1911) editions of the *Encyclopaedia Britannica*.

8. The fact that Freud made use of his work does not seem to have impressed Frazer. Just as he had been horrified at the idea of visiting exotic places, so, according to Malinowski (1944, p. 182), did he refuse to venture onto strange intellectual shores, and he never bothered to read anything by Freud or his school.

9. An abridged version of the ten-volume series (Wundt, 1916) is also available and contains the essentials of the argument.

10. Moscovici actually began his work on social representations some two decades ago when studying the public image of psychoanalysis (Moscovici, 1961). He also outlined his views in a preface to the work of Herzlich (1973), but his fullest exposition is to be found in the book cited. While this is not the place for an extensive critical appraisal of his ideas, a few comments may be appropriate.

   The most salient contrast between Durkheim's 'collective representations' and Moscovici's 'social representations' is probably that the former encompassed the global thought and belief systems of a society, while the latter has been focused on more limited issues such as psychoanalysis or illness; this is partly due to the fact that, as Moscovici explains, representations in modern society are neither static nor monolithic, but shifting and fragmented. While this is a sound enough argument, it raises a question regarding the logical status of social representations: how, if at all, do they differ from what are commonly known as ideas, beliefs and attitudes shared by sections of modern populations? Moscovici also insists that social representations are the products of individual thinking, thereby avoiding Durkheim's quasi-mystical attributions of representations to the collectivity; on the other hand Moscovici is not very clear about the nature of the processes involved—he and his followers seem more concerned with the products of such thinking.

11. This is a statement of fact and not a value-judgement. It could justifiably be argued that the social sciences currently suffer from excessive and too often trivial fact-finding research, and could benefit from a greater concentration on pure theory.

12. There is now a biography of Rivers by Slobodin (1978), which presents a more well-rounded picture of an astonishingly many-sided man.
13. For an outline in the context of the present state of knowledge, see Deregowski (1980).
14. McDougall's interest persisted longer: he went from the Torres Straits to Borneo, where he worked with another anthropologist, Charles Hose. They published a book entitled *The Pagan Tribes of Borneo* (London: Macmillan, 1912).
15. Westermarck's (1906) well-known work, *The Origin and Development of Moral Ideas*, was very psychologically orientated. For instance, he tried to explain the institution of the blood feud in terms of the 'emotion' of revenge, a line that was strongly opposed by Rivers (1926, pp. 8–9).
16. At the same time his posthumously published diary (1967) revealed not merely the amount of stress entailed by the isolation but also hitherto unsuspected personal attitudes.
17. Presumably he was familiar with the work of Galton, who had written that "the Eskimos are geographers by instinct, and appear to see vast tracts of country mapped out in their heads" (Galton, 1883–1928, p. 72).
18. In this connection he conducted a famous study of the changes of head form of the descendants of American immigrants, which disposed of the cephalic index (skull measurements used by physical anthropologists) as a reliable indicator of genetic history and established the influence of environmental factors on bodily form. This research is summarized in Boas (1955).

2 | Anthropologists and Psychology

The preceding historical summary has shown that nineteenth-century evolutionism in anthropology rested largely on explanatory principles of a psychological nature, above all on the doctrine of 'the psychic unity of man', which is still with us. Since then psychology and anthropology have not merely diverged, but each has undergone fundamental changes in theory and method. Psychology has moved away from anthropology, focusing essentially on aspects of the behaviour of people in modern industrialized countries; and, apart from the small but growing specialization of cross-cultural psychology, little if any attention is devoted to the wider socio-cultural framework of behaviour. By contrast, psychology continues to run as a vital thread through much of anthropological theorizing, especially in the United States, and anthropologists from time to time engage in debate and controversy over the place of psychology in anthropological work. The reasons for this, and the nature of the debate, will now be examined.

The most common textbook definitions of anthropology are remarkably similar to those found in psychology texts, namely, some variant of 'the scientific study of man'. One major branch, physical anthropology, deals with biological aspects and is closely akin to physiology and anatomy—this will not be further considered here. By far the major effort is devoted to social or cultural anthropology. Its broad goal is "the development of a body of reliable knowledge about sociocultural phenomena—how those came into being, how they are maintained or altered over time, and how they interrelate" (Manners and Kaplan, 1968, p. 5).

Socio-cultural phenomena are obviously supra-individual, yet a human community or society that embodies these phenomena is composed of individuals in interaction. This is the simple source of the basic anthropological dilemma as to how far the intra-psychic characteristics of individuals need to be taken into account for the purpose of understanding and explaining socio-cultural phenomena. From a broad historical perspective there are two main strands in anthropological thinking. The classical expression of one is to be found in Malinowski, who explicitly advocated psychological explanations. The other originated with Durkheim, whose follower Radcliffe-Brown took a radically anti-psychological stand; subsequently Lévi-Strauss, in the same tradition, reversed this (with a vengeance!). These and related positions will now be outlined.

Fortes (in Firth, 1957) had this to say about Malinowski's functionalism:

> Everything he wrote was riddled with psychological explanation partly because his functionalism meant seeing custom as motive, partly because its instrumental and utilitarian form led back to psychological needs, and the simplest way in which these can be visualized as emerging into action is as driving forces behind instincts, sentiments and emotions.
>
> p. 170

Malinowski postulated a set of basic human needs including nutrition, reproduction, safety, and so on. These were conceived as needs of the *individual*, and culture as the instrument whereby they were met. He insisted that both the emotional and intellectual aspects of mental processes must be considered in the analysis of culture. Preliminary mention might also be made here of Roheim (1943), who went even further than Malinowski in stressing the primacy of individual psychology. A psychoanalyst trained in anthropology, though outside the mainstream of anthropological theory, he sought to reduce the origins of culture, as well as its varying forms, to the vicissitudes of the libido. As will become apparent later, such a crude statement is somewhat unfair to a man of lively and combative intellect, but it essentially characterizes his position.

While Malinowski has been called a psychological functionalist, Radcliffe-Brown was known as a 'structural–functionalist' as he concentrated his concern on social structure and advocated the complete exclusion of any psychological elements. He modelled his theory closely on the ideas of Durkheim (1895/1947), one of whose basic rules of sociological method was that "the determining cause of a social fact must be sought among the antecedent social facts, and not among the states of the individual consciousness'' (p. 109—my translation). Radcliffe-Brown (1952) indicated that in his theory a person is regarded ''not as an organism but occupying a position in a social structure'' (p. 10). Thus, if we take two hypothetical persons, X and Y, Radcliffe-Brown was interested neither in the psychological needs they had in common, nor in their personality characteristics, but only in the fact that X is, say, Y's mother's brother. In other words, they are considered solely as occupants of certain positions within the social structure, positions to which bundles of rights are attached which determine their social relations.

A totally different heritage was taken from Durkheim by Lévi-Strauss, whose 'structuralism', as explained in the previous chapter, relates to the structure of ideas. Hence, it will perhaps not be surprising to learn of his dictum that ''l'ethnologie est d'abord une psychologie'' (1962, p. 174). In his more recent writings, to be discussed later, Lévi-Strauss has made extensive reference to psychological research in order to support his thesis that modes of perceiving relations underlie the origins of social institutions; ultimately, he contends, these are traceable to fundamental properties of the human mind. Were it not for the fact that Lévi-Strauss operates at different levels, drawing inspiration from linguistics and biology as well, he might also be regarded as a reductionist on a par with Roheim, albeit a rationalist one.

A somewhat related though distinct approach is known as 'symbolic anthropology'. While it cannot be said to encompass a coherent body of theory at present, much of its work has a strongly psychological, or at least quasi-psychological, flavour. Then there is the movement variously known as 'the new ethnography' or 'cognitive anthropology', which is rather less directly psychological than its name might suggest; nonetheless, it has given rise to debate about the extent to which its findings correspond to something rather quaintly termed 'psychological reality'.

Lastly (but chronologically prior to symbolic and cognitive anthropology), there is the field that used to be known as 'culture and personality' but has recently been re-christened 'psychological anthropology'. Within it the psychological aspects are of course direct and explicit, involving mainly psychoanalysis and, to a lesser extent, learning theory. Some anthropologists, especially in America, have had a strong predilection for Freudian theory, for reasons that will be considered later.

This brief overview is merely intended to indicate that a great deal, though by no means all, anthropological theory is shot through with psychological elements. Similarly, numerous fieldwork reports—even by anthropologists firmly opposed to psychological theorizing—can be shown to contain (unwittingly, and in spite of their denials) some kinds of psychological assumptions or interpretations. Yet, as will have become evident, many anthropologists are by no means favourably disposed towards psychology; much of the writing by anthropologists about psychology is characterized by a profound ambivalence, and this applies particularly to some of the British social anthropologists in the Durkheimian tradition. A fairly typical statement is the one by Needham (1962). ". . . in not one case or respect that I have been able to discover has psychology afforded in itself a satisfying or acceptable answer to a sociological problem." (p. 126.) Then there is a conciliatory footnote attached to the sentence:

> This is not to say, however, that psychological considerations are never of interest in relation to problems in social anthropology . . ., still less to deny the intrinsic importance or fascination of psychology.

It will be instructive to examine anthropologists' attitudes more closely, especially with a view to bringing out their conceptions as to what psychology is about.

Evans-Pritchard (1951) devoted a few pages to a discussion of the relationship between psychology and anthropology, concluding that the "attempt to construct social anthropology on the foundations of psychology has proved to be . . . an attempt to build a house on shifting sands" (p. 44). His reasons, in summary, were that psychology is concerned with psychical, and anthropology with social, systems; and even if they make the same observations of behaviour, they deal with them at different levels of abstraction. He gave as an example a trial by jury, which for anthropologists would constitute an instance of the operation of legal institutions, while for psychologists the area of concern would be the feelings, motives, and opinions of the actors.[1]

A more detailed discussion was published at the same time by Nadel (1951), himself originally trained as a psychologist and thereby in a better position to form a judgement. He identified two problem areas where psychology might help the anthropologist to understand social regularities. One concerns what he called 'innate action potentials', which roughly correspond to the 'biogrammar' in our current jargon; the problem is to discover what social behaviour or institutions are directly or indirectly determined by it. The second area relates to the so-called 'principle of psychological linkage', put forward earlier by Rivers, which holds that psychological processes may be treated as intervening variables between social antecedents and consequents. The task of psychology here would be that of helping to establish the nature of the link. Nadel (1951) also made a shrewd general remark which is as applicable today as it was then:

> Not infrequently, then, the anthropologist or sociologist is apt to treat psychology (whether he accepts it openly or not) as a stopgap rather than a discipline whose potentialities he has carefully assessed. His is often the emaciated, non-committal everyman's psychology, or some conventional psychology which he can adapt as it is expedient. Conversely, he will credit psychology with a convenient omniscience, and burden it with tasks which that science is incapable of executing.
>
> pp. 289–90

This is a very pertinent comment in view of the fact that most of the anthropologists who reject psychological explanations resort very freely —and it might be added, unavoidably—to statements about thoughts, beliefs, and feelings in their writings. The paradox has been noted by Firth (1964), who appealed to his fellow anthropologists to abandon what he termed a "ritual avoidance" of psychology. The tendency to make a virtue of the use of psychological language, coupled with a reluctance to consider more formal psychological approaches, has been defended by Gluckman (1964). Rejecting a hierarchical conception of the various sciences dealing with man, as proposed by Comte, Gluckman put forward the now widely accepted view that all these sciences share a common concern with the behaviour of humans but concentrate on different aspects of it. There is thus no need to assign an exclusive sphere to each of them, since they all employ essentially the same raw material. They are distinguished "not by the events they study but by the kinds of relations between events which they seek to establish . . . psychology looks at the interrelations between the acts of behaviour and the feelings and thoughts of individual men and their reactions to the psychical and social environment" (pp. 160–1).

The fact that the raw material is common means that social scientists of different disciplines may study exactly the same behaviour, but deal with it in different ways. Hence—and this is the burden of the argument—anthropologists are not precluded from concerning themselves with psychological aspects of behaviour:

> Thus a social anthropologist, like a psychologist, may study events of mental and emotional life—the actions and thoughts and feelings of individuals . . . The psychologist seeks to find the relations between these events as they occur *in the life of single individuals* [my italics], what Radcliffe-Brown called 'individual mental or psychical systems'. The social anthropologist seeks to find relations between these events as they

link together mental systems within a physical environment, i.e. he studies them within social systems.

p. 160

While anthropologists of the older school stressed that psychology concentrates on the *innate* features of behaviour, Gluckman is typical of a later trend to accentuate the *individual*. Given this line of reasoning, the anthropologist is perfectly entitled to 'psychologize' as much as he wishes, provided only that he is aware that he is "treating as simple facts events which for . . . other scientists are full of internal complexities" (p. 173). When it comes to actual examples, however, these are far removed from the 'naïvety' modestly claimed; it emerges that Gluckman attributed extraordinary psychological sophistication to the anthropologist in the field, which psychologists might well envy:

> But when studying a single social situation, the anthropologist has to analyse how the varying mental abilities and temperaments of individuals affect the working of institutions, without in general concerning himself with the internal relations within the psyches of these individuals.

p. 181

In practice, most anthropologists, while accepting Gluckman's central argument, would not go so far. By the 'naïvety' assumption, they merely understand that certain psychological categories like love and hate are self-evident and thus not in need of further explanation, which seems reasonable enough. However, one American anthropologist (Kennedy, 1967) took strong exception to Gluckman's position and wrote a sharp critique of it. Kennedy argued that all sociological analyses rest at least ultimately on psychological assumptions, and these ought to be made explicit. In his reply, Gluckman (1968) tried to distinguish between two senses of the term 'psychological' and claimed that he had used it in the strict sense of statements within the framework of the science of psychology, as distinct from ideas and emotions in individual psyches which are fair game for the anthropologist. While it would not be profitable to pursue the details of this dispute, Gluckman (1968) did provide a concrete example of what he regarded as the business of the psychologist, which is worth quoting; this relates to an analysis of circumcision ceremonies observed by him:

> It is the duty of the father to hold his son's penis during the circumcision. At one ceremony I watched, the first father's hands shook so much that he had to be replaced by a quite inappropriate relative, the mother's brother—but that was considered better than having the boy injured; the second father's hands were very steady and he kept his eyes

fixed on the circumciser's hands throughout the operation; the third
father's hands were equally steady, but he turned his head and gazed
steadily over his shoulder. It seemed to me that the circumcision of a son
signified something quite different to each of these men, and that those
differences presumably could be explained within the psychical system of
each of them, and not by general theories about how individual psychological mechanisms account for why societies have circumcision ceremonies . . .

p. 25

In his last sentence Gluckman distinguished two levels of motives,
namely, a general, whereby certain motivational constellations are
common to members of a certain culture (or even beyond), and a
specific one relating to individual variations. The former is presumably
within the domain of psychological anthropology, i.e. a specialization
within the discipline of anthropology. On the other hand, it is evident
that he viewed the psychologist's business as that of uncovering the
particular motivations of *individual* persons. While it may seem astonishing to psychologists to find such a view held by a distinguished anthropologist, it would be wrong to consider this as a singular aberration; in
fact, similar views are by no means uncommon. Since the issue is an
important one, another illustration drawn from more recent work will
be offered.

Hanson (1975), another anthropologist engaged in the battle against
the menace of psychological reductionism of the kind schematically
represented in Fig. 2.1, argued no doubt justifiably, that it is not
necessary or even appropriate to move up a ladder of abstraction from
'raw' behaviour via an individual psychological analysis to the institutional level (Fig. 2.1(a)). What he suggested instead, along the lines of
Gluckman's ideas, is that these constitute two separate modes of
analysis with quite different purposes, as shown in Fig. 2.1(b). What is
of interest here is how Hanson envisaged the distinction between
individual questions, which concern the psychologist, and the
institutional ones to be tackled by anthropologists. Again he provided
an example:

> One day during my fieldwork on the French Polynesian island of
> Rapa I was helping a few men with the heavy job of turning the soil to
> prepare a taro garden for cultivation. The sun was hot and we were
> perspiring freely. I picked up a jug of cool water I had brought and asked
> my comrades if they wanted to drink. They said no. When I then took a
> drink myself, they looked concerned and one of them told me I should
> not do that lest I get sick.
>
> Now we can ask the question, why did they refuse the water and

caution me against drinking? The question admits of two quite distinct answers, depending on our aim in asking it. If we want to know the Rapans' motives or reasons for acting as they did, we are asking an individual question and the answer in this case would be simply that they wanted to avoid illness both for themselves and for me. On the other hand we may want to know about the ideas which led the Rapans to

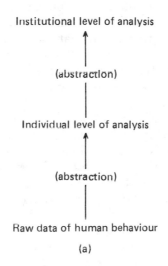

believe that drinking cold water when hot and perspiring can produce illness. This is an institutional question. It is not about people at all, but about concepts in their own right. In this case, the answer would detail the Rapan system of ideas relating health to body temperature, which in turn is affected by various foods. One implication of these ideas is that drinking cold water when the body is hot and perspiring can adversely affect bodily temperature and hence endanger health. To summarize the differences between individual and institutional questions: individual

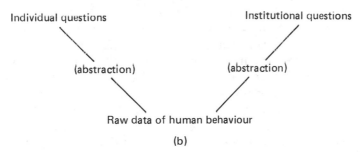

Fig. 2.1. Hanson's alternative schema of inference.

questions relate to the motives, intentions, reasons people have for doing
what they do; institutional questions concern concepts, forms of
organization, patterns of behaviour seen in relation to each other.

pp. 3–4

The so-called 'psychological' question here is so trite that an obvious
common-sense answer is entirely appropriate; no doubt Hanson, if he
were challenged on this, would say that he was merely concerned to
bring out a matter of principle so that the actual detail is secondary.
Nonetheless, it is surely no accident that examples of this kind may be
so readily found, indicating a tendency among anthropologists to view
psychology as being almost exclusively preoccupied with the study of
individual motivation.

The claim that widely held ideas and concepts fall within the
preserve of anthropology rather than psychology is one that social
psychologists especially would be reluctant to accept. It is of course true
that anthropologists refer to *systems* of ideas and beliefs, known as
'collective representations' that will be discussed more fully later; but it
might be mentioned here that the relationship between these and the
kinds of aggregate descriptive material produced by social psychologists remains somewhat problematic.

What could have led some anthropologists to have such a restrictive
outlook on psychology? I believe that there are two main answers to
this question. The first relates to the heritage of Durkheim, with whose
approach many anthropologists have been thoroughly indoctrinated.
Without wishing in any way to denigrate the seminal contributions
made by this great figure, it must be said that in the course of his
attempt to establish sociology as a science in its own right, he felt it
necessary for this purpose to pre-empt what now is the major part of
psychology. Above all, he sought to demonstrate the falsity of psychological reductionism, arguing that the interaction of individual minds
in society produced a new collective mentality *sui generis*, incapable of
being accounted for in terms of the individual psyche. Since, as
Durkheim was well aware, few psychological characteristics of individuals remain unaffected by social influences, all he left for psychology
was a very impoverished residue.[2] Thus, anthropologists as the
inheritors of the Durkheimian tradition reckon that ideas and concepts,
being largely social products, fall squarely within their sphere. There
is, of course, no point in a boundary dispute, though psychologists
would certainly reject any exclusion from the social sphere. What I
would rather like to stress is that the Durkheimian definition of their
subject-matter has led anthropologists to collect a great deal of material

about the ideas and beliefs of the peoples they studied that is of considerable interest for psychologists.

The second reason for the restricted outlook on psychology is distinct, yet not unrelated. Given the notion that psychology is concerned with individual motives, the school of thought that fits this mould most closely is psychoanalysis. Since there are other grounds (to be examined later) why anthropologists tend to be favourably disposed to it, the two factors tend to be mutually reinforcing. Hence, the image of the psychologist is often that of a specialist who probes deeply into the individual psyche. Hence, as Nadel rightly discerned, anthropologists sometimes attribute to psychologists powers of analysing individual behaviour which psychologists would not dream of arrogating themselves. This may be illustrated more concretely by a personal experience. Some years ago I attended a meeting of social anthropologists where a study of a particular group of people was presented. The speaker mentioned that the same group was subsequently subjected to personality testing by a psychologist, with the disparaging comment that the particular psychologist had not come up with any 'deeper' findings than the speaker. During the discussion I suggested that if a psychologist, after a mere few hours of testing, obtained findings about these people congruent with those of the anthropologist who had conducted intensive fieldwork over a lengthy period, then it was a matter of congratulation rather than the opposite. It was evident that this struck the anthropologist as an entirely novel standpoint, but one which, after some consideration, he was ready to accept.

The fact that psychologists and anthropologists sometimes deal with the same subject matter raises the question of the relationship between their explanatory models. The kind of scheme offered by Hanson in Fig. 2.1(b) is far too crude to be useful, and an attempt will be made to elaborate on it. A fuller model characterizing most of anthropology is presented in Fig. 2.2.

The starting point is behaviour in ordinary life, which is observed and recorded, prominently including material obtained from informants. The first step, then, is the careful marshalling of the data into an ethnographic account, followed by the analysis of the data, and finally resulting in a 'working model' of the system. The temporal sequence implied by this presentation is rather misleading because naturally the fieldworker will have the ultimate goal in mind from the outset, and this will influence the kind of material collected; moreover, the interval between fieldwork and the final culmination is typically a matter of years. The interpretation/verification occurs at several stages and can take different forms. First of all, the anthropologist will formulate hypotheses, or play hunches, while still in the field, thereby permitting immediate verification by further observation directed specifically at the problem. After the return from the field, when the anthropologist has worked out the structure of the social system, there will be checking of the field notes to make sure that the behaviour

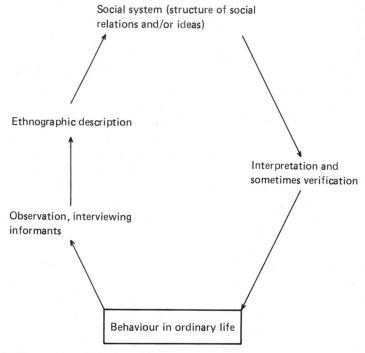

Fig. 2.2. The anthropological model. Note: The feedback shown on the right usually takes place while the anthropologist is still in the field.

observed is consonant with the system. The latter is, of course, a kind of 'hermeneutic circle' rather than independent verification. Not infrequently there is a return trip to the field for collecting additional material; or another anthropologist may work in the same community, which may be regarded as substantially, though not entirely, independent verification. It may be mentioned in passing that the unavoidable time lapse, with its intervening social changes, makes the problem of verification a difficult one. Lastly, the field material may be independently re-analysed; or if certain general principles have been deduced, these can be applied to data from other peoples in order to determine whether they fit.

With regard to the corresponding psychological models, there are at least two rather than one. Figure 2.3 shows the most widely prevalent 'experimental' model. The dotted lines surrounding 'behaviour in ordinary life' indicate that this is not normally a primary concern, nor is the relating back of the findings to such ordinary behaviour. It is true that, as has been mentioned earlier, there is an increasing demand for such concern; but so far, it is certainly the exception rather than the rule. The typical core of such work is, thus, the testing of hypotheses relating to such part-functions as perception or cognition, leading to inferences about the nature of the underlying processes and nothing further.

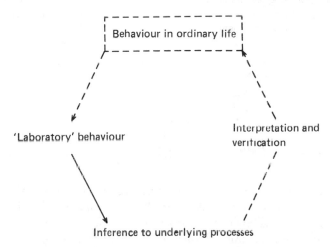

FIG. 2.3. The experimental model in psychology. The broken lines indicate that, with the exception of applied experimental psychologists, the relationships to behaviour in ordinary life are seldom considered.

The 'clinical' model outlined in Fig. 2.4 is very different. The starting point is the behaviour of the person in everyday life, as it is with anthropologists, though observation can seldom be employed. Instead, a battery of devices are deployed and the responses are analysed, leading to an inference about the psychodynamics of the individual person. In the clinical setting this forms the basis for strategies intended to bring about some modifications of behaviour, the success of which has then to be checked against behaviour in ordinary life.

From what has been said earlier, it should be evident that anthropologists are apt to consider the 'clinical' as *the* psychological model. While this is a mistake, the fact remains that it is one of the psychological models and as such may relate to the same behaviour as that studied by the anthropologist. In that case it would seem that an 'explanation' of the behaviour could be sought either by moving

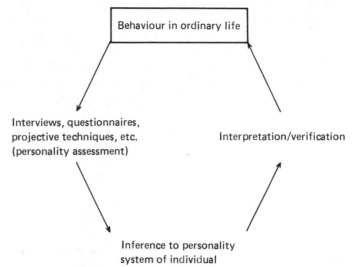

FIG. 2.4. The clinical model in psychology. Unlike the experimental, the clinical model relates to individual cases.

upwards to the social system, or downwards to the personality system. This has indeed been suggested, and the particular version I propose to examine is that of Devereux (1961a, 1978);[3] it is of special interest in the present context since Doise (1978) made use of the ideas of Devereux in an effort to demonstrate that social psychology can serve to integrate psychology and sociology (which in the present context is synonymous with anthropology).

The key to Devereux's position is the so-called 'Principle of complementarity', which he somewhat grandiosely claims to derive from Heisenberg's 'uncertainty principle':

> There exists an *inevitable* complementarity relationship between the psychological explanation and the sociological explanation of the same phenomenon . . . I subject here to a double analysis only one small raw fact . . .
>
> *The Raw Fact:* The Mohave witch Sahaykwisā incited her two lovers to kill her.
>
> 1. *Psychological Explanation:*
>   (a) *Operant Motive:* Sahaykwisā's self-destructiveness was so great that she would have managed to get herself murdered in any society;

    (b) *Instrumental Motive:* Qua Mohave witch, persuaded that it is only by getting herself murdered that she could perpetuate her hold on the shades of her (beloved) victims, she *proclaimed* herself a witch. In the Mohave socio-cultural setting, this made her murder inevitable.

2. *Sociological Explanation:*

    (a) *Operant Motive* = instrumental motive of the psychological explanation.

    (b) *Instrumental Motive* = operant motive of the psychological explanation

Devereux, 1978, pp. 10–11

Thus it would appear that an exceedingly difficult and vexing problem has been solved at one stroke by the statement of a simple symmetrical relationship, which Doise (1978, p. 56) cites with approval. But has the problem really been disposed of, or are we faced with little more than an intellectual conjuring trick producing an illusion?

First of all, it might be pointed out that an explanation in terms of 'motive' cannot be regarded as a 'sociological' explanation. One might also quibble about the label 'self-destructiveness', but I shall not do so, assuming that Devereux, as a competent psychoanalyst, has properly arrived at his diagnosis on the basis of an intensive study of the psychodynamics of the 'witch'. However, since she would allegedly have arranged for her murder wherever she might have lived, we are really faced with *two* distinct phenomena:[4] one, the fact that she gets herself murdered by whatever means; two, the particular manner in which she gets herself murdered. The former is 'explained' psychologically, the latter sociologically.

It should also be noted that no explication of the terms 'operant' and 'instrumental' is provided, so their use remains unclear. This becomes important when one wants to distinguish, as Devereux does, between the nature of psychological and sociological explanations. In the last analysis the difference vanishes, since the mere reversal of the labels attached to the identical pair of so-called 'explanations' seems to be little more than an empty formula.

The case of the Mohave witch is of course somewhat esoteric, but Devereux also illustrated the principle of complementarity with reference to the motives of the people who took part in the Hungarian Revolution (which is cited by Doise) and another, more homely, example which will be instructive to discuss. In that context he also wrote about 'predicting' and 'understanding', all of which are apparently covered by complementarity:

. . . the *more fully* I understand John Doe's anger over the arrival of his mother-in-law in socio-cultural terms (autonomy of the occidental nuclear family, the traditional stereotype of the mother-in-law, etc.), the less I can understand it *simultaneously* in psychological terms (John Doe's irritability, his wife's infantile dependence on her mother, the mother-in-law's meddlesomeness, etc.)—and vice-versa of course. It is *logically impossible* to think simultaneously in terms of two different frames of reference, especially if, in terms of one of these, the key explanation is: "All mothers-in-law are defined by our culture as nuisances", while in the other system the key explanation is: "Mrs Roe systematically interferes with her daughter's marriage." Needless to say, the same complementarity relationship also obtains between the sociological and the psychological understanding of phenomena involving large groups and nations.

Devereux, 1978, pp. 119–20; all italics in original

It is hard to see why there is so much ado about logical impossibility; while literally true, it is also trivial, since one has no trouble switching from one frame to the other in a moment—so let us leave that aside. What is worth noting is that all the examples given are of a type where psychological and socio-cultural determinants of the phenomena are *congruent*. The implication of this, which may be analysed in relation to the case of the mother-in-law, will help to clarify the problem. Devereux mentions two socio-cultural factors: autonomy of the occidental nuclear family, and stereotypes. The first of these is surprising, as the mother-in-law issue is encountered in most parts of the world and by no means confined to occidental cultures. Ever since Radcliffe-Brown (1952), most anthropologists have viewed this issue in terms of the structure of social relationships. The social roles of mother- and son-in-law (and sometimes also father- and daughter-in-law) are fraught with potential tension and conflict; this in itself has nothing to do with the psychological characteristics of the individuals occupying these roles, but relates to such issues as power and authority within the kin group. Consequently, social norms have evolved that have the function of minimizing the occasions for such conflicts and thereby protecting the common interest of the kin group as a whole. These norms frequently enjoin the son-in-law to show particular respect to the mother-in-law and restrict the kinds of communication permissible between them; sometimes they enforce what is known as mother-in-law 'avoidance', whereby they are not permitted face-to-face contact. The mother-in-law question is, therefore, regarded by anthropologists as a function of the social system as such.

From this standpoint, stereotypes are probably a secondary manifestation arising from the awareness of the potential conflict, even where no special social rules govern the relationship. Stereotypes are built into the person in the course of his or her upbringing, and they can exist in the absence of the actual object—unmarried men can have stereotypes about mothers-in-law. It should be noted that such culturally built-in dispositions straddle the boundary between the sociological and the psychological; they are, as it were, two sides of the same coin.

The primary explanation of such phenomena is therefore socio-logical, and their psychological aspects may, from one perspective, be regarded as epiphenomena. Thus the 'meddlesomeness' attributed to the mother-in-law may be merely a manifestation of the role conflict ex-pressed in psychological terms. The extent of the problem in particular instances is another matter and may require special explanation, though not necessarily a psychological one. Sheer physical distance can be an important factor: where the married couple live with the wife's family, the strain is likely to be maximal. Finally, individual psychological factors can account for unusually good or bad relation-ships between in-laws; one or the other or both may be exceptionally tolerant, tactful, and so on (or the opposite).

It should be evident by now that Devereux's principle of comple-mentarity, on which Doise relied for support, will not bear close scrutiny since it fails to give sufficient consideration to social system determinants of behaviour. Moreover, since social psychology has little if anything to say about such systems, it cannot, as Doise (1978) claims, help to integrate psychology and sociology. While Doise was thus unwise in seeking support from Devereux, he must be given credit for attempting to build bridges between the individual and social level. Moreover, he and his colleagues have conducted a brilliant series of studies concerned with social interaction, which constitute a significant contribution to our understanding of the relationships between these levels (Doise and Mugny, 1981).

There are still further lessons to be learnt by considering the several quite distinct types of examples discussed by Devereux. The Mohave witch is a unique personality in a specific cultural milieu; the partici-pants in the Hungarian Revolution were a set of people with varying individual personalities sharing a common goal and caught up also in a unique event. By contrast, the mother-in-law case is one of an enduring constellation of social role-relationships to be found in similar form in numerous cultures. Let me now take these in turn: the unique Mohave witch requires an explanation in terms of the clinical model of Fig. 2.4, made by someone closely familiar with the culture. Devereux has these qualifications, and were it not for certain problems associated with this particular case,[5] one might in principle accept such an account. The Hungarian Revolution was an event of a kind that does not lend itself to 'explanation' in terms of either varied individual motivations or the collective 'motivation' of the Hungarian people "who revolted against the system" (Devereux, 1978, p. 122), which latter is merely an uninformative descriptive statement. The analysis of such unique collective events is primarily the business of the historian. As Hofstadter (1972) put it:

> Social scientists, concerned as they are with the dynamics of behavior, are like the engineers who can tell about the dynamics of flight. Historians are concerned with such questions as why a particular scheduled flight has ended in a crash.
>
> p. 366

This leaves the mother-in-law problem to be further pursued—not that of John Doe, but of all sons-in-law in a given society. The previous formulation was in absolute terms, but this requires qualification as social institutions and social relationships change over time. Once this is taken into account, the primacy of the sociological level can no longer be asserted, since it is the feelings and perceptions of individuals in interaction that maintain particular systems of social relations. As the mother-in-law problem is tied up with a set of basic family relationships that are widespread and not usually subject to rapid change, it will be easier to illustrate the matter in relation to a marriage system. In parts of West Africa cross-cousin marriage was traditionally favoured, whereby a man had a special relationship with his maternal uncle and was usually expected to marry his daughter. With the spread of European influence, and especially education, the system began to produce psychological difficulties. In accordance with traditional practice but applied to a new objective, men would receive help with the costs of their education from the uncle, thereby incurring the usual debt of gratitude. However, they no longer readily accepted the need to marry a particular girl, especially if—as was mostly the case in the 1950s—the girl was illiterate. Yet a refusal would have caused great offence, so that for a period many young men experienced profound conflict.[6] The feelings and attitudes that had supported the system gave way to strain and both intra- and inter-personal conflict, with the result that the system began to disintegrate. Note that this can hardly be viewed as simply an instance of psychological causation in terms of 'motives', for it would be equally true to say that radical socio-economic changes were the 'real' cause. The relationship is best regarded as a dialectical or feedback process, whereby social system and psychological factors are in continuous interaction. What one can say is that there must be at least broad congruence between psychological dispositions and systems of social relationship if the latter are to remain relatively stable over time. This implies that considerable parts of the individual personality system will consist of similar characteristics within a given socio-cultural system. The manner in which such similarity is brought about and the general nature of the relationship is one of the main concerns of what used to be called 'culture and personality', but, owing to a widening of its scope, has now come to be known as 'psychological anthropology'.

While there is this specialization in (mainly American) anthro-pology, it should be evident from the earlier discussion that all social or cultural anthropologists are fully aware of the importance of psycho-logical factors, but, as already indicated, there is a good deal of uncer-tainty as to how they ought to be handled. Some anthropologists adopt a sturdy common sense view and do not allow themselves to be unduly troubled by this issue. An example would be the study by Lewis (1966) of spirit possession cults, one of which he regards as of wide significance since it relates to a situation that is not uncommon in various parts of the world. This concerns a malevolent sprite who is said to 'seize' women in Somalia and cause symptoms ranging from mild hysteria to depression or sometimes organic troubles. The sprite is said to be consumed with envy and greed, seeking luxurious clothes, perfumes, and rare foods. The cure requires the provision of these to the sprite—who of course inhabits the women and causes the symptoms—as well as the mounting of an elaborate and expensive dance.

Lewis interprets this in terms of the position of women in a harsh, male-dominated pastoral society where the woman is, or at least feels herself to be, disadvantaged, lonely, and neglected. Thus it is not sur-prising that either illnesses should be interpreted in terms of possession by the *sar* sprite, or that psychosomatic symptoms should be produced. Lewis' evidence indicates that such attacks were particularly liable to occur at stressful periods such as the husband's preliminary arrange-ments to the taking of a second wife.

One intriguing aspect is that, as Lewis observes, such insights are not a monopoly of the anthropological observer; husbands are liable to be sceptical and to suspect their wives of malingering. But the issue is complex: "Despite this sociological view of the situation, men's attitudes are in fact ambivalent; they believe in the existence of these *sar* sprites, but with true Somali pragmatism they are very sceptical when their own womenfolk and their own pockets are affected.'' (p. 314.)

This robust and in my view sensible line of argument would be repudiated by some anthropologists who maintain that it is not the business of anthropology to speculate about inner psychological states. Others maintain just as passionately that the buck cannot be passed to the psychologists, and the argument rages most fiercely in the sphere of religious belief and ritual, as indicated by the following passage:

> Just what does 'belief' mean in a religious context? Of all the problems surrounding attempts to conduct anthropological analysis of religion this is the one that has perhaps been most troublesome and therefore the most often avoided, usually by relegating to psychology, that raffish outcast discipline [sic!] to which social anthropologists are forever consigning phenomena they are unable to deal with within the framework of a denatured Durkheimianism. But the problem will not go away, it is not 'merely' psychological (nothing social is) . . .
>
> Geertz, 1966, pp. 24–5

The whole question of whether there is such a thing as 'belief' has been the subject of an entire volume by Needham (1972). This consists of analysis of the concept, mainly in linguistic and philosophical terms —psychology as an empirical discipline only crops up in a passing reference to Vygotsky. The conclusion of this fascinating if somewhat scholastic discourse is that we must ''give up the received idea that this verbal concept corresponds to a distinct and natural capacity that is shared by all human beings'' (p. 191). Far from being a general feature of human mental processes, it is ''only a psychological replication of a grammatical particular'' (p. 213). While the meaning of this last phrase is obscure to me, Needham has performed a useful service in demonstrating how nebulous the notion of 'belief' really is.[7] Psychologists tend to evade the issue by using a simple operational definition, but Needham's work shows that this will not do, cross-culturally speaking. The word is of course a useful one, and anthropologists have not abandoned it but have become more cautious in its use; some continue the effort to find a rational defence for it, as for instance Southwold (1979):

> This analysis serves to make plain why it is that ascriptions of believing . . . do not require special knowledge of the inner mental state (or psychological attitudes) of the believer. It should be evident that the verb 'believe' designates a relation rather than a state: a relation, firstly between the believer and a proposition, and secondly from the believer through the proposition to reality. What is purported to occur is doubtless mental in large part, and special psychological knowledge would

doubtless help us to assess and understand it better. But special knowledge is not necessary, since in fact we use 'believe' in a way which enables us to regard the mind of the believer as a 'black box' . . .

p. 638

What is striking about this passage is Southwold's false belief (if this expression be permitted) that his special knowledge would place the psychologist in a privileged position. Perhaps this may be true to some extent of the psychoanalyst or clinical psychologist intensively assessing the psychodynamics of a particular individual, whereby a belief could be understood within the broader personality context. However, when it comes to beliefs shared by members of a group or society, which is the anthropologist's normal concern, the social psychologists studying these will, with very rare exceptions (for example, Smith et al., 1956), also treat the individual as no more than a black box.

While some anthropologists attribute to psychologists knowledge, skills, and insights which, alas, they seldom possess, others seem inclined to declare them altogether redundant. These are the more extreme proponents of the doctrine of 'psychic unity';[8] fortunately, they are unusual, and the absurdity of their position has been pointed out by other anthropologists. One of the clearest statements of the implications of such a view is by Murphy (1971):

. . . some anthropologists have taken his Durkheim's strictures on psychological explanations to mean that the latter have no place at all in a social science. They argue that there is a psychic unity of mankind that allows us to take psychology as given—this is a negative formulation of the older doctrine of psychic unity that went on to state that the laws and stages of progress of the intellect, the order of emergence of ideas, would therefore be everywhere the same. What is advanced is a view of human nature that is negative. With the disclaimer that it attributes uniformity to human psychology, it actually attributes nothing to it. It is not so much that men are vessels filled with much the same liquids as that they are empty. Behind the rejection of the relevance of psychological processes, there is a clear psychological assumption, that man is infinitely malleable and plastic, so thoroughly shaped by his social milieu that his influence, singly or in aggregates, can be discounted.

pp. 68–8

Lest anyone be tempted to chide anthropologists who disdain psychology for their naïvety, it should be pointed out that some psychologists also seek refuge in similar notions when it appears convenient. Thus Gerard and Conolley (1972), faced with the critique that social psychological experiments conducted with college sophomores may not be generalizable to people in other cultures, fall back upon what they termed "the abiding faith in the basic universals of humankind" (p. 242), which is nothing else but our old friend 'psychic unity' in a slightly different garb. Hence, we have the amazing paradox whereby one and the same principle is invoked by anthropologists who wish to claim that all that matters is culture, and by psychologists who want to argue that culture does not matter! The paradox arises from the fact that, as Murphy rightly stated, such labels as 'psychic unity' or 'basic universals' are devoid of any substantive content. This leaves it open for people (who would find it inconvenient if particular psychological functions were to vary across cultures) simply to assume that these remain constant. In reality it is as yet far from certain, as Lonner (1980) clearly showed, what may be regarded as 'psychological universals' as contrasted to what may be functions subject to cultural or other environmental influences.[9]

Notes

1. It is of interest to note that Beattie (1964), while in agreement with Evans-Pritchard's general arguments, which he cited with approval, modified the trial illustration so as to present psychologists' interests more realistically; e.g. "What factors in the life-history of the accused might have led him to commit the offence?" (p. 26).
2. Details of his arguments may be found in Durkheim (*The Division of Labour in Society* (1893) and *The Rules of Sociological Method* (1895)).
3. Since my position is a highly critical one as regards this particular issue, I should like to record here my considerable respect and admiration for many other aspects of Devereux's work.
4. Such a claim is at least open to some question, for it assumes that in another culture the life-history generating the self-destructive impulses would have been the same.
5. When one refers to the full account of the case in Devereux (1961, pp. 416ff.), it transpires that this was a story told to Devereux by an informant through an interpreter about the life of a witch who lived and died in the nineteenth century! The story has in many respects the character of a myth, and a causal interpretation based on it seems highly hazardous, if not far-fetched.
6. Some enterprising graduates in the then newly independent countries managed to escape the problem by joining the diplomatic service!
7. If one looks it up in the *International Encyclopedia of the Social Sciences*, the entry reads merely: "Belief—*see* Attitudes, Ideology, Myth and Symbol, Norms, Religion, Values."

8. One of its most crass expressions is as follows: "How is human behaviour to be explained? . . . Man's behaviour is *fully* [my italics] explained by culture. Man learns to think, feel, believe and strive for that which his culture considers proper." (Freilich, 1972, p. 1.)

9. Since this chapter was written Cole (1981) has published two thoughtful essays dealing with historical and contemporary relationships between psychological and anthropological approaches to the study of cognition. Being exclusively concerned with cognition, the focus of the discussion is considerably narrower than the present one. Within this context Cole proposed a common unit of analysis that could serve psychologists and anthropologists alike, variously labelled as an 'activity', 'task' or 'event'. Conceived as an intersection between social structure and individual psychological processes, it is offered as a joint framework for both disciplines. The overall theoretical sweep of Cole's argument is impressive, but the concrete detail rather less so. Thus the notion that "the acquisition of culturally appropriate behaviour is a process of *interaction* between children and adults . . ." (2nd essay, p. 21) can hardly be regarded as a novel insight. Nonetheless Cole is surely right in suggesting that a joint empirical attack by both disciplines on the details of such processes is desirable.

3 | The Craft and Science of Anthropology

In the preceding chapter some misconceptions about psychology prevalent among many anthropologists have been highlighted, and I have also referred to the debate that takes place from time to time about the role, if any, of psychology in anthropological explanations. On the other hand, a considerable number of anthropologists are very well informed about psychology,[1] while few psychologists have more than vague notions about the task of the anthropologist. Hence, it will be useful to provide at least a brief sketch of anthropologists' approaches to their work. It is usual for a discipline to appear monolithic to the outsider, while the inside view is more that of a set of warring factions in perpetual crisis. One of the fundamental underlying issues is whether anthropology[2] belongs to the sciences or the humanities. Evans-Pritchard (1951) was a proponent of the latter view, holding that anthropology, like history, is concerned with the study of the *unique*. According to this view, each society or culture constitutes a coherent whole that has to be understood in its own terms; while comparisons between cultures may sometimes be instructive, there are inherent limitations on what can be meaningfully compared, so that an aim of arriving at general laws would be unrealistic. At the opposite extreme are theorists like Murdock (1949), who regards comparisons as the *raison d'être* of anthropology. He maintains that the study of particular cultures is merely the means of arriving, through systematic comparisons, at high-level generalizations about cultures and social structures.

A related issue is that concerning the so-called 'emic' versus 'etic' approaches. Within British anthropology this arose well before this terminology came to be applied: Radcliffe-Brown viewed anthropology as a hard science dealing with objective facts, while Evans-Pritchard rebelled against this and emphasized the need to reach as far as possible the insider's perspective on a culture. The naming of this kind of dichotomy was first proposed by a linguist, Pike (1954, 1966), and derived from the terms 'phonetic' and 'phonemic'. The phonetic analysis of the sounds of a language deals with the body parts involved in the production of speech utterances, while the phonemic analysis is based on the system of sound contrasts native speakers have stored in their heads and by means of which they identify meaningful utterances. This kind of distinction was then transferred analogically to the study of cultures. In that context, the etic approach can be characterized as an external one, so that behaviour is studied in terms of criteria brought in by the external observer. Such criteria are often implicitly regarded as scientific, objective, and universal, though this is disputable. In any case, the external observer who comes into the culture brings these with him and creates a system with the aid of these criteria. Thus, etic statements are those whose meanings can at least in principle be verified by independent investigators using similar operations.

By contrast, the emic approach treats behaviour as part of a pre-existing structure and the purpose is to describe that structure in its own terms and without reference to externally imposed criteria. Thus, emic statements concern meanings and distinctions that are part of the cultural system being studied. Pelto (1970), in a book on anthropological methods, made a great deal of the difference between 'eticists' and 'emicists', and it certainly continues as the topic of lively debate. Cross-cultural psychologists also tend to worry about it, but in my view quite unnecessarily since they never study cultural systems as wholes, so that a truly emic approach is simply not open to them (G. Jahoda, 1977). In practice many fieldworkers tend, with varying emphasis on one or the other, to use both approaches—sometimes floating unawares between them. There are, of course, those who are very clear as to what they are aiming at; thus the proponents of the so-called 'new ethnography' concentrated deliberately and exclusively on emic study; other workers, especially Harris (1968), whose theoretical stance is materialist (though not Marxist), feel that an undue emic bias runs the risk of what they call 'mentalist' (i.e. psychological) interpretations to which they strongly object.[3] The same problem is sometimes conceptualized as the contrast between the 'observer's model' and the 'indigenous model' of socio-cultural phenomena, especially as a result of the influence of Lévi-Strauss, whose work highlighted the natives' constructions of their own models.

While these issues are primarily theoretical, though with important implications about the kinds of data to be collected, there is of course also a great deal of discussion concerning methods. Psychologists with a merely superficial acquaintance with an anthropology are, as has already been shown, apt to dismiss the methods of the sister-discipline as 'soft'. While there is some truth in this, much of the criticism is a result of misunderstanding. Anthropologists themselves have frequently acknowledged certain shortcomings, such as a somewhat cavalier attitude about numbers, common failure to specify the type and frequency of the observations on which generalizations are based, treating preliterate communities as more homogeneous than they in fact are, and the related fault of stressing dominant modalities of behaviour and glossing over variant and deviant forms (Kluckhohn, 1959). Such flaws were more glaring among past generations of workers than they are today.

Accusations of neglecting random sampling of populations and questions of representativeness often miss the point, since anthropologists quite deliberately and for good reasons follow another strategy, as Leach (1967) showed very clearly:

> . . . the sociologist must operate with a random sample of the population. This means that *by definition* the units of population must be assumed to be unrelated to one another. It follows that no characteristics of the population which emerge can possibly be attributed to the interrelationships existing between different units. In contrast, the anthropologist explicitly concentrates on data which are *not* random. He purposely chooses a small field within which all the observable phenomena are closely interrelated and interdependent.
>
> p. 87

This is because the major aims of such anthropologists is that of studying the functioning of a social *system* rather than to obtain a general picture of population characteristics. The two objectives are, of course, not mutually exclusive, being sometimes combined in work on such specific institutions as marriage. However, the primary task of the field anthropologist is ethnography, the descriptive account of a community or group of people. The key methods employed are direct observation combined with the interviewing of 'informants'.[4] Depending upon the theoretical orientation of the fieldworker, the relative emphasis on these two methods will vary: those interested primarily in the structure of ideas, norms, and rules will rely more on what people say, while workers more concerned with the patterning of actual social behaviour will depend relatively more upon observation of what people do. In the past, psychologists were somewhat scornful of 'mere observation', and while it has recently gained favour—especially among developmental psychologists[5]—the old attitudes tend to persist. This is regrettable, for one of the weaknesses of psychology is a failure to appreciate the importance of careful description of natural behaviour, which biologists as well as anthropologists recognize. It must be admitted, of course, that the opportunities for fruitful observation are much greater in a tropical village setting than in a northern urban environment. The anthropologist sitting in a matrilineal village can build up a map of social structure by just noting who carries food from one compound to another.

In addition to observations and interviews, many anthropologists also make use of some of the sophisticated tools now available in the social sciences; yet for all that, it remains generally true that data collection is not normally standardized. This issue is sometimes discussed (see, for example, *The Craft of Social Anthropology*, edited by Epstein, 1967), and anthropologists are divided over it as may be illustrated by a recent debate. Moles (1977) advocated more operationalization of concepts, standardized data collection techniques and measurements, and more attention to problems of reliability and validity. In fact, he pointed to psychology as a model to be emulated! One of his main arguments, which has considerable substance, is that the lack of standardization is hazardous. In the ensuing discussion Moles found few whole-hearted supporters, though there was widespread recognition of the need for some improvements. However, many comments were to the effect that Moles, in his reforming zeal for standardization and measurement, was in danger of losing sight of the basic objectives of anthropological inquiry. All methods have virtues and drawbacks, and Moles had given insufficient consideration to the latter.

It is difficult to describe the strengths and weaknesses of the traditional style of fieldwork in the abstract to anyone not familiar with it. Hence, it will be necessary to try and convey a reasonably full picture of the nature of fieldwork, which is unique in the social sciences. It has been said that fieldwork is a *rite de passage* for becoming a fully fledged anthropologist—and not without reason. It is in fact often a gruelling test, involving at the outset loneliness and anxiety, occasionally coupled with actual physical illness. Ideally, it required infinite tact and patience, and the fieldworker is faced with moral as well as scientific problems.

In order to convey something of the 'feel' of the start of fieldwork, two different accounts will be cited. The first describes, with a poetic touch, the day of arrival at a beautiful Polynesian island—on the whole a pleasant experience, merely tinged with some apprehension about the problems ahead:

In the cool of the early morning, just before sunrise, the bow of the *Southern Cross* headed towards the eastern horizon, on which a tiny blue dark outline was faintly visible. Slowly it grew into a rugged mountain mass, standing up sheer from the ocean; then as we approached within a few miles it revealed around its base a narrow ring of low, flat land, thick with vegetation. The sullen grey day with its lowering clouds strengthened my grim impression of a solitary peak, wild and stormy, upthrust in a waste of waters.

In an hour or so we were close in-shore, and could see canoes coming round from the south, outside the reef, on which the tide was low. The outrigger-fitted craft drew near, the men in them bare to the waist, girdled with bark-cloth, large fans stuck in the backs of their belts, tortoise-shell rings or rolls of leaf in the ear-lobes and nose, bearded, and with long hair flowing loosely over their shoulders. Some plied the rough heavy paddles, some had finely plaited pandanus-leaf mats resting on the thwarts beside them, some had large clubs or spears in their hands. The ship anchored on a short cable in the open bay off the coral reef. Almost before the chain was down the natives began to scramble aboard, coming over the side by any means that offered, shouting fiercely to each other and to us in a tongue of which not a word was understood by the Mota-speaking folk of the mission vessel. I wondered how such turbulent human material could ever be induced to submit to scientific study.

Vahihaloa, my 'boy', looked over the side from the upper deck. "My word, me fright too much", he said with a quavering laugh; "me tink this fella man him he savvy kaikai me." *Kaikai* is the pidgin-English term for 'eat'. For the first time, perhaps, he began to doubt the wisdom of having left what was to him the civilization of Tulagi, the seat of Government four-hundred miles away, in order to stay with me for a year in this far-off spot among such wild-looking savages. Feeling none too certain myself of the reception that awaited us—though I knew that it would stop short of cannibalism—I reassured him, and we began to get out the stores. Later we went ashore in one of the canoes. As we came to the edge of the reef our craft halted on account of the falling tide. We slipped overboard on to the coral rock and began to wade ashore hand in hand with our hosts, like children at a party, exchanging smiles in lieu of anything more intelligible or tangible at the moment. We were surrounded by crowds of naked chattering youngsters, with their pleasant light-brown velvet skins and straight hair, so different from the Melanesians we had left behind. They darted about splashing like a shoal of fish some of them falling bodily into pools in their enthusiasm. At last the long wade ended, we climbed up the steeply shelving beach, crossed the soft, dry sand strewn with the brown needles

of the Casuarina trees—a home-like touch; it was like a pine avenue—
and were led to an old chief, clad with great dignity in a white coat and a
loin-cloth, who awaited us on his stool under a large shady tree.

Even with the pages of my diary before me it is difficult to reconstruct
the impressions of that first day ashore—to depersonalize the people I
later came to know so well and view them as merely a part of the tawny
surging crowd; to put back again into that unreal perspective, events
which afterwards took on such different values. In his early experiences
in the field the anthropologist is constantly grappling with the intangible.
The reality of the native life is going on all around him, but he himself is
not yet in focus to see it. He knows that most of what he records at first
will be useless: it will be either definitely incorrect, or so inadequate that
it must later be discarded. Yet he must make a beginning somewhere.
He realizes that at this stage he is incapable of separating the pattern of
custom from the accidentals of individual behaviour, he wonders if each
slight gesture does not hold some meaning which is hidden from him, he
aches to be able to catch and retain some of the flood of talk he hears on
all sides, and he is consumed with envy of the children who are able to
toss about so lightly that speech which he must so painfully acquire. He
is conscious of good material running to waste before him moment by
moment; he is impressed by the vastness of the task that lies before him
and of his own feeble equipment for it; in the face of a language and
custom to which he has not the key, he feels that he is acting like a moron
before the natives. At the same time he is experiencing the delights of
discovery, he is gaining an inkling of what is in store; like a gourmet
walking round a feast that is spread, he savours in anticipation the
quality of what he will later appreciate in full.

Firth, 1957b, pp. 1–2[6]

The second passage, at the opposite extreme, vividly describes the
shattering first encounter with a South American Indian group:

My first day in the field illustrated to me what my teachers meant
when they spoke of 'culture shock'. I had traveled in a small, aluminum
rowboat propelled by a large outboard motor for two and a half days.
This took me from the Territorial capital, a small town on the Orinocco
River, deep into Yạnomamö country. On the morning of the third day
we reached a small mission settlement, the field 'headquarters' of a
group of Americans who were working in two Yạnomamö villages . . .
We picked up a passenger at the mission station, James P. Barker, the
first non-Yạnomamö to make a sustained, permanent contact with the
tribe (in 1950) . . . He agreed to accompany me to the village I had
selected for my base of operations to introduce me to the Indians . . .

We arrived at the village, Bisaasi-teri, about 2:00 p.m. and docked
the boat along the muddy bank at the terminus of the path used by the
Indians to fetch their drinking water. It was hot and muggy, and my

clothing was soaked with perspiration. It clung uncomfortably to my body, as it did thereafter for the remainder of the work. The small, biting gnats were out in astronomical numbers, for it was the beginning of the dry season. My face and hands were swollen from the venom of their numerous stings. In just a few moments I was to meet my first Yąnomamö, my first primitive man. What would it be like? I had visions of entering the village and seeing 125 social facts running about calling each other kinship terms and sharing food, each waiting and anxious to have me collect his genealogy. I would wear them out in turn. Would they like me? This was important to me; I wanted them to be so fond of me that they would adopt me into their kinship system and way of life, because I had heard that successful anthropologists always get adopted by their people. I had learned during my seven years of anthropological training at the University of Michigan that kinship was equivalent to society in primitive tribes and that it was a moral way of life, 'moral' being something 'good' and 'desirable'. I was determined to work my way into their moral system of kinship and become a member of their society.

My heart began to pound as we approached the village and heard the buzz of activity within the circular compound. Mr Barker commented that he was anxious to see if any changes had taken place while he was away and wondered how many of them had died during his absence. I felt into my back pocket to make sure that my notebook was still there and felt personally more secure when I touched it. Otherwise, I would not have known what to do with my hands.

The entrance to the village was covered with brush and dry palm leaves. We pushed them aside to expose the low opening to the village. The excitement of meeting my first Indians was almost unbearable as I duck-waddled through the low passage into the village clearing.

I looked up and gasped when I saw a dozen, burly, naked, filthy, hideous men staring at us down the shafts of their drawn arrows! Immense wads of green tobacco were stuck between their lower teeth and lips making them look even more hideous, and strands of dark-green slime dripped or hung from their noses. We arrived at the village while the men were blowing a hallucinogenic drug up their noses. One of the side effects of the drug is a runny nose. The mucus is always saturated with the green powder and the Indians usually let it run freely from their nostrils. My next discovery was that there were a dozen or so vicious, underfed dogs snapping at my legs, circling me as if I were going to be their next meal. I just stood there holding my notebook, helpless and pathetic. Then the stench of the decaying vegetation and filth struck me and I almost got sick. I was horrified. What sort of a welcome was this for the person who came here to live with you and learn your way of life, to become friends with you? They put their weapons down when they recognized Barker and returned to their chanting, keeping a nervous eye on the village entrances.

We had arrived just after a serious fight. Seven women had been abducted the day before by a neighbouring group, and the local men and their guests had just that morning recovered five of them in a brutal club fight that nearly ended in a shooting war. The abductors, angry because they lost five of the seven captives, vowed to raid the Bisaasi-teri. When we arrived and entered the village unexpectedly, the Indians feared that we were the raiders. On several occasions during the next two hours the men in the village jumped to their feet, armed themselves, and waited nervously for the noise outside the village to be identified. My enthusiasm for collecting ethnographic curiosities diminished in proportion to the number of times such an alarm was raised. In fact, I was relieved when Mr Barker suggested that we sleep across the river for the evening. It would be safer over there.

As we walked down the path to the boat, I pondered the wisdom of having decided to spend a year and a half with this tribe before I had even seen what they were like. I am not ashamed to admit, either, that had there been a diplomatic way out, I would have ended my fieldwork then and there.

Chagnon, 1968, pp. 4–5

Who could have blamed Chagnon for giving up? However, he did not; and although no statistics are available, it would seem that few anthropologists do. They gradually come to adapt, the initial confusion and bewilderment give way to a sense of order as things fall into place, until an intimate knowledge of the community had been achieved. At the same time, no two fieldwork experiences are alike, as may be seen from Spindler's (1970) useful collection of case studies that provide a lively picture of life in the field as well as the wide range of both variations in circumstances and in the fieldworker's modes of adaptation. It is important to stress this variety, because I shall present in some considerable detail the account of his fieldwork by one particular anthropologist, namely, Middleton (1970a). The reason for this choice is that his is a most thorough and insightful description, specifically intended to convey to fledgling anthropologists the problems, procedures, and also the flavour of fieldwork. He studied the Lugbara of northern Uganda between 1949 and 1953, his main concern being with the aspects of methodology as viewed by a social anthropologist primarily interested in understanding the pattern of social relations. While Middleton does not claim that his experience is 'typical', other anthropologists have told me that his story struck a very familiar chord and is therefore unlikely to be unrepresentative.

Right on the first page there is a statement that psychologists are likely to read with surprise, if not a sense of shock: ". . . what I did was decided largely by the Lugbara themselves; another people might have led me to do a different kind of research." (p. 1.) This at once sharply highlights a fundamental contrast between the approaches of the two disciplines, for it is hardly conceivable that even a clinical psychologist doing research would say that about his or her subjects. Admittedly there are other anthropologists who would not express themselves in quite such absolute terms. Even Middleton himself, who went into the field with an open mind, was inclined to think in retrospect that it may perhaps have been too open. Yet he is against projects with fixed hypotheses since these are apt to act as a constraint and may prevent the pursuit of important issues that remain unrecognized if the hypotheses act as blinkers: "The people themselves open the doors to their culture, and since one does not know what these doors are or where they lead once opened, one can only wait and hope that this will be done." (p. 6.) If the doors are to be opened, one first has to be accepted; this is not easy, since people remote from western culture find it hard to understand the role of such an incomer. Nowadays, when few people remain untouched by the wider world, many of the peoples studied grasp quite readily that a book is to be written about them (which presents problems of its own); but this did not apply to the Lugbara when Middleton was there.

At the outset he merely walked about, acquiring impressions about the superficial aspects of everyday life. People's reactions were a mixture of curiosity, fear, and suspicion. For instance, coming across a death dance being performed in the course of a walk, he was met with open hostility as an intruder. As time went on and it became obvious that his behaviour did not conform to the local stereotype of the 'European', and as his command of the local language improved, closer contact was established, but he still remained a stranger. The Lugbara reckon that a stranger is not a person, but a thing, in much the same way as they regard a new-born baby. It is only when the stranger understands this that he can become a person by recognizing his obligations to his hosts, and they, in turn, acknowledge his rights. Middleton agrees with the Lugbara and says that "the fieldworker is like a young child and learns about the culture of the people in very much the same way as does a growing child in that culture" (p. 6). There is no doubt in my mind that this is an important truth, and I could cite several personal experiences in illustration, but one will have to suffice. Not long after my arrival in West Africa I went to a market and bought something from a 'mammy'. When she tendered me my change, I stretched out my left hand to receive it, the right one holding the purchase. As soon as I did so, she withdrew her arm, frowning; I thought she had realized that the change was wrong and wished to check it. However, she merely held it out again, only to withdraw it when I reached for it with my hand, and this (to me) silly game went on for quite a while. Ultimately exasperated by the obvious stupidity and ignorance of manners shown by the European, she touched my right hand to show that this was the one with which to receive money. Later I frequently observed women teaching their children the use of the appropriate hand in precisely the same way.

This kind of learning, although of course essential, is merely the first step. Middleton describes the gradual stages whereby he moved from being a stranger regarded with suspicion to being accepted by the Lugbara and having a recognized place in their community. The anthropologist can never become fully integrated, for even if it were possible it would be at the cost of his objectivity as an observer. Nonetheless, he became first 'more Lugbara than European' and later formed a close association with one particular lineage until he was regarded for most purposes as a full member of it, thereby finding a niche in the community that enabled him to take a full part in most aspects of their social life. A willingness to enter into all kinds of valued activities, even at the cost of one's dignity, is of great help. Thus, relatively early during Middleton's stay a dance was arranged in his honour which really constituted a kind of test, since missionaries in those days condemned many traditional dances:

> The dance given for me meant that I had to take part, and finally, helped on by one or two glasses of gin and much urging by my friends, I entered the dance. I forgot my own sense of dignity and did the best I could. Despite my clumsiness, this was greeted with much approval and enthusiasm . . . Although it is dirty and sweaty, noisy and dusty, it was great fun, and I always enjoyed it despite the foolish impression I must have given while doing so. One response was that I was known far and wide as the European who danced, and often walking down a pathway I would meet people who at the sight of me would throw down their hoes and start dancing as a sign of welcome.

p. 22

In return for Lugbara hospitality, Middleton—as is usual for anthropologists—rendered such services as he could, prominent among them the provision of medical aid. The whole process of transformation from rank outsider to quasi-member of the community is a fascinating one deserving the close attention of social, and perhaps also developmental, psychologists. For the anthropologist it is merely an essential preparatory phase prior to becoming fully effective as a fieldworker.

In attempting to provide some insight into the nature of fieldwork itself, there is a dilemma: the burden of Middleton's argument is that everything is interconnected, and in order to show this adequately one would have to paraphrase virtually everything he had to say; but such an enfeebled version would neither do justice to his lively account, nor convey much of the 'feel' of the experience. I have, therefore, chosen the alternative of presenting a few issues in greater detail and to a large extent in Middleton's own words, trying to select themes that at least indirectly bring out the overall patterning. At the outset, of course, the information collected was piecemeal:

> I began by learning the Lugbara words for any object that they used and that I saw on my daily walks and visits. I then learned of what it was made, who made it and under what conditions, who used it and under what conditions, whether it was sold and if so, what was its price, and so on. From this work I learned several things: that the 'price' was usually determined for occasional market sale and had little or no relation to the 'prices' of other objects; that time and labour were not counted in determining the price; that the price varied according to the social relationship between seller and buyer, or maker and buyer. In addition, some objects could be widely sold, others not at all or very rarely, the distinction being that of the ritual or ceremonial value of the object and not the difficulty of making it or of obtaining its raw materials.
>
> p. 23

Thus, objects had both a material and symbolic aspect, the latter not being as yet intelligible since Middleton at that stage did not know enough about their social organization. The same applied to such other important practical activities as farming, whose techniques were related to rules of inheritance. Similarly, the division of labour between men and women was a function of Lugbara cosmology which the anthropologist at that time did not yet understand. He also attempted to measure the sizes of fields and their yields, but at first this frightened the people because it was interpreted as a threat to their land, and only later did they trust him enough to raise no objections. Quite apart from these initial practical difficulties of measurement, there is also the problem of the meaning of what is being measured:

> It was clear that I should also try to estimate the volume of exchange of various commodities at markets, the composition of household budgets, and use of food and other goods. I soon found that I could easily collect a great deal of information, which could be added up and correlated in almost any way I wanted. But when I later got to know more about the ever-changing composition of families, households and settlements, and about the kinship and lineage systems associated with them, I realized that these figures were largely useless. I had merely counted things, without realizing that 'things' are also vehicles of

communication which acquire much or most of their significance because of the social relations represented in their use and exchange. I was on more than one occasion later to witness various brief visits by economic and agronomic experts, who did the same kind of brief study and returned home to produce largely erroneous conclusions without being forced later to revise their first findings in the light of more intensive understanding of the social fabric of the people whose economy they had tried to separate out as something to be observed in isolation.

pp. 24–5

As is well known, one of the important avenues towards the understanding of the social fabric is via kinship; what is less well known is that there is usually a great deal more to this than asking people about their relationships. Among the Lugbara, the residential units were clusters of compounds inhabited by small close-knit groups, under the authority of an elder man, the so-called 'joint' or 'extended' family. This local group sometimes consisted of less than a joint family, at other times of several families. Although it might seem easy to establish this, it was in fact far from obvious since the territorial groupings of compounds did not necessarily coincide with social boundaries. Middleton, therefore, had to map all the compounds within a restricted area, to obtain the genealogies of more than a thousand people living in what he later came to label two 'sections', and to check with the people themselves that all members had been included. The collection of these genealogies was a massive task, partly because the Lugbara themselves saw no sense in merely listing relationships but were very interested in telling the stories of the individuals concerned. This provided useful information about the history of various lineages, including tensions and conflicts leading to segmentation and the formation of new lineages. Apart from being extremely laborious, there were other problems:

. . . people of the same group would give me different versions of the same genealogy. At first I found this confusing and even annoying, and then realized there must be some reason for it. To write down the genealogy of a family cluster would sometimes take me several hours. I would start by asking one man with whom I was talking for the names of his brothers, the name of his father, the names of his father's brothers, of his grandfather, of his grandfather's brothers, and so on. This was usually easy enough. I would then ask for the names of the wives of all these men and from where they had come. This was usually not difficult except in the case of wives who had been divorced and returned to their natal homes. I realized very soon—as one might expect—that the names of girls born to the family cluster seemed to be very few. Since girls

marry at the age of twelve or thirteen and go to live with their husbands
five or ten miles away, their names would soon be forgotten in later
generations. In addition, since women have lower status in terms of
lineage responsibility, men would frequently say that I was wasting my
time writing down the names of women. When I would ask for the
names of members of the group in this way, the names of attached men
—sisters' sons, sisters' husbands, and clients who might be living in the
family cluster although of a different lineage ancestry—would frequently
be omitted. I had therefore always to draw first a sketchmap of the
compounds of the cluster to make sure that no one was left out.

p. 33

Some time after having constructed this elaborate kinship chart,
Middleton observed that some people did not address each other in the
way they ought to have done in the chart. This led to the discovery that
people could in some respects change their kinship relations in the
course of their lives. In order to show one way in which this can
happen, it will be instructive to move back in (Middleton's) time to the
first occasion he attended a Lugbara funeral rite.

The salient facts were that when the body had been put into the
grave, several men in turn shouted at the corpse in an angry tone.
Then the grave was filled in and drumming and dancing by various
groups in turn continued all evening. The anthropologist did not then
know the identities of the social roles of the people involved, and in
particular completely failed to understand the meaning of behaviour
that seemed to imply that people were glad the person was dead.
Inquiry confirmed that the corpse had in fact been cursed and the
dancing was said to show 'joy' at the death. If the dead man had been
the scourge of the community and the event unique, the behaviour
would be readily comprehensible; but it was a regular feature of all
funerals witnessed subsequently. At the time the scene appeared
chaotic and senseless, yet the dominant aspects sketched above that
had been so striking to Middleton led to further observation and
inquiry that gradually elucidated a meaningful pattern:[7]

The important elements, of course, are those the participants themselves take for granted, so that they are not likely to remark upon them
in conversation . . . After visiting the funeral I realized how important
were the collective emotions that were being expressed, which seemed to
me out of place and unexpected . . . It was clear, therefore, that I did not
understand the motives for the display of these emotions and would have
to check very carefully whether or not I had in fact recognized them
correctly. Later, when talking with people about these matters, I
realized the obvious fact that they were unable to translate what I had

seen into words that were adequate for my purpose . . . I was later to understand . . . that the Lugbara term refers not so much to joy in our sense, as to a satisfaction at recognizing and reordering a social relationship that had been broken by death. The death causes a period of chaos and confusion. This is brought to an end when it is restructured, by the recognition of new ties of relationship between the various people and groups concerned. Such a remark . . . has a host of implications for the ways in which we see relations of kinship, lineage and clan. So that again it became obvious to me that I could not get very far without an understanding of the basic social relations . . .

p. 49

Let us return now to the changes in kinship relations, one of which is brought about by a dead man's kinship position being taken over by his successor. But the matter is complicated, since this may hold only for some situations and purposes and not others. Thus, a man who has succeeded his dead father would in ordinary everyday contexts call his father's brother by the word for 'father'; however, in some special contexts each might address the other as 'brother'. Thus the kinship system is not necessarily rigid and monolithic, but flexibly woven into the changing webs of social relationships.

In addition to lineages, Lugbara also have clans, and the problem for Middleton was to discover how these are related into an overall functioning system. It has already been mentioned that when questioned about their genealogy people would often differ in their accounts, but when asked about clans they would respond in terms of myths about remote ancestors who were the founders of particular clans, and these myths were always the same. It became clear that while people always remain members of the lineage into which they were born, wives move into the lineages of their husbands and many men chose to live for various reasons with other lineages. Moreover, the sizes of the lineages themselves changed relatively rapidly with varying births and death rates and moves to new land resulting in segmentation. On the other hand, Middleton reported:

> . . . clans are regarded as permanent and give the Lugbara a pattern of order and regularity in terms of which they can conceive their own society and its neighbours. When I asked Lugbara about the functions of these various groups they began to talk in terms of feud and warfare, of intermarriage, of sacrifices, and of the various conflicts and disputes that led to violence and sacrifice and which in time culminated in the splitting of lineages into their constituent segments. Traditionally the Lugbara jural system was based on the recognized and formal sanctions of feud and warfare. They lacked kings, chiefs and police, so that organized self-

help was the main sanction between groups. Within the small groups themselves the main sanctions were and still are the use of various religious processes, such as the invocation of the dead and accusations of witchcraft and sorcery. I soon discovered that people quarrel mainly on account of the sharing of land and particularly about the distribution of the irrigable plots along the stream beds; and they quarreled over women, over the sharing of bridewealth to get new wives, over the behaviour of wives once married and over the rights in their children. Of course, since it is the wives who used the irrigable land and who could only be married by the giving of cattle, the distribution of women, of land, and of cattle were all very closely linked. Since one could not marry one's kinswomen it follows that the relationship of affines was that of unrelated men who lack ancestors in common. They could not observe mutual good behaviour as part of their duty to common ancestors, and the only recourse open to them was that of fighting.

p. 42

In fact fighting had been very frequent before the advent of colonial rule, and Middleton was given highly coloured accounts of glorious wars which after close questioning turned out to have been minor affrays involving mere handfuls of men on either side and consisting of occasional flare-ups lasting perhaps a week or two. Nonetheless, these affairs together with the other mechanisms described constituted a means of social control over a variety of behaviours ultimately linked to relationships of lineage and clan. It was, therefore, obviously important to examine how these two were linked, and for this purpose Middleton scrutinized the genealogical tables so laboriously assembled. This material, however, yielded no consistent pattern with the clan names being apparently randomly distributed over different localities.

Since this is not an account of Lugbara social structure, there is no need to discuss the solution to the problem in detail; suffice it to say that the Lugbara categorized social units in flexible terms relative to any given social situation. What is of primary interest here is that the Lugbara questioned by Middleton, who themselves had the notion of a fixed ordering, were able to conceptualize the system to some extent in accordance with the way that Middleton saw it, as revealed by the manner of his questioning. However, it became apparent, after some time, that this was not their own perspective; and thus Middleton came to realize that the Lugbara thought of clans as fixed once and for all by a particular ancestor, while lineages were related to the changing experiences of living people as described earlier.

It has been said that the clans were traced back to mythical ancestors, and people would relate these myths with dramatic gestures. Now it is of course not surprising that they attributed to these figures of the misty distant past all kinds of extraordinary qualities and behaviours; though it should be noted that anthropologists regard such statements as having continued meaning and significance which it is their task to elucidate. It is quite another matter when such 'myths' concern persons within living memory. As I can testify from personal experience, being told such stories in such a manner gives one a powerful feeling of absolute conviction on the part of the teller and can be extremely puzzling and somewhat disturbing. At any rate, it constitutes also a fascinating psychological problem, and I shall therefore deal with two such cases encountered by Middleton.

The first concerns the great prophet, Rembe, an historical figure among the Lugbara during the early period of European contact. Middleton knew about him from the official archives, which recorded that he was deported and hanged in the Sudan. Middleton heard his name mentioned occasionally and decided to attempt to find out more. After some initial reluctance, five old men who were contemporaries of Rembe told their story freely and with increasing excitement:

> Rembe was regarded by them as a mythological figure, and they spoke about him in the same mythopoeic idiom as they would describe the two hero-ancestors, Dribidu and Jaki. They did not tell of his activities in the terms they would use to describe an ordinary person, despite the fact that they had all known Rembe as closely as anyone could have. For example, they described in detail the immediate source of his power, a many-coloured snake or lizard with a man's face, that dwelt in a pool at Oleiba that I was taken to see; I was told that Rembe climbed to the tops of trees and there walked across the top of the paths of forest in the area; and many other wonders. I knew that when these events took place in 1916, the participants had often been under the influence of drugs, but they were certainly not so when they spoke about them to me in 1951. It was impossible for me to discover how they themselves really intended these statements to be understood, but they certainly believed in what they told me. They were using a mythopoeic form of speech so as to indicate Rembe's divine qualities. At first I found it difficult to accept such language when used of actual persons whose actual behaviour had been witnessed by my informants . . . But once I realized that they would relate to me certain events that had taken place thirty-five years before, referring to all personages except Rembe in terms of 'ordinary' people, and reserving the mythopoeic idiom for Rembe's behaviour only, then I grasped that they were showing that he was an emissary of Divine Spirit and therefore not an ordinary man at all. They saw him as a divine agent coming to lead them back to a happier Paradise they had lost because of the impact of the outside world.

p. 58

Middleton went on to explain that the events were not told in any kind of chronological order, and the relationship to the revolutionary events that occurred at the time was implied rather than expressed. Thus the Lugbara did not seem to have a Western concept of historical time in terms of which events are ordered, and they related a great many 'facts' as refracted through a mythopoeic prism. Middleton added:

> . . . although by 'common sense' the 'facts' hardly made sense . . . being neither apparently truthful nor put to any kind of chronological order, once I grasped the idiom used, they fell into meaningful place at once.
>
> p. 59

One in led to wonder whether this would have happened if Middleton had not been in possession of independent information of these same events; and in any case the psychological problem of the conditions for this kind of mythopoeic thinking is thereby not resolved.

The second episode occurred when Middleton asked people about the beginning of colonial rule. He was told that Europeans came to the country walking upside down, and only when they became aware of being observed did they change to right-side up. They were also supposed to have been able to move across the country at fantastic speeds (this at a time before motor transport, when Europeans had to walk across the bush). But the most interesting account is that based upon first-hand information:

> The man who first told me about the Europeans in any detail was my cook's father, who had himself worked as a servant for the first Belgian administrator in 1900. He would tell me of their everyday activities, saying that they were in fact quite pleasant men although they had some unusual habits: they ate strange foods and consumed enormous quantities of gin and tea. But he would always repeat emphatically that they walked upside-down and had miraculous powers. And this was confirmed by other men who had actually been present when the Belgians first appeared. At first I could not understand what was being said to me: I tried to work out a 'correct' version of these stories, then wondered whether I was not hearing the relics of distant tales of medieval giants and the like. But finally I realized that when the old men used this particular idiom they were doing so for a definite purpose—although not perhaps a self-conscious one: they were trying to tell me that these were people who came into their society from the outside world. I looked again at the myth of first creation and of the hero-ancestors and realized that the same idiom was being used there. The people, the personages of the myth before the hero-ancestors, the brothers and

sisters who committed incest, were also 'upside-down', although their inversion was moral rather than physical. That is, they committed incest and cannibalism, the very negation of socially responsible behaviour towards one's own kin.

pp. 38-9

Middleton then went on to say that when his Lugbara friends insisted on telling him these and numerous other myths, frequently in response to what were for him factual questions about the topology of homesteads or their farming techniques, they were really making symbolic statements about the fundamentals of Lugbara culture. In other words, they were telling him as best they could the aspects they considered essential if he were to understand properly what was going on around him. The meaning of the previously quoted saying—i.e. that it was the Lugbara themselves who showed him the way to conduct his research—becomes fully elucidated in the following passage:

> In telling me, at least by implication, that I should not understand the organization of their society unless I first comprehended its basic principles and cosmological notions, the Lugbara were far more correct and sophisticated than I realized at the time. A social structure is not, after all, an object that is directly observable in any objective sense; one cannot count or measure it. It is an abstraction, used by the people themselves to comprehend relations of power and authority. To understand the particular way in which any given people do this necessitates that the observer tries, as best he can, to see the patterns of relations of power and authority, as do the people he is studying. If he assumes that he can do otherwise, then he is merely assuming that the society he is observing is a variation or aberration of his own, and that will not get anyone very far. I was shown—although it took me many months to realize it—that the Lugbara were making statements to me, as they made to themselves, of the nature and distribution of power and authority; those about power were made in terms of myth, those about authority were made in terms of genealogy . . . When I saw this, I had learnt something that opened the doors to their culture to me in a way that I had not imagined possible.

p. 39

The lesson Midleton hammers home throughout is that a culture constitutes a unity transcending change—and he certainly does not underrate the extent and importance of changes. This also comes out very clearly in his discussion of religion and ritual already touched upon, where he insists—as all anthropologists would—on the relationship between religious belief and action to all the other elements of the culture which together form "a single system of thought and belief"

(p. 51). This has important implications for the research strategy of the fieldworker:

> One of the difficulties of anthropological fieldwork is that one cannot really understand what one is observing unless he sees every detail as an element in a structure, but the structure cannot be discerned until most of the elements have been collected. To have the structure or pattern complete with every detail in place would appear in fact to be an impossibility. The reason is obvious: no society is totally unchanging, so that there are always discrepancies and contradictions of detail in the organization of social life. What the fieldworker does in essence is to build up hypothetical structures or patterns as he goes along. Every new fact that he gathers can either be fitted into the structure, or if not, he is forced to change the structure. I return here to the point made at the beginning of this book: One cannot order one's field research according to a program, but must be led by the nature of the culture one is observing along a path which may lead very far from one's original aims and hypotheses.
>
> p. 47

The account given here is inevitably a selective and abbreviated one and is thereby probably misleading in some respects. While it is true that Middleton's bias is in the emic direction, he certainly did not see it as his task merely to discover and record the members' collective image of their own society. For him as for most anthropologists engaged on that kind of enterprise, such images (which often have a symbolic form) constitute merely the raw material on the basis of which successive approximations to a working model of the society are constructed. The final model of the system emerging from such an analysis-and-synthesis more often than not bears little resemblance to the participants' own perceptions of their culture; of course, the latter may be studied for its own sake, and on occasions used as a check on the model (cf. de Jong, 1967).[8]

Another misleading impression that may have been created by the mode of presenting Middleton's experience is that of progressive revelation complete by the end of fieldwork. Actually, it may be that Middleton saw rather more of the various connecting threads than usual while he was still in the field, but the final synthesis has to await the return; and it is often years before the task is finally accomplished. It is not uncommon for anthropologists not being able to see the wood for the trees when they first come back, and only a lengthy and painstaking sifting through the masses of material collected finally leading to the construction of a model:

> When I left Tongaland after a three years' stay, I could see the main

outlines of their social and political system. But I had not perceived the integrative factors amongst this welter of small groups with their opposed interests and apparent lack of unity although order was clearly present. To put it more colloquially, I had not found what made this society 'tick' in spite of so much dissension. It was not until I began to analyse my records of disputes, in courts and elsewhere, that I received my first clues.

van Velsen, 1964, p. xxvii

The work of the anthropologist might be compared to the task of a subject faced with an immensely complex Street Gestalt figure; once the figure is discerned, all the mass of detail falls into place as part of the pattern making up the whole picture. From such a standpoint the call for more standardization, which psychologists with no understanding of fieldwork would no doubt applaud without hesitation, should now appear in a somewhat different light. Middleton, in common with most anthropologists, is not averse to counting and measuring—in fact he did a great deal of it. Yet he would contend there is no virtue in measurement as such unless the entities counted can be meaningfully interpreted within a broader context; otherwise, there is a risk of ending up with spurious quantification. These remarks concern the study of socio-cultural systems as wholes—there are other approaches to be considered later that are based on quantification.

The simile of the Street Gestalt figure used above is not merely oversimplified, but begs the question as to whether there is a single unique figure that could be found by anyone possessing the necessary skills. In fact probably no anthropologist would maintain that there is *the* true model, since such models are not discoveries but constructions. Where two or more fieldworkers study the same or closely related societies, the final outcome will certainly show important similarities but there will invariably be differences. Fieldwork is a craft that requires subtle inferences bound to be affected to varying degrees by the individual style of the researcher—the data are refracted through the prism of the anthropologist's personality. There is a widespread recognition of this problem (Nash and Wintrob, 1972) which can be alleviated by greater self-awareness but can never be completely eliminated.

All this may sound as though such models were in all respects unique and thereby incommensurable, but this is not the case because a whole set of structural and organizational principles of an etic nature are embodied; these include, for instance, modes of reckoning descent, types of political authority, forms of ritual, and so on. Hence, it is not only possible to compare different models but to extract certain empirical generalizations which in turn may be applied to other field material and tested for goodness of fit. A concrete example will help to clarify how this can be done.

The story centres on a mode of gift exchange in Melanesia called the *kula*. Even before Mauss (1925/54) wrote his classical study on the subject, anthropologists have looked upon practices connected with the giving and receiving of gifts not as trivial social habits, but as important clues to social relationships. Who gives what to whom, the relative values of the items in the gift exchange, the time interval separating it—all these provide indications of the nature of the relationship between the partners, e.g. whether they are of equal or unequal status. If someone gives me a gift and I immediately find something of equal value to return to him—or worse, insist on paying for it—that person will be offended. This is because I have displayed anxiety to be rid at once of the obligation he has created, and possibly also because of my crude (and perhaps unjustified) assertion of equality of status.

In his classical studies of the Trobriands, Malinowski described the *kula* system which operates among individuals within as well as between a group of island communities. One partner gives necklaces and will receive in return armshells, the former circulating clockwise and the latter anti-clockwise through the chain of islands. Hence these transactions are known as the '*Kula* ring', and are of course entirely distinct from the purely economic barter exchanges that also took place.[9]

In other parts of his work Malinowski gave an account of what he regarded as chieftainship in the Trobriands, reporting that a father would introduce his son to the *kula* without expecting anything in return, which he attributed to fatherly love. For reasons that cannot be spelled out here in detail, these and some other aspects of the analysis did not seem to hang together in a coherent fashion, it being apparent that Malinowski's theoretical analysis had somehow gone astray.

The issue was taken up by Uberoi (1962), who studied the original field reports in detail and came to the conclusion that Malinowski had misunderstood the character of political institutions in Melanesia. This is quite understandable, since little attention had been devoted to such institutions at the time Malinowski was in the field. Since then there has been extensive work on 'stateless' or 'segmentary' societies, especially in Africa, showing that political order in such societies was maintained in a totally different manner in the absence of any chiefs with political power. Uberoi formulated the hypothesis that Malinowski's so-called 'chiefs' were in fact not chiefs at all, but merely men of high rank without specifically political power, of the type identified in the African work; the hypothesis further postulated a particular set of connections between wealth, *kula* eminence and high rank which dispensed with Malinowski's *ad hoc* psychological interpretations.

Thanks to the immense richness of detail of Malinowski's field reports, Uberoi was able to re-analyse the material, taking great pains to bring together references to particular individuals scattered over several distinct episodes (which was the then prevalent style of recording) so that their involvement in a related set of events could be traced. In addition, evidence provided by other such workers in Melanesia as Fortune and Seligman was considered. The outcome was a clear vindication of the new hypothesis, in the sense that everything now fell into place and a set of coherent relationships were demonstrated whereby the *kula* ring emerged as an important element in the political process.

So far the aim of the anthropologist has been characterized as that of constructing a kind of working model of the socio-cultural system that will encompass the maximal range of social behaviour and account not merely for those aspects where they smoothly intermesh, but also account for the areas of tension and conflict. In the case of many theorists, however, this description of aims is too restrictive, and they also feel obliged to attempt some answer to the question· What factors have brought about the particular form taken by the social system? It will be recalled from Chapter 1 that nineteenth-century anthropologists sought an answer in terms of either a rather crude evolutionism, or diffusion. In any case it remains true that in order to answer such a question it is necessary to move to a different level of explanation.

The types of explanatory schemes are diverse, but they may be broadly divided into external and internal ones. The external ones include Marxist anthropologists postulating some form of economic determinism, though this may be quite subtle and indirect (Godelier, 1977). A related and very important trend has been analysis in terms of ecological factors, which may be regarded as a return to aspects of evolutionary theory with a modern emphasis on modes of adaptation; a particularly interesting example of this is the work of Rappaport (1968), who interpreted certain forms of rituals related to the ancestors and associated conflicts between neighbouring communities as instrumental in ensuring continuity of food supply. I propose to return later to some aspects of the ecological approach that are relevant for psychology.

The division between external and internal explanation is bridged by Bateson (1972), who was a biologist as well as anthropologist and worked in psychiatry, introducing such concepts as 'deutero-learning' and the famous 'double-bind theory of schizophrenia', taken up and popularized by Laing. Bateson, who incidentally also inspired Rappaport, elaborated a remarkably broad theoretical scheme, essentially cybernetic in character, which he also applied to the study of culture. Since Lévi-Strauss ultimately traced back all anthropological problems to the nature of mind, his structuralism should probably be classed as 'internal'. However, the most prevalent 'internal' attempts at explanation over the past half-century have probably been in terms of psychoanalysis, and thus of most direct concern in the present context. This theme will be taken up at the beginning of Part 2.

Notes

1. Several prominent British anthropologists have had a training in psychology, and at American universities anthropology students are usually expected to take courses in psychology; it might also be mentioned that it is not uncommon for anthropologists, especially those in 'psychological anthropology', to undergo psychoanalysis.
2. In the present context 'anthropology' always refers to social or cultural anthropology; physical anthropology has always been firmly located within the biological sciences.
3. See also Harris (1976).
4. This contrasts with the term 'subject' applied by psychologists to the people they study, and the difference in terminology reflects underlying philosophies.
5. For a cross-cultural example, see Nerlove et al. (1974).
6. It should be understood that this is something of a 'period piece', dating back more than half a century. Sir Raymond's approach to the field in later conditions was, as he pointed out, more prosaic.
7. Lest any reader be sceptical about this, it is worth mentioning that rather similar behaviour is not uncommonly found elsewhere. I had taken a number of photographs of people at various stages at a funeral in West Africa (not featuring the corpse or grave itself) and asked a class of Scottish students to guess what the occasion was; not a single one correctly identified it as a funeral, most of them suggesting some kind of happy celebration such as a marriage.
8. It must be acknowledged that my treatment of 'models' is inevitably much oversimplified. There has been a great deal of debate in anthropology about the nature and functions of models, which still goes on (Gluckman and Eggan, 1965; Holy and Stuchlik, 1981).
9. Systems that bear at least a remote resemblance to kula can be found in our own culture. Doctors do not charge fees to their colleagues for professional

services, but it is customary to return a gift of some kind on suitable occasions such as Christmas. A doctor friend of mind told me that he was once sent an unusual and highly distinctive bottle of liquor from abroad; having forgotten to buy anything suitable for the purpose, he gave this bottle to a colleague who had rendered him a service. Several years later he was astonished to receive what was unmistakably the same bottle from another colleague!

PART 2

Mainly Social–Emotional

4 | Psychological Anthropology and Personality

> Personality psychology has sometimes been seen as the domain of a little group of rational technicians who specialize in criticizing each other's measures of the insignificant, then conclude that the existence of the obvious is doubtful, then doubt whether the study of personality is worthwhile.
>
> Helson and Mitchell, 1978

This chapter will be concerned with anthropological studies that seem to highlight some shortcomings of the currently dominant personality theories in psychology. Neither the treatment of psychological anthropology nor that of personality from an anthropological perspective purports to be exhaustive, but both themes will be further elaborated in subsequent chapters.

During the 1930s there developed within American anthropology a branch that came to be known as 'culture and personality'. Its aim, in somewhat oversimplified terms, was to explain what appeared to be intra-cultural similarities and inter-cultural differences in personality. Several good accounts are available,[1] and I therefore intend to provide merely a broad sketch necessary for the present argument. Studies of 'culture and personality' had two quite divergent roots, which later coalesced. Students of Boas wished to gather evidence showing that culture can shape what they regarded as extremely malleable human nature into whatever form required for the proper functioning of society. Neo-Freudians (as opposed to such orthodox ones as American 'revisionists') insisted, on the other hand, on the importance of the biological foundations; hence, they viewed cultural differences in personality as the outcome of limited variations grafted upon common developmental trends.

Two students of Boas were prominent in this sphere, Benedict and Mead. Benedict (1935), influenced by Gestalt psychology, pictured cultures as tightly knit, coherent configurations. She adopted an opposition (originally due to Nietzsche) between 'Apollonian' (moderation) and 'Dionysian' (frenzy), applying it equally to the conceptualization of cultures and personalities, which she treated as more or less synonymous. This dramatic contrast, while it captured the imagination (and resulted in the book becoming an anthropological bestseller!), did some violence to the facts by greatly exaggerating the internal homogeneity of cultures. Thus Benedict wrote of the Apollonian Zuni that they disapproved of heavy drinking, drunkenness being repulsive to them; but other fieldworkers reported a more Dionysian tendency towards uncontrolled drunkenness and fighting. Hence her contribution, while highly influential at the time, is today mainly of historical interest.

The early work of Mead was also largely inspired by the views of Boas about the dominance of culture over biology, though she later became more psychoanalytically oriented. Margaret Mead has long been the psychologists' favourite anthropologist, and all too often she is the only one with whose work they appear to be familiar. Even this is an exaggeration, for in her long and distinguished career Mead has written about a variety of different peoples; this includes a re-study of the Manus (some two decades after she had first worked with them) which documents the effects of social change during the intervening period. Yet almost the only peoples featured in psychological texts which execute a ritual bow in the cross-cultural direction are the Arapesh, Mundugumor, and Tchambuli! These are, of course, the subjects of her famous *Sex and Temperament in Three Primitive Societies*, and it is interesting to note that in the later paperback edition (Mead, 1950) she described this as her "most misunderstood book". The reasons for this are pertinent to the present discussion.

Mead was greatly concerned with the question of sex differences, which constitutes a major thread running through most of her voluminous writings. In fact her first monograph, *Coming of Age in Samoa* (1928), had the significant subtitle, "A psychological study of primitive youth for modern civilization", indicating her view that the study of adolescent development in pre-literate cultures had important lessons for modern societies. She was not only a forerunner of the women's liberation movement, but she saw it more generally as one of her aims to utilize anthropological findings for the purpose of stimulating social change at home. The fact that some of her interpretations continue to be quoted in psychological texts—especially those that fit in with the currently fashionable denial of most of the differences between the sexes—testifies to her success. At the same time awareness that she had an axe to grind should lead to some caution when considering her conclusions. In so complex a sphere as culture, sex, and personality, it is all too easy to select (and not necessarily deliberately) aspects that support a particular thesis. It was precisely this that some critics accused her of—hence the plea that she had been misunderstood.

Her first complaint concerned the suggestion that the book was about sex differences when she had stated quite clearly in her original introduction that it was not about that, but rather that "it is, very simply, an account of how three primitive societies have grouped their social attitudes towards temperament about the very obvious facts of sex-difference" (Mead, 1935, p. xvi).

Readers, however, may be forgiven for thinking that this was precisely the primary aim of the book in terms of the amount of space devoted to it. Moreover, and in spite of her protests to the contrary, Mead tended to minimize biological determinants of sex differences as indicated by the following conclusion:

> The material suggests that we may say that many, if not all, of the personality traits which we have called masculine or feminine are as lightly linked to sex as are the clothing, the manners, and the form of head-dress that a society at a given time assigns to either sex . . . The differences between individuals within a culture are almost entirely to be laid to differences in conditioning, especially during early childhood, and the form of this conditioning is culturally determined. Standardized personality differences between the sexes are of this order, cultural creations to which each generation, male and female, is trained to conform.
>
> 1950, pp. 190–1

The second accusation to which Mead took exception was that her results were too neat, made too beautiful a pattern to be credible. This issue cannot be examined in detail, but one example will show that the critics seem to have a case. Mead claimed that among the Tchambuli there was a total reversal of sex role, with women being dominant and men dependent. However, being an outstandingly able and conscientious fieldworker, Mead faithfully recorded that women nursed the children, prepared the food, and generally performed the tasks commonly allocated to women in other societies; she also stated that the women's attitude towards the men was "one of kindly tolerance and appreciation" (1935, p. 255). Yet in her general conclusion she conveyed the impression that relations between the sexes were totally unlike what is found in most other societies.[2]

Thus in her early work Mead, believing that "human nature is almost unbelievably malleable" (1935, p. 280), also tended to exaggerate the internal homogeneity of cultures and the contrasts between them; and the facts she carefully presents are sometimes open to somewhat different interpretations. The reason for labouring this point is not any wish to carp at Margaret Mead, a formidable woman who has made an outstanding contribution; rather, it is intended as a warning to psychologists that it is somewhat perilous to quote relatively old anthropological findings in support of a particular psychological position without informing oneself about the critical discussion of given interpretations by other anthropologists.

Another instance of the same kind relates to the issue of the universality of the Oedipus complex, where Malinowski is sometimes cited by psychologists as having shown conclusively that it cannot be universal. The actual story is not quite so simple. As already mentioned in Chapter 1 Malinowski showed that in the Trobriands it was the mother's brother and not the father who was the main authority figure; hence, he argued, the nuclear complex postulated by Freud depends upon a particular type of social structure. However, far from having delivered a mortal blow to Freudian theory, this was merely the start of a continuing debate. Defenders of psychoanalysis claimed that Freud's formulation did not necessarily imply that it was the actual genitor who had to exercise authority. An even more telling point made was that, in Malinowski's own description, the change in the authority pattern did not take place until the child was at least eight years old, by which time the Oedipal constellation is already well established; until that age, the child was brought up entirely by the nuclear parental pair.

Among those who took a prominent part in the debate was Roheim (1947), then uniquely qualified as a practicing clinical psychologist as well as a trained anthropologist with extensive fieldwork experience. An important though somewhat quixotic figure, he was a Freudian fundamentalist who held that cultures have their origins in defence mechanisms against certain dangers arising in specific infantile situations. He was apt to irritate his fellow anthropologists not merely by his extravagant interpretations,[3] but by attributing their reluctance to accept them as evidence of their own unresolved complexes. Roheim took a lively interest in the work of others concerned with personality and culture, such as Benedict and Mead, against whose cultural relativism he argued shrewdly; yet his most acid comments were directed at that Neo-Freudian revisionist, Kardiner. In the 1940s Kardiner, a psychoanalyst without anthropological training, ran a seminar jointly with Linton, a prominent anthropologist, on what they called 'psycho-

logical analysis of primitive cultures.' Since their influence was considerable until the early 1950s, including some impact on psychology at
the time, some discussion of their work is necessary.

Kardiner's (1939) first formulation of the relationship between personality and culture was worked out together with Linton on the basis of
the latter's Marquesan data, and subsequently modified and expanded
(Kardiner, 1945) in a version relying heavily on a study of Alor by Cora
DuBois (1944). In this later version Kardiner proposed that each culture
contains two distinct sets of components, called 'primary' and 'secondary'
institutions, respectively. The primary institutions comprise the socio-
economic framework of the society and the child-rearing practices viewed
as resulting from it. The particular nature of the child training determines
what Kardiner called the 'basic personality structure' consisting of
elements common to all or to most members of the society. These
personality features give rise, in turn, to 'secondary institutions that are
derivative projective systems expressing personality needs in terms of art
and religion while at the same time providing a means of satisfying them.
Personality is thus conceived as mediating the relationship between these
two types of institutions. The virtue of this model is its dynamic potential:
changes in subsistence will alter child-rearing practices, which leads to
adaptive modifications of basic personality structure.[4]

Kardiner applied this general mode of analysis to material from
several cultures provided by anthropologists, without directly under-
taking any fieldwork himself. This fact is not without significance, for
what emerged were images of cultures and personalities refracted
through his theoretical lenses, without the perspective and insight that
can only be gained by first-hand experience of a culture. The
application of his method will be illustrated with the case of Alor, which
he himself regarded as an outstanding example of successful analysis.

Alor is a small island between Java and New Guinea, which had a
population of some 70 000. Cora DuBois, who conducted the fieldwork,
concentrated on a cluster of mountain villages with a population of
about five-hundred. The subsistence was agriculture, which was
mainly the responsibility of women, while the men concerned themselves with pigs and chickens. When the women went out to work in
the fields, infants were left behind to be cared for by older siblings or
elderly relatives. There is, of course, a mass of other ethnographic
information which it is neither possible nor necessary to provide. The
stages of the analysis were summarized as follows by Kardiner himself:

> The first step of the experiment was a study of the institutions, mores,
> and folklore of Alor, on the basis of which a hypothesis was formulated

concerning the impact of the institutions on ontogenetic development. The second step was a test of this hypothesis by the study and analysis of the eight native biographies that had been secured by the ethnographer through extensive life history interviews. The third step was a comparison of the results of the psychodynamic analyses of the eight biographical subjects with the results of the psychologist's study of thirty-eight Rorschach protocols and a collection of children's drawings. Kardiner and Oberholzer conducted their studies of DuBois' data independently and did not know of each other's conclusions until each study was completed. The correspondence of the results of these two methods of analysis was remarkably high, and quite beyond the range of chance.

Kardiner and Preble, 1961, p. 252

The salient features of Kardiner's analysis will now be outlined. The starting point is the particular mode of subsistence (women working in the fields), which led, according to Kardiner's interpretation, to a child-rearing pattern characterized by maternal neglect. This interfered with the integrative processes and produced a basic personality which was not only emotionally constricted but suffered from an impairment of cognitive functions. The secondary institutions, religion and folklore, reflect these personality deficiencies by their distinctively negative features. The gods or ancestors are mainly feared for the harm they can do, indicating that they do not incorporate any positive aspect of the parental image. Similarly the folklore themes are redolent with aggression, or at least with animosity, often said to symbolize unconscious hatred against the mother.

Kardiner's scheme thus appeared to offer the prospect of explaining not merely the overt behaviours of people in different cultures but also such subtle and elusive aspects as religious beliefs and forms of art. Thus, at the time it was hailed as a breakthrough. Unfortunately, various weaknesses soon became apparent. I shall give only one specific example, which is fairly typical of psychiatrically biased characterizations of personality but particularly evident in Kardiner; this is the tendency to describe the 'basic personality' of a whole people in terms implying that they are all emotional cripples. Here is his grim picture of the Alorese:

The basic personality in Alor is anxious, suspicious, mistrustful, lacking in confidence, with no interest in the outer world. There is no capacity to idealize parental image or deity. The personality is devoid of enterprise, is filled with repressed hatred and free-floating aggression over which vigilance must be exercised . . . [and so on, in much the same vein].

Kardiner, 1945, p. 170

Personally, I felt some revulsion when reading so utterly damning an account of people whom Kardiner never met in the flesh. Although they were said to be incapable of cooperation, affection, and trust, the Alorese did welcome and readily help the anthropologist Cora DuBois, and it would seem that some of them paid with their lives during the Japanese occupation in World War II when they predicted victory for the 'Hamerika' about which she had told them.[5] Perhaps Kardiner himself had some doubts, for he ruminated on the fact that Alorese culture had managed to survive, seemingly for a long time, though he qualified this by saying that their continuance "must hang on a very thin thread" (1945, p. 253). He was obviously puzzled by what Cora DuBois had reported to him that the Alorese have lots of good times and engage in a great deal of socializing. This led him to ask whether they are happy, and while unwilling to give a straight answer he confidently asserted that "it is certain that they are not aware of their wretchedness" (1945, p. 253). This condescending phrase reveals the lengths to which Kardiner sometimes went to impose his theoretical preconceptions on recalcitrant facts, even when this led to patent absurdity.

While numerous weaknesses could be pointed out, the fatal flaw of Kardiner's (and other similar) schemes was the inability in practice to make really independent assessments of the two major sets of variables relating to culture and to personality, respectively. Owing to this contamination, the claim that the psychoanalytic delineation of the personality is congruent with the major features of the culture becomes very doubtful because the dice have been heavily loaded in favour of such an outcome. What one is left with at the end, therefore, are some interesting descriptions[6] and occasionally useful insights, but no general principles that could be applied in comparative studies.

Lest any erroneous conclusions be drawn, I should like to point out that the ultimate failure of Kardiner's approach cannot be simply regarded as a failure of psychoanalytic theory as such. Kardiner's version was highly unorthodox, allowing for far more cultural variation than most psychoanalysts would concede, with the result that they were also among his critics. It should be remembered that my harsh evaluation is the product of hindsight—at the time Kardiner's ideas seemed fresh and exciting. One important effect that the work of Kardiner and his associates had was that of inspiring a considerable number of young anthropologists to pursue studies in culture and personality. In this connection another contemporaneous but independent figure should be mentioned, namely, Hallowell. His fieldwork was mainly with American Indians and was concerned with personality and problems of

acculturation. Hallowell had wide psychological interests among which
the cultural aspects of perception were included, and his writings have
stood the test of time better than have those of Kardiner.[7] Hallowell
encouraged his students to take courses in psychology, usually with
considerable emphasis on projective techniques but also in the areas of
psychometrics and statistics. Among those he influenced were Wallace,
who was later to give a more cognitive and biological twist to the
culture and personality problem (Wallace, 1961), and Spiro, who
abandoned his early flirtation with Kardiner to become one of the foremost psychoanalytically oriented anthropologists. It should also be
mentioned that several of that generation of rising anthropologists also
had intellectual contact with Dollard and Miller, thus becoming aware
of social learning theory.

The result of all this intellectual ferment was a bifurcation of efforts
along very different lines. One group of workers sought to pursue the
broad aims of cross-cultural comparisons with a more effective strategy
than Kardiner's, namely the use of the Human Relations Area Files
(HRAF). I shall return to this in more detail later. Others abandoned
the lure of a single, grand scheme and concentrated instead on the
relationship between personality and culture within particular
societies. Initially some attempts were made to patch up the tatters of
Kardiner's conceptual framework by referring to 'modal' rather than
to 'basic' personality. Projective techniques remained in favour for a
considerable period, although the increasing awareness of their shortcomings in cross-cultural contexts (Lindzey, 1961) caused their
popularity to wane. There also occurred a gradual shift from the earlier
treatment of 'personality' and 'culture' as distinct entities towards an
emphasis on personality as being merely instrumental in understanding the nature of socio-cultural processes. At the beginning of the 1960s
the field was accordingly renamed 'psychological anthropology'; a
useful general survey of its problems and findings may be found in the
book of that title edited by Hsu in 1961 and later updated by him in
1972. More recently this approach has been illustrated, reflecting a
broader range of topics, in Williams (1975).

What remained constant throughout a period of change in psychological anthropology was the predominance of psychoanalysis. Moreover, interest in Freudian ideas was by no means confined to anthropologists who regarded themselves as primarily 'psychological'; and
some of the latter, as well as a substantial proportion of the former,
underwent analysis themselves (see, for example, LaBarre, 1958).
There are, of course, many opponents, sceptics, and critics; but no one
is prepared to deny that psychoanalysis has had a profound influence

on anthropology as a discipline. My purpose in examining this issue in some depth is to show that it holds some important lessons for the academic psychology of personality. It might also seem odd that I have chosen to discuss this theme now, rather than to subsume it under the relationship between anthropology and psychology. The reason is that in my opinion the attraction of psychoanalysis for many anthropologists cannot be properly understood without knowing at least something about the nature of the fieldworker's experience.

At the outset, different kinds of applications of psychoanalytic theory may be distinguished. I would suggest four types, as follows:

1. efforts to account for the *origins* of social institutions;
2. attempts to explain unusual features of field material;
3. 'depth' descriptions of personality in culture—still a major concern of psychological anthropology; and
4. the elucidation of symbols.

Here only the first three will be discussed, since the last is better dealt with in the context of symbolism in general. Let us take the first three applications, then, and consider them in more detail.

1. *The origins of social institutions.* This usually takes the form of psychological reductionism, of which Roheim was the foremost exponent. He proposed an ontogenetic view of culture that contained a strong biological component. According to Roheim (1943), culture in general is a defence system directed against the fear of object loss and separation anxiety; he also regarded specific institutions as being traceable to unconscious sources (for example, I have already cited the Trobriand gardening pattern). Similarly, differences between cultures were attributed to differences in the form of infantile nurturing; for instance in Central Australia, where he had worked, Roheim observed that the mother lies on top of the small boy (one is not told what happened in the case of girls). This fact he sought to link by means of the Oedipus complex to a variety of cultural features, including a phallic ceremonialism that excluded women and the practice of phallic sub-incision. This will be enough to convey the flavour of what Roheim himself called the 'undiluted Freudian wine' (1947, p. 29) that he offered to his fellow anthropologists—who generally refused to swallow it, although they did acknowledge its contributions in selected areas. The reason for this overall rejection was probably not so much Roheim's psychoanalytic interpretations as such, but rather the fact that he avowedly went into the field in order to validate Freudian theory; and as far as anthropology is concerned, this is definitely putting the cart before the horse.

Others since Roheim have begun with conventional fieldwork and ended up with psychoanalytic speculations. There is, thus, with the exception of Roheim and a few others like him, no sharp boundary between types 1 and 2. The ideas of Meyer Fortes, however, since they are concerned with possible origins, may be briefly mentioned, although brevity unavoidably detracts from the persuasiveness of the arguments that Fortes backs with extensive documentation. He began as an educational psychologist, prior, as he said, to the "opening up of more exciting intellectual prospects that eventually tempted me away into anthropology" (1974, p. 81). The theme of that (1974) paper is the special position of the first-born child, and Fortes shows that among the Tallensi, whom he studied intensively over many years, there are a variety of taboos relating to the first-born, whether male or female, and to the parent of the same sex. As an example, he quotes a small boy of about six years who was already able to rattle off the major rules of avoidance: "I share my mother's dish of food. I never eat with my father. If I did I might die of a wasting disease. It's because I'm his first-born. We first-born sons may not eat chicken, we may not look into our father's granary, we may not wear his cap or his tunic or carry his quiver or use his bow." Similar rules are binding on first-born daughters in relation to their mother. With the death of the parents and their translation into the ranks of the ancestors, the first-born child of the parent's sex—who is, after all, the ideal replacement for the deceased parent—ceremonially looks, for example, at the father's granary. Similar taboos govern mother–first-born daughter relations. In discussing these Fortes points out that the Tallensi are perfectly well aware of the conflicts and rivalry between parents and children, but the critical feature is that the avoidance rules focus on the *first-born* of a particular sex and not on the eldest surviving child.

A similar emphasis on the first birth can be shown to exist in a wide range of cultures in every part of the world. Furthermore, Fortes cites the psychological literature on birth order and various medico-social studies, all of which appear to indicate that there is something unusual about first-borns. One can assume that this is probably the consequence of special treatment on the part of the parents. From all this Fortes concludes that "the setting apart of the first born reflects experiences deeply rooted in the relations of parents and children in every society" (p. 95). In the latter part of the same paper Fortes seeks to relate these experiences to the Oedipus complex, but the discussion is lengthy and somewhat indirect, not lending itself readily to a summary that conveys the coherence of the various strands of the argument.

Therefore I turn to a later paper (Fortes, 1977), where in one place the case is presented in a tighter form:

> Now a person's Destiny is ruled by the ancestors who reveal themselves as its guardian . . . . The individual exercises no choice, the initiative lies with the ancestors. Thus, though fathers and first sons apparently experience and often even express their presumed antagonism, they do not feel responsible for it, for it is imposed upon them from the outside by Fate that made them ineluctably father and son, at the mercy of their ancestors.
>
> This is Tallensi dogma. From the observer's point of view, it is the controlled ambivalence in the relations of father and first son, mother and first daughter, that arouses attention. Is it far-fetched to see in this an oedipal conflict between consecutive generations of the same sex, symbolically focused on the first-born? Significantly, the mutual trust and affection that are essential for successful child rearing are identified with younger children, thus, as it were, splitting up the intergenerational ambivalence. Does not attributing the latent antagonism between father and first-born to their Destinies suggest that the taboos make sure that the temptation to destroy each other is kept in check?
>
> To speak of this situation in terms of an oedipal conflict takes us back to the problem of how to justify such a deduction from the observation of custom. For me, the justification lies in the insight this afforded to connections between different items of custom that would not otherwise emerge. Take the rule that the first-born may not wear his father's clothes or use his tools. The Tallensi explanation is that their 'body dirt' must not mix; if this happened one would die. Brothers by contrast may borrow each other's clothes and tools. 'Body dirt' refers to sweat, bodily odours and other such exudations. It is, in Tallensi thought, uniquely representative of the individual himself and is particularly associated with adult sexuality. Does not the taboo make better sense if we suppose the antagonism between father and son, mother and daughter, to have a sexual undercurrent though this is not overtly admitted?
>
> 1977, p. 141

There are just two things I should like to add here. First, Fortes also explained that when he first started in anthropology, it was precisely his training in experimental and 'test' psychology that was partly responsible for his initial scepticism about any psychological explanation of custom and social organization; he frequently voiced objections to 'psychologism', criticizing Malinowski on that score (Fortes, 1957). It was his thinking about relationships between various aspects of culture (or 'customs', as he prefers to call them) that led him to speculate about origins. This brings me to the second comment, where I wish to draw attention to the question marks punctuating the quoted passages: far from being presented with dogmatic assertions, we are merely invited to consider the possibility that Freudian mechanisms might be underlying certain widespread customs.

2. *Unusual features of field material.* As an example of an attempt to throw light on unusual features of field material, I shall refer, even more briefly and thus inadequately, to a study by Epstein (1979) of the Tolai, a New Guinea people. When first encountered by Europeans during the latter part of the nineteenth century, they seemed, in the fashion of the day, to be the prototype of 'savages': men and women went around naked, head-hunting and cannibalism were practiced, and they lived in scattered hamlets without any chiefs or other visible political authority. However, there was one remarkable exception: they had a true monetary system of a standard value. This shell money known as *tambu*, which is deeply embedded in the Tolai social fabric, intrigued first missionaries and then professional anthropologists.

By the time Epstein came to study them in the 1960s the Tolai had long donned clothes, become members of various Christian denominations; the better-off among them owned stores, had cars and bank accounts (for ordinary cash); but remarkably they also still had their *tambu*, the shell money. The reason why this is remarkable is that over most of the world such indigenous currencies simply disappeared with the introduction of a Western cash economy. Thus one problem was to discover how and why it managed to survive. At one level Epstein is able to show that it continued to subserve important social functions related to various rituals of the life cycle, a pointer being the verbal association between the name of the shell money and the category of *tambu* (= taboo). When tracing all the numerous threads linking various aspects of the economic and symbolic usage of *tambu*, Epstein became increasingly aware of "a number of seeming discrepancies and contradictions within the *tambu*-complex as a whole, that shell money itself is a focal point of conflict" (p. 165). Moreover, some of these conflicts appeared to be intra-psychic as there were several indications that the notion of *tambu* carried a heavy affective charge. Since a purely social–structural analysis left a number of curious features unresolved, Epstein considered the possibility that the Freudian concept of anal eroticism might throw further light on the problem. Accordingly, he looked for evidence that the shell money might symbolize faeces and as such play a critical part in the Tolai psychic as well as social economy. By juxtaposing the Freudian delineation of the anal-erotic character and Tolai traits, practices, and values, Epstein demonstrates what is at least a fascinating correspondence. For instance, the coexistence of the condemnation of the careless spendthrift (the 'retentive impulse'), coupled with the opposite extreme of the obligation to give lavishly in certain contexts, was supported by religious beliefs:

> In general ideas about conditions in the Abode of the Dead are extremely hazy, save in one notable regard—the treatment of the niggardly. Brown (1910) comments: "So far as I could gather, the punishment for this was the only kind of which they seemed definitely assured." Niggardly people had their ears filled with filth, and their buttocks were dashed against the buttress roots of a chestnut tree . . . in terms of the preceding analysis, one meaning that can be reasonably inferred seems fairly patent: in his mortal life the victim had refused to part with his faeces (his possessions); now, to adopt the common vulgarism, they were beating the shit out of him.
>
> pp. 172–3

What is of particular interest is that Epstein relies for his evidence of anal-erotic character traits mainly on old documentation that could not have been contaminated by Freudian notions. Thus he cites reports from before or around the turn of the twentieth century about the almost obsessional orderliness and cleanliness of the Tolai, which greatly impressed the observers because it was in such contrast to what they regarded as their general 'savagery'. Epstein believes that such an interpretation not merely sheds light on Tolai society in the past, when the behaviour engendered by anal-erotic character traits subserved the harmonious functioning of their form of social organization but also shows how, with the passing of the old order, *tambu* has become the focus of conflict because it symbolizes an old identity they are reluctant to abandon while at the same time aspiring to a new 'modern' one.

It only remains to add that Epstein, unlike Fortes, had no prior formal contact with psychology or psychoanalysis, being originally a specialist in the anthropology of law. It was his puzzlement with the observed phenomena that led him towards psychoanalysis; the interpretation, while necessarily speculative, appears to make sense of the data.

3. *'Depth' descriptions of personality and culture.* My example for the third type is drawn from a study of Hindu villagers by Carstairs (1957). Born in India where he spent his early life, with Hindustani as his first language, and trained in both psychiatry and anthropology, Carstairs was uniquely qualified to conduct such research. One should add that his medical skills not merely enabled him to render service but occasionally to pass through the so-called purdah barrier otherwise tightly closed to a male anthropologist. He lived in the community

observing behaviour, conducted intensive interviews with a variety of people, and even applied some psychological tests (although these contributed little of value). The picture of village Hindu personality which he portrays is many-dimensional, bringing out the relationship between ideals of conduct prescribed by Hindu religion with the notion of an 'inner light' to which one turns for guidance; how these signs are uncertain and sometimes lead to callousness and at other times to seemingly bizarre changes of behaviour; how the Hindu pantheon mirrors many of these conflicts; and finally, he seeks to trace these phenomena to unconscious roots by applying a somewhat eclectic version of psychoanalysis.

One cannot tear the pieces out of such an intricate web without damaging their appearance; and yet I have no alternative. Out of the wealth of potential material I have chosen Hindu ideas and feelings about body products; the reason for this choice is to show that Epstein's speculative interpretations of the Tolai data—which might seem odd and unconvincing on their own—can be viewed in a different light when it is realized that there is a great deal of ethnographic material relating to concern over bodily products.

Carstairs discusses these in the context of two connected belief systems, namely, those about defilement by impurities and the importance of controlling instinctual impulses. The most fundamental source of defilement is excrement, but closely associated with this is the contamination resulting from contact with a person of lower caste, and in particular from eating with them. The deliberate inculcation of these powerful feelings occurs in early childhood:

> As the child learns to accept responsibility for its own bodily cleanliness, it was also taught the importance of avoiding the invisible pollution conferred by the touch of members of the lower castes. The mother or grandmother would call him in, and make him bathe and change his clothes if this should happen, until his repugnance for a low-caste person's touch became as involuntary as his disgust for the smell and touch of faeces.
>
> p. 67

Even within the family, any food that has touched the lips of a person becomes *jutha* (leavings), and it would be utterly disgusting for anyone else to eat this—*jutha* is evidently the psychological equivalent of faeces. There are two interesting exceptions: a father can favour his children by giving them food he has left over; similarly, worshippers can eat food that a God has 'tasted':

> Symbolically, these leftovers represent the faeces of the father and the

God: the act of grateful acceptance represents a submission to their authority, and is the model of the only 'good' relationship with the father.

p. 162

Once again the unconscious roots of this and other aspects of village Hindu personality are traced back to the early family constellation; but the components of the oedipal situation are very different from those found among Fortes' Tallensi. In the Hindu situation, the father remains detached from the small child, there being a taboo on demonstrative affection; when he does impinge on the life of the child and adolescent, it is as a powerful authority figure to whom unquestioning obedience is due. Even as a young mature man the son is obliged in his father's presence "to suppress all indications that he may lead an adult sexual life, and by extension he has to stifle every manifestation of his spontaneity and emotional responsiveness" (p. 160). This brake on sexual activity is reinforced by the belief, shared by every one of Carstair's informants, that there is a close relationship between semen and health. It is thought that semen is produced very slowly and stored in the head; since it determines moral and physical health it should ideally be preserved. Hence celibacy is a pre-condition of real fitness, since orgasm wastes precious and laboriously accumulated semen. In addition to sexual activity, there are other causes of loss of semen:

> . . . every sort of violation of Hindu *dharm* (rule of conduct) such as mixing and eating with people of inferior caste; acting disrespectfully towards one's elders; drinking to excess; giving way to anger or lustful thoughts, to fear or to excessive worrying. In all these cases, what happens is that a man's semen curdles and goes bad and can no longer be retained, issuing from him in the form of a thin, evil-smelling fluid. Consequently, any prurulent discharge which seemed to come from inside the body was held to be 'spoiled semen', whether it came from ears, eyes, or nose, in the sputum or in the stool.

p. 85

Such beliefs act simultaneously as a mode of social control, especially with regard to sexual[8] and inter-caste behaviours, and as sources of profound conflicts, whose manifestations in everyday life are graphically described. Throughout Carstairs is not merely perceptive, but sympathetic, and he does not make the mistake of implying (as other personality-and-culture writers have frequently done) that the underlying processes postulated are somehow more 'real' than more superficial external appearances:

> It would be an act of blindness indeed to suggest that because relations

between a Hindu son and his parents, between a man and his wife, lack
that warmth and spontaneity which is expected in Western society, they
are necessarily inferior. Each patterning of human behaviour has its
positive as well as its limiting aspects. Psychoanalysis is better equipped
to demonstrate the latter than the former; but as an ordinary responsive
observer, one must pay tribute to the serenity and calm which prevail in
a well-adjusted Hindu family. It is perhaps a precarious calm, based on
suppressing rather than on resolving of underlying tensions, but still it
reflects a gracious and civilized way of life.

pp. 168–9

Any tough-minded psychologist who has persevered so far is by now
likely to have a considerably raised blood pressure, bursting to cry out
—''All the same old speculations, without a scrap of real hard
evidence!'' Such a reaction is perfectly understandable, and my own
would have been similar at one time. I do not regard myself as a
'Freudian', I have not had the benefit of an analysis, and I would not
argue for the correctness of any of the specific interpretations cited. All
I am trying to suggest is that there are extensive and important areas of
behaviour about which academic personality theory has little if
anything to say. This conviction is not just the outcome of abstract
reflection—it was the result of first-hand experience of working in other
cultures, which I shall illustrate.

The first occasion when these shortcomings were brought home to
me was when I was teaching in a university in West Africa and came
across the problems connected with envy. During examination periods,
a number of students, including some of the most gifted ones, suc-
cumbed to a syndrome that was sufficiently common to have acquired
the local label of 'brain fag'. It was characterized by extreme tiredness
and inability to concentrate, severe headaches, and other similar
symptoms. On inquiry it emerged that most of the sufferers (or victims,
as they felt themselves to be) attributed their troubles to the *envy* of less
fortunate kinsfolk who did not have the same chances of getting on in
the world and therefore employed supernatural means to spoil the
possible success of the person in question.

Naturally I tried to find out more about envy, and the anthropological literature revealed that it is extremely widespread across the
world and is often an important factor affecting behaviour. While in
West Africa envy (and the fear of it) tends to be confined to cases where
people acquire unusual wealth or status that sets them apart from their
fellows, elsewhere even quite minor differences in status may give rise
to envy. This is very clearly brought out in a relatively recent study by
Pocock (1973), who worked in a Gujerati village in India:

Najar, the evil eye, is the eye of envy, and it is an inevitable feature of a world in which men set store by looks, or health, or goods, or any pleasant thing. Even if, as is likely, one sets no store by one's mere subsistence, the very deprivations of others give grounds for fear. Since there is no one who cannot find someone whose plight is in some way worse than his own, so there is no one who is completely immune to envy and so to *najar*. Let me describe some typical *najar* situations. Doors should always be closed while eating, otherwise hungry men may look in. Thus, if one is eating out of doors, for example in the fields, and someone passes, one should offer him food. If food is offered, and can be accepted on caste grounds, some, be it only a little, should be eaten to demonstrate good will. A man in the village once suffered a fever because when he was drinking tea outside his house a stranger to whom he had offered some, had refused it. The fever was only cured after he had given a coconut to the goddess. The stranger in this case was presumed to be deliberately malevolent . . .

p. 27

Pocock devoted a whole chapter to a variety of aspects of envy, concluding that "it is most to be feared when those who should be equal are not so in fact" (1973, p. 39), and it may well be that this principle applies very widely.

When I turned to psychology books in order to learn more about envy, I drew a blank—by and large, it is simply ignored, and the only serious discussions were to be found in psychoanalytic writings such as those of Melanie Klein (1957). There has been hardly any change in this regard during the more than two decades that have elapsed since then [9]

Let me give another personal example, this time from India. Although I spent only a short time there, it was at least in the purely Indian setting of a provincial town. I was able to observe the constraints in the relations between men and women (even a girl student was said to have spoilt her chances of a good—arranged—marriage by going for a walk with a boy). I sat through Indian films suffused by a cloying sexuality which yet was never permitted to emerge in any overt expression of bodily contact. I saw in the temples phallic *lingams* and was told by the priest that offerings of milk, melted butter, and other such semen-like substances were poured on it during rituals; and I read numerous advertisements for remedies against impotence in the local press. The work of Carstairs made all this resonate, and even if he was wrong in many details, there must be powerful subterranean processes boiling beneath the deceptively calm surface.

Such powerful emotional factors are hard to pin down, yet their behavioural manifestations can sometimes be clearly observed and call for a coherent psychological explanation. Can academic personality theories supply such explanations? Let us glance at least cursorily at some currently dominant positions. One is that of Mischel (1979), who is opposed to trait theory and who, after having stressed the influence of situational variables, now favours a more cognitive approach. One of his main opponents and an arch-critic of psychoanalysis, Eysenck (1980) argues for the retention of the trait-state approach and the crucial role of hereditary factors. What they both have in common is an emphasis on the sophisticated description of individual and group differences by means of measurement, usually employing pencil-and-paper tests. Without wishing to question the value and importance of such approaches within their own chosen sphere, I am here concerned to point out their limitations. The characterizations of 'personality' resulting from the kinds of measurement advocated by Eysenck and Mischel remain flat and two-dimensional, lacking any account of the dynamics of behaviour—the term 'dynamics' being viewed by both with grave suspicion as being psychoanalytically tainted.

It is precisely this dynamic aspect, however, which appeals to many of those anthropologists who are interested in the psychological aspects of their material.[10] The reason is probably that 'dynamics' implies that personality constitutes a functioning system of the same type as the social systems previously discussed. The models anthropologists construct in order to represent such systems cannot, of course, be tested experimentally. Hence the criteria applied in evaluating the adequacy of such models are those of internal consistency, how well all the ethnographic material fits, and whether any general principles extracted can be applied to social systems in other cultures (previously illustrated by the 'Kula ring'). Psychological anthropologists apply these same criteria to psychoanalytic interpretations and are satisfied that they not merely help to make more sense of their data but are relevant to comparable situations in other cultures.

Predictably, the response of the tough-minded psychologists would be simply to dismiss such anthropologists as 'unscientific' and leave it at that. I think that such a response would itself be unscientific, a mere evasive turning away from problems confronting us. The lesson to be learnt from anthropology is that our present approach to personality, involving a pale abstraction defined mainly in terms of test scores, is inadequate. This is indicated by the fact that academic theories are almost completely useless to anthropologists who have to deal with people of flesh and blood, in whose lives such issues as sex, aggression, or envy are extremely important. In other words, as Kluckhohn has put it, anthropologists need a 'theory of human nature in the raw', and the closest we have to that is psychoanalysis. Marie Jahoda (1977) has written a perceptive evaluation of Freud that is in many respects highly critical; yet she has also conceded that psychoanalysis is unique in at least one respect:

> . . . where it succeeds it says something about human beings; simpler models make research easier but often only result in statements about variables; they are based on a model about behaviour, not about man; or in statements about supermen, when based on a model about action and conscious choice alone.
>
> 1980, p. 283

The upshot of my argument is not that psychoanalysis is the answer, but that anthropology presents psychology with a challenge to produce a more scientifically defensible theory that will deal with the range of problems presently encompassed only by psychoanalysis. Such a theory would have to come to terms with personality as a system, which in itself presents formidable difficulties. For a complex system like personality will involve numerous feedback loops, and thus it would be vain to look for any simple causal relationships. Hence it would come up against the very troubles that have militated against the acceptance of psychoanalysis: for instance, the 'reaction formations' whereby the same factors can result in opposite effects, for which psychoanalysis has often been held up to ridicule. Nonetheless, the existence of serious obstacles in the way of a radically fresh approach is no reason for clinging to the patently inadequate theories that currently dominate the field; but it is a reason for being more tolerant of the shortcomings of psychoanalysis.[11]

Another lesson that may be learnt from anthropology is that any new 'systemic' theory of personality should deal with the need for food as well as that for sex. It is often said that psychoanalysis must be culture-bound because it was derived from the behaviour of middle-class Viennese neurotics. This does not appear to me a convincing objection, since the crucial elements of the basic family constellation have a great deal in common in all cultures, in spite of wide variations in the form of the family. By contrast, the nutritional status of Freud's middle-class patients was no doubt entirely satisfactory—at least it is highly unlikely that any serious deprivation was ever experienced. By contrast, malnutrition has been prevalent in many non-Western societies, and the number of people so afflicted has unfortunately been increasing. Long ago Audrey Richards (1932), who studied a tribe whose food supply was inadequate, drew attention to this fact:

> Nutrition as a biological process is more fundamental than sex. In the

life of the individual organism it is the more primary and recurrent physical want, while in the wider sphere of human society it determines, more largely than any other physiological function, the nature of social groupings, and the form their activities take.

p. 1

The lead given by Richards has been followed mainly by ecologically oriented anthropologists concerned with the relationship between subsistence and social organization. On the other hand, there have been few studies attempting to assess the effects of malnutrition on personality and social behaviour.[12] I shall review two very different contributions bearing on the issue.

The first of these is Turnbull's famous—or infamous—book (1972) on the *Ik*, a small and diminishing tribe in a remote corner of Uganda. Unlike the usual anthropological monograph the book is written in narrative form, being addressed to a wider audience, and has also been successfully dramatized. It carries a powerful message about the fragility of the human values we most cherish, based on a field experience which for Turnbull was evidently traumatic. The term 'personality' as such is not used in the book, but its key theme is the character and behaviour of the *Ik* (pronounced 'eek'), which Turnbull found horrifying. He described them as unfriendly, uncharitable, inhospitable, and generally mean; he said that they have abandoned love, hope, and cooperative sociality, their behaviour being governed almost entirely by crude self-interest. He also suggested that they do not form a true society but merely enter into temporary associations which constitute nothing more than a system of mutual exploitation: "This is the relationship between all, old and young, parent and child, brother and sister, husband and wife, friend and friend." (p. 290.)

The account Turnbull gave of such social institutions as there are fits in with this dismal picture. Marriage takes place only where it provides some specific cooperative advantage; sexual activity is very low (the only exception being young girls who sell their sexual services to non-*Iks*), and affection between marriage partners is exceptional. Children are only cared for until about the age of three, and then simply sent out to fend for themselves. The aged and helpless are callously treated, their distress being a source of fun; the death of others, including even close kin, is regarded with indifference or even satisfaction if it entails some advantage. In order to convey something of the "feel" of all this, one single episode culled from the many harrowing ones is related by Turnbull, which I will quote in full:

It was then that I saw Loiangorok for the first time. He had managed to get out of the ruins of his village by late afternoon, when most of the moving was over for the day, and had started down the hill. But he could not even raise his frail bones off the ground, and was dragging himself along on his side, as though he were swimming. Loiamukat, the *niampara* (headman) of that village, came out with a bundle of sticks and stepped right over the old man and continued down the path. I shouted to him to find out who it was, and he replied, "Loinagorok—don't worry, he's my father." Which, knowing Loiamukat, I thought was the best of reasons for worrying. My nerves were still on edge from the confusion and uncertainty of the night before, and my threats, combined with bribes, were so effective that Loiamukat put down his sticks and returned to pick up his father, who had barely enough strength to put his arms around his son's neck. But when he got in sight of the temporary camp, Niangasir, Loiamukat's younger brother and the old man's youngest son, shrieked with derision to see Loiamukat carrying such a useless bundle. Loiamukat promptly deposited Loiangorok on the ground and told me I could carry him myself, which I did, feeling sick, not at the unkindness, but at the feel of those bones as they wrapped themselves around me.

I carried him past where his sons and daughter were busy setting up their new compounds, to where Atum's village was taking shape. Kinimei and Lotoköi had put up a rough shelter for themselves within what was to be Yakuma's compound, and I paid them to let me use it for the old man . . . It was there, while I was nursing Loiangorok, that there was a sudden exodus from the village, distant shouts of laughter, and then someone running back to tell me to come quickly. At first I thought it was a trick to get me away from the old man while in the middle of feeding him, so I finished that first and then went to see what the excitement was about. It was someone else I had never seen before, dead Lolim's widow, Lo'ono. She too had been abandoned, and had tried to make her way down the mountain-side. But she was totally blind and had tripped and rolled to the bottom of the *oror a pirre'i* (gulley), and there she lay on her back, her arms and legs thrashing feebly, while a little crowd standing on the edge above looked down at her and laughed at the spectacle.

pp. 225–6

One also learns from the book that such utter callousness had not always been the way of the *Ik*. Originally hunters in the Kidepo Valley of Uganda, they were forbidden to hunt when a national park was established there; resettled in an adjoining dry mountain region, they were expected to turn into farmers and wrest a living from the arid soil. There was evidence that in their former existence they had possessed the kind of cooperative social morality typical of hunters and gatherers all over the world, characterized by generosity, hospitality, and mutual help. The radical change only came about when they had to struggle, with very limited success, to adapt to a totally different ecological niche.

As might have been gathered from hints in the quotation, Turnbull made no attempt to conceal either his intense dislike of the *Ik* and their ways, or the fact that in the presence of so much misery his own sensibilities had become somewhat blunted. One of his fellow anthropologists launched a bitter personal attack on him, mainly on ethical grounds: the debate[13] that followed focused more on Turnbull's interpretation of his material, some arguing that on his own evidence the *Ik* are not as bad as he made them out to be.

While most discussants mentioned the stress engendered by starvation as a vital factor, it is interesting that this aspect tended to remain in the background. Here we have a case where anthropologists might have arrived at a more balanced view if they had taken account of the work of psychologists. For when Turnbull wrote about the '*Icien*' way, or the lack of human values of the *Ik*, he largely missed the point: it is possible to show that the fact of these people being *Ik* was largely irrelevant since the behaviours so vividly depicted are those of starving people everywhere.

There is plenty of evidence for this, most of it descriptive, but a unique experimental study was conducted in America during the Second World War (Keys *et al.*, 1950). Conscientious objectors were given the opportunity to volunteer for this experiment, which involved a reduction in caloric intake of some 50 per cent over a period of six months. These were all healthy young men, screened for fitness, who had high moral ideals and hoped to serve humanity by taking part. They had to pledge themselves to stick to the restricted diet during the experimental period, but were not physically prevented from obtaining extra food—they were free to mix with the general population during the period. It should also be remembered that apart from their food deprivation, their conditions were infinitely more favourable than those of the *Ik*. They lived in clean and pleasant surroundings, were given regular medical checks, and knew that in case of danger of serious damage to health they would be released from their promise; above all, they knew that their suffering would last only for a finite period.

Only a few of the most salient and relevant findings can be mentioned here. The first fact was that food became the centre of their lives. They had exhibited a protective attitude towards it, and at table some hovered low over their tray as if to protect it. Physically they became increasingly weakened, slowed down in their activities, their interests narrowed, and they seemed to age as well as to feel prematurely old. They became hyper-irritable and had spells of elation followed by depression; some had strong impulses towards violence—and it should be remembered that they were conscientious objectors—which they controlled only with great difficulty. Those who showed the greatest degree of physical and mental deterioration became objects of aggression by the rest of the group. Social interest declined sharply; they became grossly self-centred, and barely managed to maintain socially acceptable behaviour. They allowed their personal appearance and manners to go to pieces. The only form of humour that remained was sarcasm. Sexual interest declined sharply, and romance collapsed.[14]

Allowing for the contrast in setting, many of these behaviours are strikingly parallel to those of the *Ik*. Others, such as those relating to the family, could hardly manifest themselves among this group of young men. There are, however, numerous reports from all over the world of behaviour during famine, including reports from Europe, testifying to the fragility of family bonds in periods of extreme starvation. The following is just one example quoted from a thirteenth-century Russian chronicle about a famine in Novgorod:

> A brother rose against his brother, a father had no pity for his son, mothers had no mercy for their daughters; one denied his neighbour a crumb of bread. There was no charity left among us, only madness, gloom, and mourning dwelt constantly within and without our habitations.
>
> Morgulis, 1923, p. 15

Thus, Turnbull was right in pointing to the relative fragility of human values but wrong in singling out the *Ik*; for these values are apt to break down in the majority of people whenever starvation grips a land, be it in Africa, Europe, or America.

The second study to be considered, carried out by Bolton (1973) among the Quolla Indians of Peru, is in several ways a counterpoint to the first one. Pelto (1967), writing before Turnbull's work on the *Ik* had been published, had this to say about the Quolla: "In the anthropological literature, these Andean highlanders are portrayed as perhaps the meanest and most unlikable people on earth." (p. 151.) Bolton presented a list of personality traits attributed to the Quolla by previous field workers, which reads like a catalogue of vices dominated by aggression. Their reputation is so bad that they have been used as anthropological textbook examples of a people characterized by a personality configuration of extreme hostility and violence; historical documents suggest that these unpleasant qualities were already noticeable in the sixteenth century.

The question that has intrigued anthropologists is why the Quolla

should have developed such personality traits. Some of the anthropologists who worked with the Quolla advanced what Bolton called the
'domination hypothesis', referring to the fact that for many centuries
they have had to live under highly authoritarian dommination.[15]
Bolton conceded some plausibility to the hypothesis but criticized its
failure to consider the processes whereby domination might produce
aggressive personalities.

A second hypothesis proposes that a series of such stress factors as
high altitude, excessive drinking and coca chewing, insanitary housing,
inadequate clothing, poor diet and frequent sickness may, in combination, be responsible for extreme behaviour. Again Bolton pointed out
the speculative nature of this suggestion, and the fact that for several of
them counter-examples readily come to mind—e.g. several more
pleasant peoples live at high altitude.

What particularly struck Bolton was a sharp contradiction between a
demanding moral code, enjoining compassion and cooperation, to
which most Quolla paid lip service, and their behaviour in everyday
life. The people themselves showed little awareness of the discrepancy
between their code and their actual conduct:

> In the end I came to agree with several informants who gave answers
> to my questions about why people killed one another, slaughtered each
> other's animals, burned their crops, fought with them, and so forth.
> They insisted: "Such behavior is not rational. A rational person would
> not do things like that!"
>
> p. 230

When Bolton said that he agreed with his informants, he meant that
it was necessary to search for causal factors that could account for such
irrational behaviour. In doing so, he quite deliberately eschewed the
psychoanalytical approach in favour of what he called a psychobiological one—there is no mention of child rearing practices at all. For
this purpose he scrutinized the literature on aggression and its physiological concomitants. The most promising notion for the particular
living conditions of the Quolla that he found was that of a relationship
between levels of aggressiveness and blood glucose concentration.
Hence, he proposed the 'hypoglycemia hypothesis' which postulates a
relationship between low blood glucose levels and a disposition towards
aggression.

In order to test this hypothesis he selected a random sample of male
household heads in the village, and from other key informants obtained
ratings of the extent to which these subjects were inclined to quarrel
and fight. The validity of these aggression ratings was checked against

behavioural indices such as homicide accusations and found to be satis-
factory. Then he managed to persuade two-thirds of the sample (66 men) to undergo a physiological test, which was quite elaborate since it involved 12 hours of fasting followed by a blood sample. A significant ($P<0\cdot02$) association between blood glucose condition and rated aggressiveness was obtained, in conformity with the hypothesis. More detailed analysis suggested the presence of curvilinear relationships such that moderate hypoglycemia produces maximal aggressiveness, while both normal glycemia and severe hypoglycemia were characterized by less aggression.

Fully aware of the problems of interpreting correlational data about complex phenomena, Bolton considered the possibility of aggression causing hypoglycemia but rejected it on the basis of clinical evidence. On the other hand, he envisaged a possible spiral effect whereby physiologically caused irritability releases aggression in others to which the individual responds, with the result that the hypoglycemia worsens. The next problem was to consider how hypoglycemia is related to the broader eco-cultural setting: since its exact etiology is still imperfectly understood, though undoubtedly complex, this was a difficult task. Nevertheless, Bolton constructed a tentative model reproduced in Fig. 4.1.

It is not feasible to summarize Bolton's extensive discussion of this model, which refers to a substantial volume of research evidence for most of the links and feedback loops. On the other hand, it should be mentioned that he made an attempt to test parts of the model for which measurements could be obtained. Thus in a multiple-regression

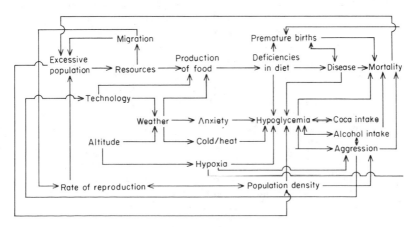

FIG. 4.1. A model of the bio-aggression system of the Quolla.

analysis two independent variables, density and protein deficiency, accounted for 20 per cent of the variance in hypoglycemia levels. On the other hand, aggression as a dependent variable failed to reach significance, indicating the indirect nature of the complex relationships.

Bolton was careful not to claim that the variable he had isolated, hypoglycemia, was *the* cause; rather, he described it as merely one element in a complex web of causes that together opened the door for other environmental, historical, or child-rearing hypotheses. His general strategy—relatively unusual for anthropologists—is more in line with that adopted by psychologists. In particular his model bears at least a family resemblance to that subsequently developed by Berry (1976), in that both relate eco-cultural factors to variations in cognitive styles, the latter having been very influential. Modes of socialization are treated as an intervening variable in Berry's model, but in psychological anthropology they are often the primary object of study. This will be our next consideration.

Notes

1. Barnouw (1973); Bock (1980); LeVine (1973).
2. It has been pointed out by Barnouw (1973) that by describing the three tribes at different phases of their history—Mundugumor in the past, before she had arrived, Arapesh and Tchambuli in the colonial era of enforced peace—Mead (at the very least) greatly enhanced the contrast between them. Thus, Tchambuli men used to be headhunters until the imposition of colonial rule, and it is possible to regard the change as one in which Tchambuli men were forcibly deprived of some previously essential components of their masculine role.
3. Here is a fairly typical example:
   > Thus we find the staple food of this culture area symbolically equated with semen, tears, blood, child, excrements, and the ground into which it is put and out of which it is taken represented as suckling or pregnant woman. The Trobriand Islanders use the following formula for planting:
   > > Boginai [name of woman] is recently deflowered . . . But your vulva, Bomigwagu [another woman] over there at the corner of the fence, has for a long time had considerable circumference.
   >
   > Evidently 'defloration' refers to the breaking of the ground and the big vulva means deep planting. We may now suggest that the unconscious meaning of taking roots out of the ground was originally the body destruction fantasy of pulling 'good body contents' out of the mother's body and that the restitution phase of this fantasy led, by chance, to the origin of the cultivation of these plants.
   >
   > Roheim, 1943, p. 57

4. A more extensive discussion of the work of Kardiner and his associates, somewhat more sympathetic than my own, is to be found in Bock (1980).
5. Reported in Honigman (1967, p. 129).
6. But it should be noted that even some of Linton's ethnographic material has subsequently been subjected to devastating criticisms (Suggs, 1971).
7. See Hallowell (1955, 1976).
8. Carstairs also discusses, though less thoroughly, the personalities of women. A more recent study of father–daughter relations in Bengal (Roy, 1975) concentrates on the problems of women.
9. Among the few early references I have been able to find is Heider (1958); he is unusual among psychologists in that he had his finger on the pulse of ordinary people. A recent empirical study by Silver and Sabini (1978) used hypothetical scenarios to find out whether their subjects would be able to interpret the characters' feelings as 'envy'; this they mostly managed to do, indicating that the layman is not lacking in insight. The tracing of relevant studies is made difficult by the significant fact that before 1973 there was no entry for 'envy' in the *Psychological Abstracts*; thereafter there is an entry that merely reads "Envy (see Jealousy)"—as though these words were the same! A useful survey of the varying manifestations of envy in a range of cultures has been provided by an anthropologist, Foster (1972); he also speculates about the psychological processes involved in both the expression of envy and defences against it; needless to say, these speculations are psychoanalytically inspired.
10. As was made clear in Chapter 1, rationalist/structuralists are less interested in behaviour as such, and even those structural/functionalists who concentrate on the empirical study of behaviour are sometimes strongly opposed to *any* explanations in psychological terms. Those not averse in principle may remain unconvinced by Freudian approaches, as, for instance, Leach (1976), who wrote: "My general conclusion is that the hunches of psycho-analysts are often correct, but the 'theory' by which they seek to justify their hunches is of such intellectual crudity and so lacking in sophistication that it has practically no value as a general tool for the analysis of ethnographic materials." (p. 96.) While I do not wish to convey the impression that anthropologists in general are in favour of psychoanalysis, it is nonetheless true that psychoanalysis is resorted to by them more than any other psychological theory.
11. In a recent series of papers entitled "Rethinking culture and personality theory", Shweder (1979a, 1979b, 1980) has critically examined various positions and proposed a new approach based on a combination of neo-Freudian and neo-Tylorian principles. While Shweder's ideas are stimulating and worthy of study, I feel that their predominantly cognitive orientation would not meet the anthropologist's need for a theory that adequately encompasses the orectic aspects of human behaviour.
    A closely reasoned defence of a modified form of psychoanalytic theory is provided by LeVine (1981), whose gist is expressed in the following summary:

> Psychoanalytic theory provides a framework for conceptualizing individual mental processes as a system of interdependent parts, hierarchically organized, with processes for maintaining a steady state, for growth and disintegration. It does not compete with the empirical psychologies of perception, cognition, memory, language, affect, and learning, with which it should be entirely consistent, but deals with a higher level they do not touch, viz., their organization in the experience and behavior of the individual. This is a level in which cultural beliefs and values are salient, providing the individual with the collective meanings, standards and expectancies that form the context of personal experience and the reference points for the evaluation of self and others. The comparative study of human development cannot do without this level of analysis, and it must bring some conceptual framework to investigation at that level; hence the relevance of psychoanalytic theory.
>
> p. 64

LeVine also makes specific recommendations of appropriate strategies of cross-cultural research, citing anthropological studies that have made effective use of these.

12. Psychologists and medical researchers have devoted a great deal of effort to examining the impact of malnutrition on mental development; a good survey of the literature is to be found in Werner (1979, Chapter 5).

13. Barth (1974), "On responsibility and humanity: Calling a colleague to account". The subsequent discussion appeared in *Current Anthropology* (1975), vol. 16, pp. 343–58.

14. The men were periodically given psychological tests, including personality measures. Some of these, such as the MMPI, at least in part reflected the dramatic personality changes that had taken place. Others, especially projective techniques (including the Rorschach), were entirely negative. This clearly indicates the shortcomings of personality measures even within Western culture.

15. It is of interest to note that one of the authors referred to Lewinian experiments on authoritarian and democratic group organization in support of the hypothesis; but Bolton points out that life in the villages, far from being authoritarian, is rather 'anarchic'. Subsequently Bolton (1979) tested some alternative hypotheses relating aggressiveness to social support and social status, but these failed to account for the incidence of aggressiveness and litigation. On the other hand a recent study of hypoglycemia (Bolton, 1981) provided further evidence of its causal link with hostility.

5 | Socialization

There is broad agreement among psychologists and anthropologists about the meaning of 'socialization'. Schaffer (1980) surveyed a variety of psychological definitions of the term, concluding that there is consensus at least about the ultimate function of the process, namely, preparing individuals for life within a particular society. Anthropologists express essentially the same notion when they say that socialization is the process whereby culture is transmitted from one generation to the next.

The first and most obvious lesson to be learnt from anthropology is the huge range of variation in socialization practices across the world. Anthropological observations are, of course, confined to global aspects and do not include the microprocesses that have increasingly become the focus of psychological studies.[1] At any rate, at the macro-level there is evidence that Euramerican socialization practices encompass only small segments of extensive continua. Taking just a few examples, onset of weaning may range from less than two weeks to several years; it may be gradual and gentle, or abrupt and traumatic, as when the mother smears hot pepper on her nipples to give the child a painful shock. The same applies to toilet training, and the general atmosphere in which socialization takes place may be permissive and easy-going to exceedingly harsh. There are also variations relevant to the current concern with the details of interactions between child and caretaker. The bulk of such work is, understandably, devoted to the mother–child dyad; and while it is true that the mother is nearly always the most important single caretaker, on a global perspective the task is typically shared with other adults[2] and with older children (Weisner and Gallimore, 1977). So far, we know little about the consequences of this for the development of the child.

Most studies have been concerned with the effects of variations in socialization practices, and there has been little emphasis on the complementary issue that has been well expressed by Blurton-Jones (1975, p. 76): ''The fact that social behaviour and child-rearing practices vary from culture to culture implies that variations in social behaviour are associated with variations in child-rearing, but it does not imply that the existence of social behaviour depends upon the kinds of features of child-rearing that are seen to vary between cultures.''

In other words, as implied by the definitions cited at the beginning, most effort has been directed at showing how children come to be adapted to a particular society and culture, rather than towards isolating those elements common to socialization practices everywhere that are necessary and sufficient to make the child into a full member of the human family. Again, this question of universals cannot be adequately answered without help from anthropology.

In this chapter I shall attempt to illustrate some of the ways in which anthropologists have studied problems related to socialization and social behaviour. In view of the immense richness and variety of such materials, the selection is bound to be somewhat arbitrary.

In the older and more traditional ethnographies designed to portray a community as a whole, descriptions of child rearing and child behaviour came in as part of the account of what used to be known as the 'life-cycle'—customs relating to birth, infancy, childhood, adolescence, and so on. Taken together, such work has yielded a mass of information scattered over numerous monographs which, as will be shown, has become available in usable form. Although there are some early examples of writers particularly interested in childhood (e.g. Kidd, 1906), most studies of this kind are of a more recent date.

A fairly representative selection of anthropological accounts of child rearing in various parts of the world has been edited by Middleton (1970b), who also provided an extensive bibliography. The detailed examples I shall cite are all drawn from Africa, illustrating the extent of variation to be found within the continent. Richards (1964) dealt with the Ganda of Uganda, her material being obtained by observations, descriptions of their childhood by informants and questionnaires administered in schools. She reports that in the past the father in the Ganda family expected, and was accorded, an extreme degree of deference by his wife, children, and other members of the household:

> Children knelt when they spoke to their father, crouching on the floor
> at the door of his room. This is still done in most village homes and
> young children kneel to greet older guests, putting their clasped hands

on those of the visitor and speaking in a high-pitched squeaky voice which is thought to be especially respectful . . . Children were expected to keep silent at meals—to sit upright with legs neatly folded under them, at the end of the long mat that served as a table. They had to refrain from yawning, giggling, or moving away from the dinner mat. Their father's chair or stool was sacrosanct and might never be touched.

p. 259

The father commanded instant and unquestioning obedience, and any failure to comply or other insolence was a very serious offence; as such it was severely (and in the past, savagely) punished. The most frequent forms of punishment were beatings, deprivation of food, or locking the child outside at night. There were indications that in the past serious injuries were sometimes inflicted, leaving the child scarred for life. Generally the father was regarded as having absolute power over the persons of his children.

The children themselves were expected to, and in fact did, accept their father's right to deal with them as he thought fit; punishment was taken without rancour or complaint. Richards quoted children as saying that they were grateful for the kindness shown by punishing them when they did wrong, and a common proverb has it that ''to beat a child is not to hate it''. Nevertheless, when questioned about their attitudes towards their fathers, the predominant response was 'fear', though not unmixed with respect and admiration. It would seem that boys were more terrified than girls. On the other hand, the mother was viewed as a good and kindly figure, one who helps to protect against the father's wrath. Given this kind of relationship to the father, Richards shows that the potential hatred and jealousy towards him is at least implicitly recognized in Ganda institutions; e.g. a son is forbidden to sit on his father's chair because this would indicate a wish to succeed him while the father was still alive.[3]

The father's unrestricted power made it possible for him to bestow favours on some children and deprive others in an arbitrary way, e.g. in nominating his heir. This inevitably caused rivalry between siblings, which is also enshrined in proverbial wisdom: ''Brothers are like dried gourds. They bang against each other.'' (p. 269.) On the other hand, the relationships between brother and sister, less directly threatened by rivalry, were often close.

In general the overriding authority of the father, which was a function of sheer physical paternity, did not cease when the children reached maturity but continued to be asserted when the offspring tried to make his or her own way in life. Richards argued most convincingly that the father–son relation closely paralleled that between chief or king and subject, so that a single model of absolute authority pervaded the whole society. A brief sketch of the rights of the former Kabakas (kings) over their subjects will illustrate this similarity.

The Kabakas were absolute rulers who required extreme deference from their subjects, who could only speak to them on their knees (''the Kabaka's secretary kneels as he hands His Highness the telephone'' (p. 274)). There had to be constant expressions of loyalty, respect, and praise. The Kabakas were owed complete obedience to the extent of an utter surrender of any subject's person if they requested it, and the subjects had no rights against them. They could and did command not merely their subjects' labour and property, but also their wives and children, if they so desired. It is an astonishing and also important fact that even in relatively recent times this does not appear to have been resented. Thus, in 1955 a middle-aged teacher told Richards: ''If the Kabaka took your wife you would just go down on your knees and thank him, and in time, if she became a favourite, she would probably ask something for you and you might get promotion.'' (p. 276.) In the past Kabakas were apt to punish people brutally, by mutilations and executions, apparently sometimes just as a whim of power if they disliked someone; and those who survived had to thank the Kabaka. In spite of all this—and perhaps also because of it—people felt that they were completely dependent on the Kabaka and owed him everything as the embodiment of the community.

The parallels are so obvious that there is no need to labour them. However, it might be pointed out that this was a culture where a client–patron system obtained such that advancement depended upon behaviour designed to elicit favours from superiors wielding arbitrary power (as typified by the teacher's statement) and where it was crucial to avoid offending such superiors in any way. Given these requirements, a home where the father is a miniature tyrant offers a most effective learning situation for coping with the kinds of problems the person is liable to encounter later. It is an intriguing question how far parents are aware of preparing their children to fit into the community, as opposed to merely following established practice. Richards found some evidence of people knowing what they were doing: Ganda fathers defended their harshness towards their offspring by explaining that only a humble and obedient child who is anxious to please superiors will get on in life.[4]

An almost totally different picture was drawn by Read (1959) in her study of socialization among the Ngoni of Central Africa. Read set out the child-rearing objectives of the Ngoni themselves, showing with a wealth of detail how they attempted to transmit the values and skills of their culture. As in practically all traditional African cultures, considerable emphasis was placed on good manners and respect towards elders and superiors; but relationships to parents and other people in the child's environment were easy and harmonious. Boys went through a tough training as cattle herders and hunters, and the puberty ritual was an occasion for the assertion of paternal authority. Yet it is clear that children were not coerced or subdued, the relationships between father and son being one of mutual affection and trust. Paternal authority among the Ngoni was not incompatible with personal dignity and self-respect.

Another fundamental characteristic of the Ngoni was their concern for the rule of law, impartially enforced; Read witnessed a court case where a chief awarded a complainant heavy damages against his own son. In this connection Read illustrated the fact that even quite young children rehearsed in their play the tasks of the adult social system:

> A perennial amusement among Ngoni boys of five to seven[5] was playing at law courts. They sat round in traditional style with a 'chief' and his elders facing the court, the plaintiffs and defendants presenting their case, and the counsellors conducting proceedings and cross-examining witnesses. In their high squeaky voices the little boys imitated their fathers whom they had seen in the courts, and they gave judgements, imposing heavy penalties, and keeping order in court with ferocious severity.
>
> p. 84

While some anthropologists brought in observations of play behaviour merely as illustrations, others devoted a great deal of study to play as part of the socialization process itself. In fact, the 'anthropology of play' has emerged as a special field in its own right, recently surveyed in two useful volumes (Lancy and Tindall, 1976; Schwartzman, 1978). Play and games are, of course, involved not merely in social and emotional development, which is our present concern, but equally in cognitive development.

Perhaps the most ambitious effort ever to demonstrate how play contributes to the shaping of a character was the work of Bateson and Mead (1942) in Bali. They took thousands of still photographs and feet of film to record, among other things, the fine-grained aspects of the relationships between parents and children in order to show the subtle ways in which cultural elements are communicated from one generation to the next. Play behaviour was also recorded in minute detail, and its analysis was used in an attempt to interpret certain typical features of Balinese culture such as their formalized style of social interaction, the value they place on close spatial proximity coupled with sudden withdrawals in the form of becoming totally unresponsive or even falling into a trance. Whatever the validity of the interpretations of the highly complex Balinese culture (cf. Geertz, 1973), such crucial features as the sudden withdrawal have been convincingly traced to their childhood origins and related to types of play.

A few anthropologists have borrowed the technique of projective doll play, but I find these less useful than simple records of observed behaviour because the workers appear to have approached the task with strong theoretical preconceptions which probably led them to influence the behaviours.[6] Hence, I shall conclude this part of the discussion with a brief extract from Hogbin's (1946) account of childhood in a New Guinea tribe, illustrating early sex role learning:

> Wanai (a girl) was now busy making mud pies and at this point begged Kalasika (boy) to build her an oven where these might be cooked. Gwa (boy) joined in the game, and, although no fire was kindled, the grubby mess was wrapped in leaves and put into the middle of a pile of stones. Wanai next made out that her water bottles were empty and told Niabula (boy) to fill them. "No, that's women's work," said Gwa. "We men don't touch such things. You go yourself." An argument would have developed had not Gabwe (old woman) interposed and persuaded them all to play a hand game with little white stones.
>
> p. 276

This brief survey illustrates the fact that even anthropologists who eschew depth interpretations often seek to demonstrate the continuity between child training and child behaviour and adult life. Although such relationships are not usually conceptualized in terms of 'personality', much of the material has obvious implications for the ways in which behavioural dispositions and values are inculcated during childhood and adolescence. The advantage of such material for the psychologist is that it conveys a much more clear-cut picture of such connections than could be discerned in modern industrial cultures, where they are blurred by the prevailing heterogeneity. This is probably also one reason why we have relatively few observations of natural behaviour in such cultures as compared to traditional ones, the other reason being the more difficult conditions of observation; as already mentioned, far less behaviour takes place in the open in temperate, as compared to tropical, settings.

The drawback of such observational studies, from the standpoint of the psychologist, is that they are mostly confined to the demonstration of a satisfactory congruence between child rearing or play and some salient adult behaviour patterns, without direct evidence of a connection.

However, it hardly behoves psychologists to complain too much about that, since their own efforts in that direction have not been very successful. With the recognition of the complexity of the early antecedents of adult behaviour, on the one hand, and the fact that feedback processes are likely to be involved, on the other, few straightforward causal links are to be expected. Instead of being critical, we should therefore make use of the anthropological offerings that are so plentifully available for the purpose of gaining greater insights into a process that is more readily laid bare for inspection in traditional cultures. At the same time, as will be shown shortly, attempts have been made to get beyond individual cases in order to arrive at broader generalizations.

The discussion so far has been entirely concerned with the socialization process as producing common adult characteristics, ignoring intracultural variations. These are, of course, recognized by the people themselves, who often have quite elaborate 'theories' of personality (Selby, 1975), a topic to be taken up again later. Here I wish to show, in relation to socialization, that indigenous conceptions of the determinants of personality should be taken seriously. This is because they may influence modes of handling children and thereby be self-validating, and in particular circumstances this can be testable.

In order to set the stage a brief outline of the traditional Akan (Ashanti, in Ghana) notions is necessary. There are two key conceptions relating to the individual, namely, *sunsum* and *okara* or *'kra*. *Sunsum* has been defined by Danquah (1944) as 'personality' or 'ego' but this is somewhat misleading, as his own discussion indicates. While corresponding in some respects to these concepts, it has properties strange to us and rooted in traditional beliefs. The common element is that *sunsum* designates the appearance and individuality of a person, a form of consciousness and also certain unconscious aspects. On the other hand a *sunsum* may wander about while a person is asleep; and if it meets other *sunsums* on such excursions it may get hurt, in which case the person will feel unwell, or it may even get killed, and then the person will sicken and die. A man's *sunsum* can catch his wife in adultery, and then deal with her so that she becomes ill and dies.[7]

While the notion of *'kra* overlaps to some extent with that of *sunsum*, it also has in other contexts a quite distinctive meaning. It is as though both were in a part–whole relationship, except that it is not always certain which is part and which is whole. There is no doubt, however, that *'kra* is a more mystical idea, related to Akan cosmological beliefs. The *'kra* of a person exists before his birth; it may be the soul or spirit of a dead relation or other person, who returns to earth and through the intermediary of a god or fetish enters a child. Now the *'kra* carries with it important elements of the person's destiny. It is not altogether an ineluctable fate, but a powerful influence shaping the child's disposition. It would appear that there are seven different types of 'kra, each associated with the day of the week on which the child is born. Accordingly, that day is dedicated to a rite called the 'washing' of the 'kra. Its function in the life of a person is a complex one. In addition to shaping character and foreshadowing destiny, the 'kra protects a person, may give him good or bad advice, help him to prosper or neglect him. Hence the need for rites to propitiate one's 'kra. Unlike the sunsum, it never leaves the person until death.

My own interest in these matters came about in an entirely serendipitous fashion. Not long after having arrived in Africa, I became involved in a discussion about the development of children's character with a group of Ashanti teachers and welfare workers. Most of the people present strongly maintained that the day of the week on which a person is born determines what type of character will emerge. Being ignorant of the traditional ideas, I remained politely sceptical. But one headmaster, whose previous contributions had proved him to be an intelligent and well-informed man, claimed that he had put the matter to the test. It appeared that he had consulted the records on corporal punishment and had found that those born on a Wednesday were by far the most frequently in trouble; and this accords with prevailing beliefs.[8]

On reflection it seemed to me quite reasonable that the expectations of other people should influence the development of a child's character. Many psychologists from McDougall onwards have put forward this idea, though without much evidence; this is probably because attitudes towards children vary greatly and irregularly in Euramerican society, so that it would be extremely difficult to track down any specific effects. In Ashanti and other Akan areas a powerful element of uniformity is introduced by the existence of socially determined beliefs about certain defined categories of children, who are named after the day on which they were born.

I therefore decided to try and put this to the test, and an objective criterion was found in the delinquency records at the court in Kumasi, the capital of Ashanti. Two appropriate day names were selected: Kwaku, the Wednesday boy already mentioned, who is held to be quick-tempered, aggressive, and a trouble-maker; by way of contrast Kwadwo, the Monday boy, is supposed to have a 'kra which makes him quiet, retiring, and peaceful. On this basis it was predicted that Kwaku would be significantly prone to commit offences against the person, whilst Kwadwo would generally have an unusually low delinquency rate. These predictions were significantly confirmed (Jahoda, 1954), showing that the ideas about personality and character held in various cultures may be of potential value when assessing personality development, and should not be neglected.[9]

The preceding discussion has been based essentially on the work of social and cultural anthropologists who analysed one particular society, including its socialization practices. Psychological anthropologists aim to go beyond this in order to arrive at generalizations valid across cultures, employing for this purpose psychological tools. In the words of Honigman (1975):

> Assuming continuity between the realms of human nature and culture, psychological anthropologists have utilized psychoanalytic, behavioristic (learning theory), ethological and other concepts, including temperament, in studying the role of motivation in cultural and social systems.
>
> p. 605

Following the decline of the older culture-and-personality school associates with Kardiner, a radical new departure was pioneered by Whiting and Child (1954) and carried on by Whiting with other associates over many years. This new approach, now known as the 'hologeistic' method, has continued to flourish and expand yet is relatively little noticed by psychologists. In order to explain the method it will be necessary to backtrack a little and briefly describe the origin of the so-called 'Cross-cultural Survey', based on the Human Relations Area Files (HRAF).

Over the years an enormous mass of ethnographic material has accumulated, buried in libraries all over the world. Anyone wishing to conduct a study comparing features across a variety of cultures would greatly benefit by having access to all these sources, but in the past that was impossible in practice. What was needed was an efficient retrieval system, and this was created through the initiative of Murdock in 1937 at the Yale Institute of Human Relations—hence, the name. The details of the method are not essential here; they are given in an appendix to this chapter since, as I shall explain later, the method is of potential value for psychologists. All that concerns us at the moment is that Whiting and Child had access to the files and extracted relevant material from them relating to 75 societies.

Such an extension of the range of comparisons was of course achieved at a cost: it was necessary to sacrifice the integrity and totality of both personalities and cultures. They deliberately abandoned previous efforts to arrive at detailed interpretations of the relationship between culture and personality in particular cases. Instead, they said, "We will deal with *personality processes* as mediating between *certain aspects of culture* which lead to them and others to which they in turn lead." (p. 3.) The phrases I have italicized show that they focused merely on some constituent elements viewed as being critical for the relationship to be studied. Their theoretical model postulated the causal chain set out below, though admitting that the actual direction of causation might be reversed in particular cases:

Maintenance systems

↓

Child training practices

↓

Personality variables

↓

Projective systems

The 'maintenance system' consists of the socio-economic and political basis of the society regarded as the major influence in determining the mode of its child rearing; this latter shapes certain specific aspects of personality. Lastly, these personality variables are responsible for the nature of the 'projective systems' which manifest themselves in forms of art, religion, or particular sets of customs. It should be noted that all the component parts of the scheme, with the exception of 'personality variables', are directly observable. In fact, ethgnographers working in a culture would normally be expected to record information about these aspects of behaviour and institutions. The personality variables, on the other hand, have quite a different logical status: they constitute hypothetical 'intervening variables' that are held to account for the functioning of the system in different cultures. Thus if child rearing builds certain motives and dispositions into the person, then corresponding adult behaviours should result. Since the link between child training and adult personality was the king-pin of the whole enterprise, its starting point was some kind of psychological hypothesis about this relationship. However, there was a further practical difficulty here, as ethnographic materials hardly ever contain sufficiently systematic descriptions of adult personality to be usable. In order to get around this problem, Whiting and Child had to make a further assumption embodied in the scheme; namely, that different kinds of adult personalities will lead to corresponding regularities of behaviour at the *institutional* level within cultures, such institutions being manifestations of projective systems.

It will be evident that the general model employed was a hypothesis-testing one. The theories from which Whiting and Child (1953) derived their hypotheses was an eclectic mixture of psychoanalysis and behaviour theory, sometimes one being pitted against the other. It was of course necessary to translate psychoanalytic concepts into types of behaviour, for it must be remembered that all they had at their disposal were ethnographic field observations, since the approach consists of secondary analysis not involving any direct study of behaviour.[10]

The early work by Whiting and Child (1953) found modest but significant support for the predictions of both psychoanalysis and behaviour theory. In subsequent studies Whiting came to rely increasingly on Freudian hypotheses, in the main finding them strongly supported. The whole series of investigations has been reviewed by Kline (1977) from the standpoint of cross-cultural research as a testing ground for the validity of psychoanalysis. Kline took the view that the results of Whiting and his associates constitute powerful evidence for Freudian theory, mainly on the grounds that it would be difficult to put forward alternative interpretations to account for the significant associations. There is no doubt some substance in this argument; yet in spite of being sympathetic towards psychoanalysis, I am rather less impressed than Kline by the evidence from hologeistic studies.

Kline cites one of the best-known studies by Whiting et al. (1958) dealing with the function of male initiation rites, considered as a means of resolving tensions due to Oedipal rivalry. Kline did not cite a subsequent paper (Burton and Whiting, 1961) where the previously central Oedipus complex slipped into the background with a shift to the notion of "sex identity conflict" which had appeared only as a footnote in the earlier article. Moreover, other workers (Cohen, 1964; Young, 1965) have put forward social-structural interpretations of initiation rites dispensing with child-rearing or personality variables altogether. Also some more recent work has thrown considerable doubt on Whiting's assumption that initiation rites necessarily have an immediate impact (Herzog, 1973). Such considerations do not dispose of the puzzle why a significant association should have been obtained, but they indicate not merely the existence of alternative hypotheses to account for initiation rites, but that the particular causal connection postulated is unlikely to be correct.

What fails to come out altogether in Kline's (1977) summaries is the sometimes inordinate length and tenuous nature of the chain of reasoning involved in the hypothesis, so it may be useful to illustrate this with a study (Whiting, 1959) that followed on from the previous one (Whiting et al., 1958), both concerned with the effects of the duration of the post-partum sex taboo. Earlier studies had indicated that a long period of sexual abstinence tends to be associated with domestic arrangements in which the infant sleeps in the mother's bed, while the husband sleeps elsewhere. The assumption was then made by Whiting that, being thus sexually deprived, the mother "may unconsciously seduce the child"—whatever that could mean. At any rate this would produce powerful sexual anxiety and therefore lead to paranoia, itself a defence against sexual anxiety. Hence, the prevalence of belief in sorcery could be regarded as a defence against sexual anxiety, itself engendered by exclusive mother–child sleeping arrangements, which in turn is a function of the duration of the post-partum sex taboo. This exceedingly tortuous hypothesis was tested by constructing a contingency table wherein 36 societies were allocated to cells according to whether they were polygamous and/or nomadic (and thus had a long sex taboo, versus others with a shorter one) and whether or not beliefs in the causation of illness through sorcery were present. The outcome was consistent with the prediction, with $P = 0 \cdot 004$.

Can such a study, mentioned among the confirmatory ones by Kline, really be regarded as validating psychoanalytic theory? There is no doubt in my mind that the answer must be negative, for the correlation obtained is subject to a whole host of alternative interpretations. There is really no need for any detailed dissection, since the author himself later admitted that "the data are not very convincing" (Harrington and Whiting, 1972, p. 482). All this is, of course, not a critique of psychoanalysis as such, but merely of the view that hologeistic studies are a royal road towards its validation—personality and social processes are far too complex for that.

While the discussion so far has been concerned with psychoanalytically inspired hypotheses about socialization, the hologeistic approach itself is entirely neutral with regard to the nature of the hypotheses, if any, that are being tested.[11] An influential socialization study was that of Barry et al. (1959), based on an a priori analysis of the characteristics of child training likely to be needed in different types of subsistence economies. It was predicted, and confirmed, that hunting and fishing societies tended to encourage independence and self-reliance, while those deriving their food from animal husbandry or agriculture placed more emphasis on responsibility and obedience. With this and similar kinds of studies, there is little or no problem concerning the direction of causality, since subsistence is related to ecology and thus most unlikely to be an effect of child training. It is not even necessary to have any hypothesis at all, merely some appropriate question about the distribution of some practices, beliefs or ideas around the world. A study by Rogoff *et al.* (1975) dealing with the ages at which children are assigned roles and responsibilities of various kinds shows how interesting this can be; the passage below summarizes the salient findings:

> From our data it appears that in the age period centering on 5–7 years, parents relegate (and children assume) responsibility for care of younger children, for tending animals, for carrying out household chores and gathering materials for the upkeep of the family. The children also became responsible for their own social behavior and the method of punishment for transgressions changes. Along with new responsibility, there is the expectation that children between 5 and 7 years begin to be teachable. Adults give practical training expecting children to be able to imitate their example; children are taught social manners and inculcated in cultural traditions. Underlying these changes in teachability is the fact that at 5–7 years children are considered to attain common sense or rationality. At this age also, the child's character is considered to be fixed, and he begins to assume new social and sexual roles. He begins to join with groups of peers, and participate in rule games. The children's group separate by sex at this time. Concurrently, the children are expected to show modesty and sex differentiation in chores and social relationships is stressed. All of these variables indicate that at 5–7 the child is broadly categorized differently than before this age, as he becomes a more integral part of his social structure.
>
> p. 367

The hologeistic method is therefore a potentially valuable tool for psychologists, deserving to be better known and more widely used. Hence, a fuller and more technical account of it is given as an appendix to this chapter. At the same time it is of course not without short-comings, the chief one being the patchiness of data on some topics which sets limits on what one can do. It was in order to overcome this limitation that Whiting determined to arrange for the collection of systematic data on socialization in a sample of cultures, embarking upon an enterprise of previously unknown scale that lasted for almost one-quarter of a century.

The preliminary stage consisted of the description of the socio-cultural background and a broad sketch of child-rearing practices in the cultures selected, that were as follows: Nyansongo (Kenya); Khalapur (India); Taira (Okinawa); Jaxtlahuaca (Mexico); Tarong (Philippines); and Orchard Town (USA). A monograph was devoted to each of these in a book edited by Beatrice Whiting (1963). A full account of the methods employed in the whole project is given in an elaborate Field Manual (Whiting *et al.*, 1966), which shows the enormous care that went into its preparation. The units of study within each culture were small so as to allow for intensive work: communities of between 50 and 100 families were chosen, and from among these were selected 24 mothers and 24 of their children. The main stress was on the systematic observation of behaviour, interviews with mothers, and some projective techniques.

One of the early products of the project was concerned with child-rearing antecedents, based on interview with mothers (Minturn and Lambert, 1964). This was largely a factor-analytic study whose aim was "to discover pancultural factors in child-training practices and to use these to describe the similarities and differences in the six cultures we have studied" (p. 43). Seven factors emerged for which intra-cultural was greater than cross-cultural variance:

1. Responsibility training
2. Warmth of mother
3. Aggression training: peer-directed aggression
4. Proportion of time mother cared for baby
5. Proportion of time mother cares for child
6. Aggression training: mother-directed aggression
7. Emotional instability of the mother.

The relationships between factor scores and a number of environmental variables were examined, including the testing of several hypotheses. Such testing was not confined to the six cultures, but checked on a wider scale by the hologeistic method. While the study yielded much interesting descriptive material, the outcome as a whole must be regarded as disappointing. Only two hypotheses were solidly established, and these were not unduly impressive:

a. when other women are available to help, mothers tend to spend less time with their children;
b. in settings where many people live together in cramped quarters, children tend to be more severely punished for fighting with each other.

Further hypotheses relating to maternal warmth and instability received only weak confirmation. All these analyses were based on the interview data and projective techniques, but the main objective had been to relate this material to the behavioural observations. In the event this turned out to be much harder to achieve than had been anticipated, and after a struggle with a mountain of complex data covering some two decades, no clear pattern seems to have emerged.

The most important outcome of the project to date has been a book based on the analysis of the observed social behaviour of the children in the six cultures (Whiting and Whiting, 1975). The method consisted essentially of collecting 14 or more 5-minute behaviour samples over a period of several months to a year for each of the children. In order to indicate what the raw material looked like, a sample observation is reproduced below:

Sample Observation

Child observed: Kamlaa, 10-year-old girl
Date: 17 March 1955
Place: Kamlaa's house
Present: Mrs Makkhan, Kamlaa's grandmother
　　　　　Nacklii, Kamlaa's year-old boy cousin
　　　　　Mrs Dhiaar, Kamlaa's aunt and Nacklii's mother
　　　　　Mimlaa, 13-year-old girl

Mrs Makkhan and Mrs Dhiaar are cooking. Kamlaa comes back from seeing if Mimlaa is going to the fields. She wasn't able to find her because Mimlaa has just entered Kamlaa's courtyard. Kamlaa comes in after her and says, "I went to your house to see you and you weren't there." Mrs Makkhan says to Kamlaa, "Now take this food to the fields." Kamlaa answers, "Let me eat mine first." Mrs Makkhan says, "Take the food to the fields and eat yours there." Kamlaa replies, "No, I will eat here."

Nacklii has been inside sleeping. He wakes up and begins to cry. Kamlaa goes inside, gets him, and brings him back out saying, "No, I will eat here, because there won't be any left for me." Mrs Dhiaar shouts, "Don't we give you any food?" Mrs Makkhan says, "All right, we'll set your food aside for you." Kamlaa says, "All right." Mrs Makkhan tells her, "Go quickly."

pp. 217–18

While such material bears a superficial resemblance to ordinary anthropological observations, there are two fundamental differences. First, it was the product of time sampling and stands as an isolated episode, unrelated to context; second, it is further reduced by coding from a narrative to an aggregate of standardized sub-units capable of being treated quantitatively.

All social acts were first grouped into seventy types, eventually reduced to the twelve major categories listed in the left-hand column of Fig. 5.1. The scores on these categories for each of the children constituted the dependent variables. The independent ones were as follows: sex, age, nature of the situation in which the child was being observed, type of learning environment provided by the culture in which the child was being reared; and to these should be added another element, namely, the differences produced between individual children by intra-cultural environmental variations. While the monograph reports on all these, I propose to concentrate on the single key one, culture.

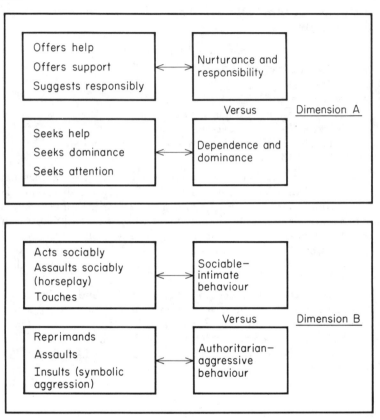

Fɪɢ. 5.1. Coding categories for child behaviour and corresponding dimensions.

For the purpose of analysing cross-cultural similarities and differences, the scores of children on each of the categories were pooled within each of the cultures, thereby averaging individual differences and yielding a net residual attributable to culture. The resulting cultural medians were then subjected to multidimensional scaling, from which two interpretable dimensions could be identified. These are set out in the right half of Fig. 5.1, where the acts corresponding to them may be seen on the left; the category 'insults' did not load highly on either dimension and was therefore omitted.

The next step, a great deal more difficult and elaborate than can be indicated here, consisted of a division of cultures according to median scores of children on dimensions A and B. The resulting groupings of cultures were then examined to discover what features they had in common that were compatible with the findings on child behaviour. The researchers asked themselves the question what differences in learning environments might lead to the observed variations in child behaviour.

The answer they arrived at as regards dimension A was 'cultural complexity', normally defined in terms of such characteristics as a cash economy, a centralized political and legal system, and the extent of occupational specialization. When the six cultures were rated on these criteria, dichotomization according to complexity did correspond to the distribution of children's scores on dimension A. This in itself does not, of course, explain how children acquire different forms of behaviour in more or less complex cultures. After further exploration of the data the authors concluded that the mediating factor was the mother's work-load: being greater in simpler societies, it leads to more training in nurturant-responsible behaviour that contributes to family and community welfare.

Classification of the six cultures along dimension B produced quite a different dichotomy, and after a similar search the conclusion was reached that household structure was the critical element here. The domestic arrangements in three of the cultures were based on the nuclear household confined to parents and children, where husband–wife relationships are close and intimate, and father–child interactions relatively frequent. The other cultures were distinguished by a patrilineal extended family, where authority is vested in a member of the grandparental generation, and the father's relationship with mother and children tends to be less close. However, it was not made very clear in this case how such differences in learning environments influence children's behaviour: Why should children from nuclear households score higher on 'acts sociably', 'assaults sociably', and 'touches', and those from the extended family on 'assaults' and 'reprimands'?

While the explanations suggested by the Whitings for the associations may be open to some doubt, the associations themselves have been firmly established (at least for these particular culture samples), and fall into the neat pattern displayed in Fig. 5.2. This model indicates that complexity and household structure are both independently associated with different aspects of children's behaviour.

The overall findings support neither those who hold human nature to be infinitely plastic and completely shaped by culture, nor believers in

overriding biological determinism. Different cultures produced differences in some behaviour patterns, while others cut across cultures.
Among the latter, the few clearly isolated were children's tendencies to
seek help and attention from adults, and to offer help and support to
infants.

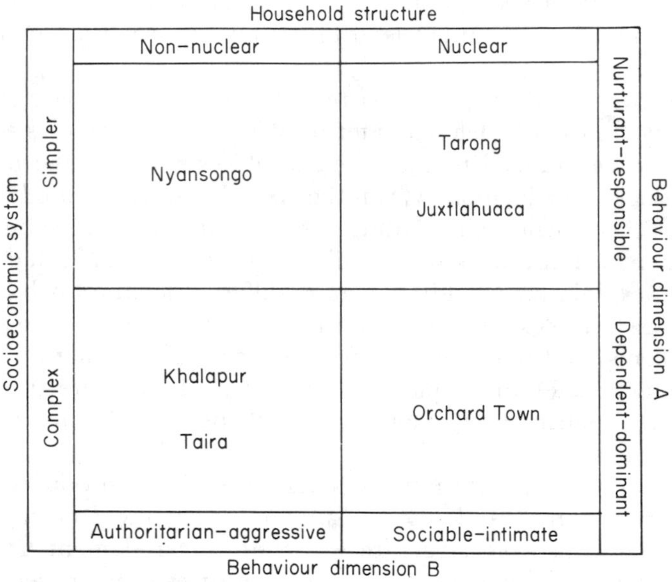

Household structure

	Non–nuclear	Nuclear	
Simpler	Nyansongo	Tarong Juxtlahuaca	Nurturant–responsible
Complex	Khalapur Taira	Orchard Town	Dependent–dominant
	Authoritarian–aggressive	Sociable–intimate	

Socioeconomic system (left vertical label)

Behaviour dimension A (right vertical label)

Behaviour dimension B

FIG. 5.2. The relationship between culture types and dimensions of social behaviour
(from Whiting and Whiting, 1975, p. 128).

While the present outline could hardly do justice to the wealth of
interesting material in the book, it should be evident that it was an
important project on an unprecedented scale, seeking to break new
ground. Hence, it merits close critical scrutiny, which I propose to
undertake from the following standpoint: we have here a team of
anthropologists who attempted to advance the study of socialization by
forsaking in the main the traditional anthropological approach and
adopted instead an essentially psychological one, aimed at generalization; the question I wish to consider is whether this new departure is
sufficiently promising to render the usual anthropological approach
obsolete.

The first aspect to consider is the nature of the raw material, i.e. the
'behaviour samples'. At first sight these appear to be ethological rather
than anthropological; but if one compares the approach with a purely
ethological one like that of Blurton-Jones and Konner (1973), it

becomes clear that it is not strictly ethological either. These authors studied sex differences in behaviour of London and of Bushman children, observing them in an outdoor situation in the presence of other children and adults. As in the Whiting project, behaviour was studied in random segments without any attempt at filling in the situational or cultural contexts but concentrating entirely on the nature of the interactions. But here the similarity ends, since the Whitings deliberately refrained from imposing any prior categories on their observers, asking merely for descriptive protocols. The ethologists, on the other hand, employed a set of closely defined categories in terms of which the observations were conducted. Admittedly, when one compares the categories used in the two approaches, there is a certain amount of overlap; in general, however, the ethological categories referred to smaller units of behaviour and require less interpretation. For instance, in the sphere of antagonistic behaviour the Whitings have categories like 'assaults on person', 'children fighting', or other behaviours that can be qualified by the adverb 'aggressively'. The ethologists' list includes the following, far more specific categories: 'hit', 'kick', 'bite', 'push', 'wrestle', 'bump', 'poke'.

Apart from the types of categories, the main contrast already mentioned is that the protocols consisted of narrative accounts that were sent to Cambridge, Massachusetts, where a set of behaviour codes was developed through a series of successive approximations by people without first-hand knowledge of the cultures. It is here that the psychological element of the approach comes in, since the Whitings' categories contain numerous psychological concepts involving inferences such as 'guilt', 'self-reliance', 'responsibility', 'achievement', and so on. While this obviously provides more information, it also runs more risk of errors of attribution or bias. It should be said that the Whitings themselves were acutely aware of this danger and made every effort to guard against it; yet insofar as it is inherent in the procedure (inferences *had* to be made from the protocols in order to be able to code them), the problem is inescapable.[12]

Apart from this important limitation, the indications are that the coding was reliable. Yet there remains the doubt about the validity of the psychological inferences made, it will be remembered, remote from the field. It might be argued that the successful elaboration of a model that appears to make sense of the behaviour patterns constitutes evidence in favour of the validity of the psychological inferences, but some caution is indicated here. This is because the model had not been envisaged at the start of the vast enterprise many years ago, and was arrived at inductively. The data underwent an extremely lengthy process of analysis, whereby various patternings were tried out in order to find the 'best fit'. Now there is, of course, no reason why hypotheses should not be the outcome of a project, but it must be stressed that they are hypotheses and the normal requirement is that they should be tested with fresh data. Given the scale of the work, this could hardly be expected in the present case. Hence, it would be wise not to regard the model as firmly established, since one can only judge it in terms of its inherent plausibility. I would here distinguish between the two parts of the model. Behaviour dimension A, contrasting 'nurturant–responsible' with 'dependent–dominant', seems to me both coherent and intelligible in terms of the requirements of the cultures displaying these patterns. On the other hand, dimension B, which juxtaposes 'authoritarian–aggressive' and 'sociable–intimate' does not seem to me to be convincingly related to the relevant learning environments. The implication that children from cultures with extended households are comparatively less sociable and more aggressive is one which I would be reluctant to accept on the basis of both personal observation and anthropological reports.

These reservations regarding some of the conclusions should not be allowed to obscure the fact that the work of the Whitings is the most extensive and ambitious study of certain critical aspects of socialization ever undertaken. Its value resides not only in the findings, but in the lessons it can teach us about further work in this sphere. The single outstanding one is that one needs a more systematic scrutiny of the 'learning environments', which the Whitings brought in only *ex post* in order to substantiate the model. This brings us back full circle to the need for a more directly anthropological approach, which alone can satisfy this requirement. Ideally such studies should be conducted by researchers competent in both psychology and anthropology, and there is at least one investigation that satisfies this requirement, providing a penetrating analysis of the learning environment within a particular culture. This is the study of Wolof socialization by Zempleni-Rabain (1973), herself trained in both psychology and anthropology, which will fittingly conclude this chapter.

Perhaps it will be best to begin with a short extract which strikingly brings out the contrast with the Whitings' approach:

A quite violent altercation took place between Yirim (4 years and 6 months) and his grandmother over a small box belonging to the child which the grandmother wanted to give to his small brother. Yirim cried wildly and his mother protested to the grandmother. After the child had remained disconsolate for more than half an hour, the grandmother calls out to him suddenly, in a lively way, saying: "Come and give me some big mangoes!" Everyone burst out laughing.

p. 228

Now this little episode is rather similar in scale and type to the sample observations used in the Whiting and Whiting (1975), one of which was given on p. 123, and the reader is invited to look at it again. The fragment of exchanges which took place at Kamlaa's house constitutes merely a 'behaviour sample', a specimen of the observed child's interactions. It is not related to any background, and most aspects remain obscure: for example, why is Kamlaa afraid that there will be no food for her? However, this is really beside the point since for the Whitings it constitutes merely an example of their raw material, relegated to an appendix. By contrast, the episode of little Yirim was specifically selected because it can throw light on Wolof culture and socialization practices. The key feature is the fact that the grandmother succeeds in consoling this very small child by *asking him* to make her a gift, instead of giving him something. This is discussed in detail, show-ing how the symbolism as well as the actual giving of food is, in Wolof culture, closely tied to the nature of relationships between different kinds of people, and can effect changes in such relations.

This whole process is traced right back to the period of weaning, which Zempleni-Rabain viewed from a standpoint quite distinct from that of most previous workers in this area:

> Studies made by the culture and personality school have found a difficulty in making sense of this weaning period, since they sought to understand it on the level of the events themselves, which were isolated and described along the lines of Western psychological models hastily transposed to fit the situation. In our opinion results will only be achieved by studying this crucial period *in the light of the child's ulterior relationships*, not only with its mother but with all those people with whom it comes into contact. It seems to us that only in this way will we be able to judge the significance of the fact of separation and the way its supposedly harmful effects are overcome or canalized.

pp. 221–2

Zempleni-Rabain then went on to analyse the mother–child rela-tionship in terms of two component systems, namely, mother-as-food and mother-as-support; and in her view neither of these is totally broken up at a given moment among the Wolof. The suckling relation-ship is closely associated with bodily contact with the mother, but both food and support systems come to be extended well before weaning. In the first place (and this probably applies to most traditional African

cultures) the child experiences from its earliest age close bodily contact
with different members of the community, so that the mother-as-
support tends to become more widely diffused. Secondly, solid food is
provided by the mother and other caretakers before weaning; the child
at that time has already ventured away from close proximity to the
mother, though always able to return for shelter and comfort. After
weaning there is highly permissive feeding, allowing the child considerable autonomy unrelated to adult meal times, whereby independent behaviour is encouraged. After weaning children are apt to
increase their demands for intimate physical contact, which are readily
granted by both mother and father. Moreover, the feeding relationship
continues for some time to parallel closely that which obtained before
weaning, as shown by the observation quoted below, where the child
was tied to the mother's back:

> Lying against his mother's back Abdou is whispering slightly and then
> clearly asks for something to eat. An elder brother brings him some rice.
> The mother tries to lift the child onto her lap. But he grumbles, pushes
> her away and spontaneously presses himself against her back, becoming
> immediately quiet. She hands him the bowl of rice over her shoulder; the
> child takes it and begins to eat all by himself, still leaning against her
> back. The mother lifts her left arm and passes the child a small tin of
> water; he leans over, grabs the tin which the mother still holds and
> drinks it in the same position.
>
> p. 224

Zempleni-Rabain also commented on the relatively casual nature of
the latter feeding relation, contrasting it with that of Western cultures
where it tends to be a focus of maternal anxiety, so that the acceptance
or refusal of food may be a primary channel for the expression of
emotional tensions. On the other hand, food is of great importance in
Wolof culture in an entirely different way, since together with clothing
it plays a predominant part within a system of ritual exchanges.
Mutual gift-giving is rigidly codified and serves to define the individual's position in a stratified society. Within the same stratum it is a
basic norm that generosity must be shown, and there are strictly
codified rules about hospitality.

Now a major part of the study was concerned to show how, from
weaning onwards, these fundamental rules began to be transmitted to
the children. The chief way in which this is done is by associating the
child with the sharing-out process, directly in the course of interaction
with his own group and indirectly by adults jokingly bringing him into
exchanges between different categories of adults such as kinsmen or
host and guest. For example, a father has given his two-year-old child a

sweet, and invites him to give some of it to a visiting kinsman. Or again, a mother asks her three-year-old child if she has a fiancé, and she names her maternal uncle who lives in the compound. On being asked what she will give him, the child said, "some rice and some *laax u bissap*", which, astonishingly for one so young, was the correct type of food prestation.

Rules and prohibitions relating to food are rarely enunciated directly, behaviour being instead controlled by relating it to the framework of exchange which binds siblings together. Thus, when a small boy took some sugar from his mother's hut, she did not scold him or tell him to return it. She merely said that his little brother is going to eat it, or that the older brother is going to look after it. Zempleni-Rabain then demonstrated how with increasing age the informal teaching of the sharing and exchange norms passes more and more into the hands of the sibling and age-mate groups themselves: "A mechanism for self-regulation exists in the fraternal group, due to the power inherent in the word of the adult, whose direct intervention is no longer needed." (p. 233.)

There are three points to be specially noted about this excellent study. In the first place, it throws fresh light on the weaning process by looking at it from a broader perspective, analysing its antecedents as well as what follows. It should not be thought, of course, that the particular case of the Wolof is in all, or even most, respects typical of African cultures—the Wolof are probably relatively more gentle in their weaning practices than some others. Nevertheless, the general element of continuity stressed by Zempleni-Rabain in opposition to the conventional 'traumatic' interpretations is likely to be the rule rather than the exception.

Secondly, the work shows in a more compelling manner than the present summary can convey that among the Wolof some of the fundamental social norms of the culture begin to be systematically and, in the main, painlessly instilled into the children almost immediately after weaning. Moreover, the powerful role of the sibling group in this process is spelt out in considerable detail; and it would be surprising if similar processes could not be found elsewhere.

Lastly, these important insights could not have been achieved without a method which consisted of carefully detailed observation of child and parental behaviour. These observations were guided by, and interpreted in terms of, a combination of psychological and anthropological approaches. While it required psychological skills to conduct the observations of child behaviour, such behaviour could only acquire a richer meaning within the framework of an anthropological insight into the cultural characteristics of the Wolof and the way in which their society functions.[13]

Notes

1. On the other hand, cross-cultural psychologists have begun more fine-grained studies of that kind, reported in Munroe *et al.* (1981).
2. Among these, grandparents are probably exceptionally important. See Epstein (1978, chapter 3).
3. But it should be noted that similar prohibitions exist where the father–son relationship is much more amicable, as it is among the Tallensi described by Fortes (see p. 91). Unlike Fortes, Richards did not relate the pattern of relationships to the Oedipus complex, though the Ganda would seem to provide an unusually clear setting for its powerful manifestation.
4. One is tempted to speculate that Amin, though not a Ganda himself, may have modelled his behaviour on that of the old Kabakas while ruling over a country of which Buganda forms the most important part.
5. Ages are often difficult to assess in traditional cultures, and I imagine that Read may have somewhat underestimated them in this case.
6. An extreme example is that of Roheim (cited in Schwartzman, 1978), who openly encouraged the children to make their dolls enact coital games, drawing conclusions about their reactions to the 'primal scene' that are, to say the least, far-fetched.
7. The *sunsum* is also invoked in an indigenous version of psychosomatic illness, which originated long before this idea became accepted in the West. An old high-priest gave the following account of the reasons for the *Apo* ceremony to Rattray (1923, p. 153):

> You know that every one has a *sunsum* that may get hurt or knocked about or become sick, and so make the body ill. Very often, although there may be other causes, e.g. witchcraft, ill health is caused by the evil and hate that another has in his head against you. Again, you too may have hatred in your head against another, because of something that person has done to you, and that too causes your *sunsum* to fret and become sick. Our forbears knew this to be the case, and so they ordained a time, once every year, when every man and woman, free man and slave, should have freedom to speak out just what was in their head, to tell their neighbours just what they thought of them, and of their actions, and not only their neighbours, but also the king or chief. When a man has spoken freely thus, he will feel his *sunsum* cool and quieted, and the *sunsum* of the other person against whom he has now openly spoken will be quieted also. The King of Ashanti may have killed your children, and you hate him. This has made him ill, and you ill too; when you are both allowed to say before his face what you think, you both benefit.

8. The traditional calendrical system of the Ashanti, unusually for Africa,

also had a seven-day week; but this was part of a 42-day cycle in terms of which time was mainly reckoned (Rattray, 1923).

9. Perhaps a small postscript is desirable. While the outcome was satisfactory in confirming the hypothesis about expectations, my Ashanti friends were quick to point out that the results equally supported *their* views about the effects of *'kra*, and it was difficult to give a convincing reply. Theoretically it might be possible to strengthen the argument by collecting evidence about the actual processes involved, though this would be extremely difficult in practice. Even then, it is doubtful whether the believers in the traditional view would have been convinced. The lesson is that science itself rests on a set of assumptions, themselves at some stage unverifiable, about the nature of the universe and our place within it. Other assumptions are possible, not necessarily in logical conflict with the scientific ones.

10. It may seem redundant to labour this, but I have found that students who read the literature often came away with the mistaken impression that actual people had been studied.

11. While the growth in hologeistic studies has been rapid (Schaefer, 1977), the resort to Freudian hypotheses appears to have declined.

12. If one compares the findings of the Whitings with those of Blurton-Jones and Konner in the sphere of sex differences, where they overlap, there is a broad congruence: boys tend to be more aggressive. The main discrepancy concerns 'seeking dominance', a psychological notion of the kind ethologists normally eschew.

13. A fuller account of Wolof socialization, in French, may be found in Rabain (1979).

Appendix: Resources for the hologeistic method

The Human Relations Area Files (HRAF) are designed as a data archive incorporating an efficient retrieval system. The two fundamental classifications are those of cultures and features relating to the cultures. The first of these raises the vexed question as to how a 'culture' might be operationally defined. Naroll (1973) suggested the notion of a 'cultunit', by which he means ''people who are domestic speakers of a common distinct language and who belong either to the same state or the same contact group'' (p. 731). In practice the necessary information for assigning peoples to such 'cultunits' is not often available; and realizing this, Naroll came to regard his notion as mainly a conceptual norm that can only be approximated in reality. The actual classification employed in the HRAF and embodied in the *Outline of World Cultures* (OWC) (Murdock, 1975) is a pragmatic one. The world is divided into eight major geographical regions, which are then subdivided, usually on a political basis; within each sub-region more specific cultural units are designated, employing an alphanumerical code. Thus, FE 12 indicates the *Twi* speakers (12) within Ghana (E), which is part of Africa (F). The OWC lists several thousand cultures, of which over 300 are actually represented in the Files. This may sound a small proportion, but even so the Files total well over half a million pages of text! The OWC is given on top of each File unit, and the onus is still on the individual researcher to define a 'culture' for a particular purpose.

The second classification is contained in the *Outline of Cultural Materials* (Murdock *et al.*, 1971) that was arrived at empirically, with the needs of social scientists uppermost in mind. It consists of 79 major subject headings, each subdivided into more specific content categories totalling more than 700. Here only numerical codes are used, and there are many helpful cross-references. As an illustration, the subdivisions of the major heading of 'socialization' are shown below:

  86 *Socialization*
  861 Techniques of inculcation
  862 Weaning and food training
  863 Cleanliness training
  864 Sex training
  865 Aggression training
  866 Independence training
  867 Transmission of cultural norms
  868 Transmission of skills
  869 Transmission of beliefs

These two major classifications form the basis for the preparation of the Files. For any given cultural group, primary source material is incorporated, most commonly consisting of anthropological monographs; but the writings of other social scientists or even journalists are sometimes drawn upon. In the case of older sources it is usually reports by travellers, missionaries,[1] or administrators, non-English publications being translated. The whole of the material relating to a particular culture is processed by coders applying the OMC categories, whose numbers are marked in the margins adjacent to the relevant passages. A sample File page is shown in Fig. 5.3, where it will be seen that it consists of extracts from the original text, the code numbers providing a ready means of locating the required material. The heading on top of each File unit gives a great deal of useful background information: the author's name and training, an evaluation of the quality of the sources (from 1 = poor to 5 = excellent primary data), dates of fieldwork and of publication, the OWC code of the culture and the name of the society.

It will be evident that the HRAF is a unique store of retrievable information, but it is certainly not free from inherent weaknesses. Thus it must not be imagined that materials for all OCM categories are to be found in the File for each culture. The File can only be as good as its sources, and a nineteenth-century traveller who recorded his impressions of the tribe he visited could hardly have been thinking of the needs of twentieth-century social scientists when doing so! Hence the information is usually patchy and sometimes poor and unreliable. It is for this reason that the quality control rating is made available, based on such criteria as length of stay in the field, familiarity with the native language, and completeness and length of the report. Unfortunately such shortcomings tend to be particularly acute as regards data of special interest to psychologists: not merely is the relevant material relatively scarce, but even where present in the source the general

OCM categories tend to be too coarse for effective utilization (some remedies will be mentioned later).

There is always the option of using the HRAF merely as a pointer to the original sources, thereafter selecting and coding the material according to one's special requirements, as was done by Whiting and Child (1953). Quite apart from the immense labour that would be entailed, there are also pitfalls in the sampling of cultures. A major one was identified long ago by Galton, who raised it at a meeting of the Royal Anthropological Institute in 1889 when Tylor read a paper that set out for the first time the possibility of a cross-cultural survey method; accordingly, it has come to be known as 'Galton's problem'. As Tylor discussed 'adhesions'—what we would call correlations—between certain cultural traits, Galton pointed out that such correlations would not necessarily constitute evidence of an intrinsic evolutionary connection, since cultural traits often spread by diffusion, through borrowing or migration; in other words, the correlations might be

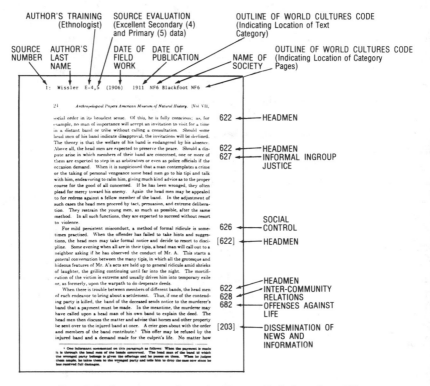

FIG. 5.3. Sample page from the Human Relations Area Files.

spurious. While this error could have vitiated much of the earlier cross-cultural survey work, there are now several different 'solutions' to this problem (Naroll, 1973). What these methods have in common is that they make use of geographical propinquity in order to assess the extent to which diffusion is likely to have contributed to similarities. Since human societies are rarely completely independent, Galton's problem can never be completely disposed of (hence the inverted commas when referring to a 'solution'). However, for the purpose of arriving at confident decisions about the nature of associations, the methods seem to be perfectly adequate.

In fact a Standard Cross-Cultural Sample of 186 cultures has been developed, as well as a stratified probability sample of 60 cultures, both of which have been constructed with a view to minimizing Galton's problem. These Files, held at various institutions (mostly, it must be said, in the United States) can be on ordinary paper or in the form of microfiches. Material coded for previous studies is available on computer cards; while very labour-saving, the proportion of codings dealing with features of direct psychological interest is rather limited.

Fortunately there is also the *Ethnographic Atlas*, derived from the HRAF but distinct from it, which consists of ready-made codifications of ethnographic data that are published from time to time in the journal *Ethnology*. Several of these relate to child training and socialization (Barry and Paxson, 1971; Barry, Josephson *et al.*, 1976, 1977), based on the Standard Cross-Cultural Sample that consists of cultures for which good quality ethnographic data are available. The format of the *Atlas* may be illustrated by the main headings from Barry and Paxson (1971), listed below:

1. *Sleeping proximity* of mother and father to infant
2. *Bodily restrictiveness*, i.e. any common type of physical restraint
3. *Bodily contact* with caretakers—proportion of the day
4. *Carrying technique*
5. *Crying:* (a) Reward—attempts to gratify needs expressed by crying;
          (b) Amount—frequency and duration
6. *Pain infliction*, such as rough handling, punishment, etc.
7. *Post-partum sex taboo*
8. *Special procedures:* (a) ceremonialism, e.g. naming or baptism
          (b) magical protectiveness—symbolic actions, rituals, etc.
          (c) physical protectiveness
9. *New foods* and ages at which given
10. *Five aspects of development:*
          (a) Weaning: early *vs.* late, mild *vs.* severe
          (b) Motor skills: encouraged or not

      (c) Autonomy: attaining independence of caretakers
      (d) Elimination control: early *vs.* late
      (e) Covering genitals: age of training

11. *Age of weaning*
12. *Ranking of age for five aspects of development*, referring to column 10 in terms of relative age of onset
13. *Non-maternal relationships:* importance of other caretakers and companions
14. *Role of father*
15. *Principal relationships:* (a) infancy caretakers
              (b) early childhood companions and caretakers
16. *General indulgence:* (a) infancy
              (b) early childhood.

The behaviour under each of these headings is rated on a quantitative scale; for example, in the case of number 3, bodily contact, the scale is as follows:

1—Limited to routine and precautionary care
2—Only occasionally
3—Up to half the time
4—More than half the time
5—Almost constantly

The *Atlas* contains this information on ratings for each of the cultures (insofar as the information was available in the original sources, of course). The coverage is apt to vary considerably according to topic. Thus, for number 1, sleeping proximity, scores may be found for some 90 per cent of the sample, while 5(b), frequency of crying, is shown for less than a quarter of it. Yet in spite of numerous unavoidable gaps, the amount of material assembled in readily available form is impressive, especially when one considers also the other *Atlas* contributions dealing, respectively, with the traits inculcated in childhood and the agents and techniques for child training.

The existence of this carefully processed set of data enables one to discover, for instance, how widespread a particular socialization practice is across human cultures. In fact, the *Atlas* data makes it not only possible but easy—perhaps too easy—to conduct cross-cultural hypothesis-testing research while sitting comfortably in one's office. If a slightly sour note has crept in at this point, it is because the predigested nature of the data offers a temptation to play around or go for quick and easy results that has not always been resisted. This is not the place for a critical evaluation of the hologeistic approach.[2] My limited aim here is to encourage psychologists to explore the use of the method.

though not indiscriminately. The optimal way, in my view, is when a hypothesis concerning relationships (between, say, child-rearing variables) has been established intra-culturally, and one wishes to ascertain whether similar relationships also hold cross-culturally. Such combination of the hologeistic with other more direct methods is also favoured by some anthropologists (Rohner, 1975). Alternatively, the ascertainment of the prevalence of a particular set of norms, beliefs, or practices, as in the example cited on p. 121, appears as a defensible objective.

Readers wishing to obtain more detailed practical guidance in the use of the hologeistic method should consult Naroll *et al.* (1976) or Barry (1980).[3]

Notes

1. In case any readers might scoff at such a source, I should mention that reports by missionaries—who have often spent decades in a place as . compared to the years spent by anthropologists—are frequently very rich and valuable.
2. Many anthropologists have been highly critical of the hologeistic approach (e.g. Barnes, 1971; Vermeulen and de Ruijter, 1975) for reasons rooted in anthropological theory and not germane to psychology. As far as I know, it has not been critically assessed from a psychological standpoint.
3. The full HRAF on microfiches are not widely available in Europe; only France, Germany, and Sweden have copies. There is no complete set in Britain, but a copy of the 60 cultures probability sample is located in the Library of the University of Strathclyde, Glasgow. Copies of the journal *Ethnology* containing parts of the *Ethnographic Atlas* can, of course, be secured through the usual library channels. Up-to-date information can be obtained from Human Relations Area Files Inc., P.O. Box 2054, Yale Station, New Haven, Connecticut 06520, USA.

6 | Social Behaviour

Psychologists are apt to pay a good deal of lip-service to the social aspects of human behaviour, but neither theories nor practices reflect this to any great extent. As Farr (1978) commented, "models of man within psychological traditions . . . are, in fact, non-social models" (p. 511). This is quite understandable in such fields as physiological psychology, where humans have to be treated as organisms rather than as persons. Surprisingly, however, it also applies to the other end of the continuum, namely, social psychology, which led Moscovici (1972) to ask what is 'social' about social psychology.

The individualistic bias that characterizes much of social psychology is epitomized in the definition given by Allport (1968) in the *Handbook of Social Psychology*, some variant of which has been adopted by most text-book writers: "an attempt to understand and explain how the thought, feeling and behaviour of individuals are influenced by the actual, imagined or implied presence of others" (p. 3). Thus 'social' here means simply that one is concerned to study people, as opposed to non-people, as stimulus objects. This bias is most pronounced within the tradition of experimental social psychology, the chief target of Moscovici's critique. Another protester against the aridity of such social psychology is Tajfel, much of whose work is closely concerned with real-life social problems, especially concerning inter-group relations (Tajfel, 1981). However, objections are by no means confined to the European side of the Atlantic. Thus Neisser (1980), among the most prominent American cognitive psychologists, scathingly complained about the narrowness displayed in a symposium on 'social knowing' on which he had been asked to comment: ". . . the combined bibliographies of all the papers include not a single reference to Freud, no mention of Erving Goffman, virtually nothing on the entire field of non-verbal communication, no ethology, no ethnology or anthropology . . ." (p. 602). Neisser concluded by suggesting that the object of study ought to be closer to social reality.

Anthropology, by contrast, has an essentially social perspective without thereby neglecting the individual in cases where the characteristics of particular persons are important. However, the individual is invariably viewed in his or her social context, since the aim is not so much to understand the individual as such but rather behaviour as part of a social process. From the standpoint of the psychologist, such an approach seems to have the drawback that it rarely results in generalizations relating to individuals or even groups. Anthropologists would probably take the view that generalizations of this kind, abstracted from specific settings, are liable to be of limited value. This issue can be more fruitfully pursued in the course of the following discussion, where it can be related to types of social behaviour. In any case, whatever one's position on this problem of generalization may be, I would argue that even the most tough-minded experimental social psychologist might find it beneficial to look at social behaviour in a broader cultural perspective. It is, therefore, proposed to review some examples of what appears to be relevant anthropological work, which has bearings on various aspects of social psychology.

At the outset a central theme in social psychology will be selected, namely, the study of group behaviour. When this began with Lewin about forty years ago, it was mainly oriented towards practical problems and usually conducted in real-life settings. Thus the studies of the effects of different 'social climates' (Lewin et al., 1939) were carried out in experimentally created youth clubs; or again, the early work on the influence of group discussion (Lewin, 1947) was a type of action research designed to change people's eating habits. Thus, while the methods were experimental, subjects were ordinary people in normal surroundings. Since then there have been thousands of investigations of group behaviour, but mainly in laboratory settings and with student subjects—Lewin's original ideals came to be abandoned for the sake of tighter control. Yet taken as a whole, the product of all these labours is less impressive than one might have hoped. When one of the social psychologists most actively involved in group studies summed up the state of the field, some disappointment is evident:

> In its 30 years of development, research into group behaviour has concentrated on a dozen major topics while many other potentially promising subjects have been ignored. Studies have also more often been focused on the *behavior of individuals* [my italics] in group settings than on the properties and outcomes of groups as a unit.
>
> Zander, 1979, p. 447

While Zander's point regarding undue concentration on the behaviour of individuals is certainly a valid one, he wrote as though it had been merely a matter of experimenters not selecting the best dependent variables; in fact, the very framework of such experiments makes an individual emphasis almost inevitable. The typical setting for such studies is a collection of strangers assembled for a limited time and given some joint task to perform. It therefore follows that such artificial 'groups', with neither a past nor a future, yield findings that can only be analysed in terms of either such mechanical parameters as sheer size or sex and age composition,[1] or of some selected characteristics of the component individuals. Many of the most interesting phenomena of group life simply cannot occur under such restricted conditions. Some social psychologists, like Doise (1978) or Farr (1978), have been acutely aware of this problem, and what they have advocated in order to overcome it is some *rapprochement* with sociology. Yet in many respects anthropology is much closer to psychology, for it tends to be much more directly concerned with actual behaviour than most of sociology. This fact is not readily apparent from the occasional references in social psychology texts to anthropology, and a closer look at actual studies is needed to appreciate it. The anthropological approach to social behaviour in groups could be exemplified from a wide range of monographs. My particular illustration deals with a small village of barely a dozen huts, chosen because all the people were in face-to-face contact; in that respect, at least, they constituted a group like those studied by psychologists. Otherwise, it was very different, for not merely was it a natural group with a history behind them and a future to shape, but also a small community in the sense that most people's lives were centred on it. Moreover, the central theme of the study has to do with something like the 'leadership' problem so extensively discussed in social psychology. Lastly, the work will serve to show that kinship charts, which outsiders are apt to regard as an odd quirk of anthropologists, are sometimes indispensable for the understanding of social behaviour.

The study by V. W. Turner (1957), concerned with a small Ndembu village located in what was then Northern Rhodesia (now Zambia), is relevant in the present context. The key facts one needs to know about the Ndembu are as follows: they reckon descent matrilineally, and they regard matrilineal kin as the primary and essential element in the composition of a village. Maternal descent also determines succession and inheritance. It will be easier to explain this in relation to a (greatly simplified) kinship diagram of Turner's village. In Fig. 6.1, G stands for 'generation' and the common ancestress is arbitrarily labelled as 'G0' (generation zero), one of whose daughters (G1.2) originated lineage A (LA), while her two granddaughters G2.1 and G2.2 marked the beginnings of lineages B and C, respectively. Now a headman is usually succeeded by his uterine (i.e. same mother) brother; or, failing that, by his so-called classificatory brother (matrilineal parallel cousin).

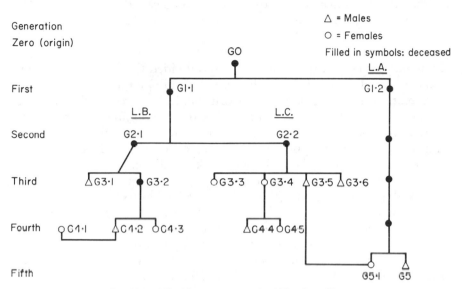

FIG. 6.1. Kinship structure of a Ndembu village.

This is a good deal simpler than it sounds: for instance, in Fig. 6.1, G3.5 and G3.6 are uterine brothers, while G3.1 is a classificatory brother in relation to them. If all these have died off or—and this is important—there is no suitable candidate among them, the right to succession passes down to the next senior generation of sisters' sons (see, for instance, in Fig. 6.1: this might be from G3.1 to G4.2).[2] After building up a picture of the system, Turner came to the conclusion that there were lines of stress between successive generations, and especially between the specific positions of mother's brother and sister's son. The reason is that the rule giving priority to succession within the older generation is apt to try the patience of ambitious younger candidates in the line of possible succession. Initially Turner treated that as a hypothesis to be tested: Do such struggles in fact take place? One strong test he applied was to look at cases where village groups actually broke up (regarded by the Ndembu as an undesirable outcome because it weakens the community). If the hypothesis is correct, one would expect the relationship of leaders of seceding groups to their previous headmen to be that of sister's son rather than brother, a prediction that was clearly confirmed.[3]

Having established that struggles for succession occur frequently, Turner went on to investigate how these are handled by the members of the village community. A recurring set of conflicts, he argued, should in due course acquire its own pattern of norms. He thus embarked upon a series of case studies of what he called 'social dramas'. I shall outline one of these, as well as Turner's analysis:[4]

A social drama

Sandombu (G4.2) trapped a duiker and divided the meat between his village kin. His own mother's brother Kahali Chandenda (G3.1) was headman of the village and by custom should have received a back leg or the breast of the animal as his share, but Sandombu gave him only part of the front leg. Kahali refused to receive it, saying that Sandombu had shown that he despised his uncle. A few days later Kahali himself snared an animal and sent it back to the village, where Sandombu again divided it contrary to accepted custom. When Kahali returned, he asked Sandombu's wife (G4.1) for some food as he had no wife of his own at the time; while not refusing outright, she temporized; and so in the end, Kahali went to his classificatory sister, Nyamwaha (G3.3), who gave him beer as well as food. At night Sandombu's sister and Kahali's own niece Mangalita (G4.3) came to him in private and told him in anger and shame how the meat had been divided.

Next morning Sandombu went off early to a place some 25 miles away, where he had seasonal employment. Kahali spoke bitterly in the village forum about Sandombu's behaviour, and the latter's wife wept at this public shaming of her husband. When Sandombu came back a week later, she reported Kahali's criticism. A fierce dispute arose between uncle and nephew, in the course of which each threatened the other with sorcery. Sandombu ended by saying, "I am going to Sailunga area. The people of this village are worthless. Some people must look out." This was a common expression of a threat, understood as such by the villagers who took him to mean that he was going to seek out the services of a notorious sorcerer to kill Kahali.

Some time later Kahali, an old man, fell ill and died shortly thereafter. Some village people, especially Mukanza Kabinda (G3.5) and Kanyombu (G3.6), classificatory matrilineal brothers to Kahali, said that Sandombu had condemned himself out of his own mouth. Generally a consensus emerged in the village that Sandombu must not succeed Kahali, for he had shown himself a selfish man and sorcerer. Sandombu was not expelled from the village, as there was no positive proof of his guilt such as might be obtained through a diviner—he had only spoken in heat, although good men did not speak that way. The question of succession was left over for a while, and then Mukanza Kabinda was made headman with the general approval of the village people.

In his analysis of this episode, Turner considered 'social personalities' of the actors in relation to the kinship structure. While it was normal and encouraged within the culture for senior men to aspire to headship, special factors fuelled Sandombu's ambition to an unusual and objectionable extent. One was his sterility, and sterile people 'die forever', unless remembered as occupants of political positions. Another factor was the possibility perceived by Sandombu that if one of the classificatory brothers of Kahali in lineage C (G3.5 or G3.6) obtained the headship, the subsequent succession might jump right across his generation[5] to G5.2 in lineage A; this gave a desperate urgency to his quest, and such excessively blatant ambition was not well received by his fellow villagers. Hence, when the struggle for succession began, his breach of custom reflecting the tension between himself and his maternal uncle (a tension, it should be noted, rooted in the kinship structure) was remembered and held against him. On the other hand he was not without considerable social assets. These included being a highly successful agriculturist who also brewed beer from his millet, which he gave away free; he also managed to get labouring jobs for some fellow villagers and helped to finance the education of some village boys. On the other side of the ledger, both his exceptional industriousness and his sterility[6] marked him out as a person connected with sorcery.

These idiosyncratic factors combined, according to Turner's analysis, with his structural position in explaining why Sandombu failed. If he had won, members of one lineage segment of different generation would have succeeded to headmanship, while a senior of another lineage was available. Since no lineage should have a monopoly of headmanship, this would have threatened the unity of the whole structure and secession might have followed, thereby 'killing' the village. On the other hand, Mukanza (G3.5), who secured the office, was, through his marriage to Nyamukola (G5.1), in a pivotal position for maintaining the unity of lineages A and C. Thus, in by-passing Sandombu while at the same time officially ignoring his sorcery and keeping him in the village, unity was maintained, together with the benefits Sandombu provided. He in turn was willing to remain, sustained by the hope of being able to fight again another day, as he in fact did.

This greatly abbreviated version fails to do justice to the detailed nature of Turner's account of social and kin relationships within and between villages, thereby weakening the force and persuasiveness of his analysis. From a series of 'social dramas of this type, he was able to show that they did in fact display a regular pattern, which may be summarized as follows:

1. A breach of customary norms regulating relationships between parties.
2. A crisis which, unless it can be sealed off rapidly, sets off a factional struggle which reveals the lines of fissure within the social unit.
3. Adjustive mechanisms are brought into play by the leading members of the relevant social groups; these may range from informal arbitration to formal judicial machinery or the performance of public ritual.
4. The final stage is either a reintegration, as in the present example, or a recognition of schism with consequent irreparable breach.

Turner's analysis was thus based on the nature of the kinship structure, together with particular aspects of the social personalities of the actors involved. Turner was, of course, well aware of the possible objection that he tended to ignore the individual personalities of the participants. His reply is worth quoting in full:

> It may be objected that such factors as innate psycho-biological constitution and personality variations determined by differential training in the early years of childhood take precedence over sociological factors in shaping the events to be described. But it is clear that the different personalities involved occupy social positions that must inevitably come into conflict, and each occupant of a position must present his case in terms of generally accepted norms. A person can avoid disputes over succession only by renouncing the claim to office vested in his position. In a society governed by rules of kinship, he cannot abrogate his position, into which he is born and by virtue of which he is a member of the village community. Personality may influence the form and intensity of the dispute; it cannot abolish the situation in which conflict must arise. A person who endeavours to avoid pressing his claim to office when the position of headman falls vacant is subject to intense pressure from his uterine kin and from his children to put it forward. If he fails to do so, there occurs a displacement of the locus of conflict, not a resolution or by-passing of conflict. Instead of leading a group of kin against the representatives of other pressure groups, he becomes the target of criticism from members of his own group. At some point in the social process arising from succession he is compelled to turn and defend himself, whatever his temperament or character.
>
> p. 94

Thus, in this kind of analysis, which has become widely adopted in anthropology, the simplicities of the old rigid conceptions of roles and rules are transcended. Thereby justice can be done to the dynamic character of social processes, including the effects of social change. The analysis is conducted at different levels so as to take the influence of the particular social actors into account; but it is contended that group structure is ultimately the decisive factor.

It could no doubt be objected that an argument based on social behaviour in an African village is not particularly relevant for social psychology, since tight structures of the type to be found in that setting are rare in modern industrial societies. While this is certainly true, there are a number of answers to such an objection. First of all, it is important to recognize that this is not an all-or-none issue, but one that is concerned with a continuum. At one extreme there is the small traditional community whose structure reaches into most aspects of people's lives, largely shaping behaviour in most situations. At the other extreme there is the one-shot collection of unrelated people coming together into what is known as an 'experimental group'. In between there are all kinds of groups ranging in inclusiveness from the family to voluntary associations impinging only marginally on people's life-space, and quasi-groups like networks (to be further discussed shortly). It ought surely to be of interest to social psychologists what processes may be common to all these various types of groups, and for this purpose anthropological material can provide valuable clues.

This leads to the second point—namely, that comparative anthropologists have themselves sought to isolate both structural elements and rules of behaviour which show similar patterning across a wide range of human cultures. An example would be the work of Bailey (1969), who was concerned with 'political' groupings in a broad sense. His aim was to demonstrate underlying structural regularities of behaviour in quite disparate settings: untouchables in an Indian village struggling against the efforts of the 'clean' castes to keep them in their place was shown to have certain features in common with the contest within the British cabinet during the First World War that led to the fall of Asquith.[7] Or again, the violent manner in which the American *casa nostra* arranges for succession in leadership was shown to have a close parallel among the Swat Pathans of Pakistan. It is of particular interest for social psychology that the theoretical framework of the analysis, known as 'transactionalism', is related to exchange theory (Chadwick-Jones, 1976) and shares some of its basic postulates.

The last point is that anthropologists themselves have had to come to terms with the fact that tightly knit traditional systems are breaking up in many parts of the world, with people drifting to the cities. This means that new groupings have emerged so that kinship, while remaining important, ceases to be the key organizing principle of social behaviour. Under these changing circumstances, conventional anthropological techniques of study had to be modified so as to allow for the nature of city life, where people from villages form fresh contacts with other individuals of different origins and join occupational, political, or other associations. How can all this be tracked? The simple answer is: by following what people themselves do. Let us imagine a common occurrence in an African city. An illiterate woman from a remote village arrives at the town bus terminal in search of her husband; she has no address, and all she knows is that he is working in the town. What she will do first is to find someone from her own tribe, who in turn will pass her on to someone from, or at least with links to, her own village; and that person will most probably be able to direct her to her husband. This process usually works with remarkable smoothness, even in large conurbations. The various channels follow what is known as a 'network', and the method consists of mapping the actual and potential links that persons have with each other.[8]

One of the best examples of this line of approach is the set of studies edited by Mitchell (1969), dealing with social networks in Central African towns. One of the investigations consisted of following particular individuals in their movements around the town, noting their various contacts, from which the structure of their networks could be identified. It was shown that people had different roles, some derived from the tribal system, others from the wider social system characterizing the urban environment. Thus, from an accumulation of mainly dyadic interactions of various kinds, it was possible to throw light on the manner in which new norms are created and the sanctions by which they are maintained. The chains of transmission of gossip about a case of adultery also revealed the network structure. One study conducted in a work setting provided a picture of the operation of networks in a conflict situation, showing how some of the oppositions even in a modern context were viewed by the participants in terms of witchcraft. Another study concentrated on crisis situations, especially deaths, when the whole of the available network is mobilized in order to get help; hence, these are among the few occasions when the whole network becomes clearly visible.

Networks are, of course, not confined to urban areas of the Third World, though the extent to which they play a part in social behaviour varies considerably. Their importance in Mediterranean cultures was brought home forcibly to Boissevain (1974) on a chance occasion in Sicily, where he was at the time engaged upon field work. On a walk

with a *Professore* (a secondary school teacher), he learned about the truly
byzantine machinations, involving even the Mafia, by which the man
sought to ensure the entry of his son into university (a matter of family
honour)[9] and defeat an enemy who was trying to keep the son out. The
initial stimulus prompted Boissevain to look at social networks as kinds
of opportunity structures, and the role of the person within them as an
entrepreneur who attempts to manipulate them. He presented
numerous analyses of individual networks in Malta and Southern
Italy, and also their functioning in relation to groups. One amusing
case will show how networks can be manipulated.

A student (S) from Syracuse had a problem: he wanted to submit a
thesis to a professor at Palermo personally unknown to him, but the
latest date for registration was two months past. The network he
exploited is outlined in Fig. 6.2. His first move was to go to Leone and

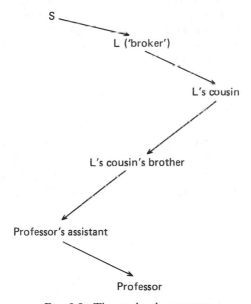

FIG. 6.2. The student's progress.

see a notorious 'broker', a secretary of the Christian Democratic party
to whom S himself had rendered a service at a time when he had
worked in the town. This man (L) sent him to his cousin in Palermo
and also offered him a copy of his own thesis which, as he pointed out,
would save a lot of labour. S declined this offer and went to see the
cousin, who passed him on to his brother as someone who knew many
people at the university. The brother introduced him to the professor's

assistant as his 'dearest friend'. The assistant said that he might arrange things, provided S volunteered to help the professor with his forthcoming election campaign, to which S agreed (though in doing so he was cheating since he lived outside the relevant electoral district). The assistant then made an appointment with the professor, who initially was cool; but when S played the political angle, the professor warmed at once, indicating that there would be no difficulty about the thesis, which was in due course accepted.

Boissevain also speculated on the reciprocal relationship between type of network structure and personality characteristics. This is an instance of the kind of problem sometimes raised by anthropologists but not pursued, since they regard it as outside their sphere of competence. Some of these ideas might be well worth considering by psychologists who have the necessary skills to test them empirically. There is another, more important, reason why social psychologists in particular would benefit from a better acquaintance with anthropological literature: when elaborating theories of social behaviour that are intended to be of universal validity, prior knowledge of the cross-cultural range of relevant behaviours is necessary. Otherwise, one might be vulnerable to critiques like that of Harré (1980), who wrote that "it seems never to have dawned on the vast armies of social psychologists working the Ph.D. machines of American universities that they were not discovering universal laws of human nature but reflections of local culture" (p. 207).

This can be illustrated in connection with Zimbardo's (1969) theory of de-individuation, postulating that individuals who are anonymous and whose personal identity is concealed will be more liable to engage in behaviour transgressing legal and moral norms. He adduced a great deal of rather dramatic evidence to this effect, mainly based on empirical studies carried out in America.

Yet there exists a category of people always de-individuated in public who certainly do not have a reputation for proclivities to transgress social norms; on the contrary, they are regarded as being extremely restricted in their behaviour, if not oppressed. I am, of course, referring to Arab women wearing the veil. Anthropological work reveals that the reality is a great deal more complex than this popular image; and one might add that a topic of this kind can only be tackled by observational studies and getting the reports of informants. Preferably it should be participant observation, which requires a woman anthropologist. Such research was conducted by Makhlouf (1979) in Yemen.

Discussing the 'depersonalizing' aspect of the veil she wrote:

Of course, one probable consequence of the veil is that the veiled person is experienced as a 'non-person', to use Goffman's term, by those not acquainted with the culture. But it is not a necessary consequence that the veiled persons themselves feel depersonalized or are treated by men as non-persons. One should take into consideration not only the objective reality of veiling patterns, but also their subjective reality, not only what veiling consists in, but also how it is experienced by the women themselves.

p. 30

There are several different kinds of veils, some for indoors (the *lithma*), worn all the time by unmarried girls and on certain occasions by married women, and some for outdoors, of which there are two main types corresponding to higher or lower rank of the female wearing the veil. Within these general types further differentiations are possible, based on quality of material, so that once again we have a status indicator (this, of course, applies equally to the compulsory black skirt, the cut of which may be more or less fashionable). While such women are generally anonymous in the street, relatives and close friends can usually recognize each other by gait and by movement patterns.[10] Women must always cover their face in the presence of a man who is not her husband or covered by the incest taboo, such as a brother. There is, in fact, one aspect of the veil to which Zimbardo's theory is at least indirectly relevant: since the veil makes all women look more or less the same to outsiders, it does provide some freedom for those who wish to break the rules: thus, a woman who has an extra-marital affair can walk with the man in public, as it will be assumed that he is covered by the incest taboo. Moreover, she can go to places of assignation incognito: "In other words, even though a woman who breaches the moral code may be recognized by friends or relatives, her veil can be used as a disguise, to provide an element of doubt against accusations." (p. 33.) This is, of course, not to say—as Zimbardo's theory would seem to require—that the veil as such releases immoral behaviour!

Makhlouf described how the veil can be manipulated by girls in a playful manner to enhance their attraction—for the total concealment does, of course, make any revelation all the more exciting. Thus, they may delay raising the veil just enough to make it seem accidental when a man enters the house, or take advantage of the fact that it is per-mitted to lift it under certain circumstances. The veil can also be used for the opposite purpose, namely, to discourage unwelcome attentions.

Paradoxically, the seclusion pattern of which the veil is an inte-gral part can also serve to give women important decision-making powers:

> Since men cannot know girls outside the immediate kin group, they are completely dependent upon their female relatives for advice. Women can influence their brothers and sons by controlling the circulation of information about other females through gossip, through access to the reports of children[11] who run errands and hear things from their play-mates, and, most importantly, through visiting.
>
> p. 42

It is through such channels that marriages are arranged, though officially it is the father who makes all the decisions. This is due to the fact that only a man's mother and sister actually know the bride-to-be, so that their advice is crucial. When in due course the bride lifts her veil, this will be the first time the bridegroom sees her. However, the bride herself will not see a stranger, because she will have been shown her future husband through a window blind or from behind a door. If he has been previously married, all the gossip about his private life will have been conveyed to her.

This account has wandered away a little from the 'de-individuation', but it will at any rate be clear that such an interpretation is not readily applicable to veiled Arab women. This indicates once again that if social psychologists wish to claim universality for their findings, they must be tested outside the confines of the 'local culture'.[12] In addition, this research showed that the common stereotype about Arab women's helplessness in a male world is at least exaggerated.

Anthropological material can also be valuable as exemplifying certain psychological principles in a striking manner. However, it is necessary to dig out such material since anthropologists present their findings for a different purpose and are probably as a rule unaware of their psychological interest. Perhaps one of the most rewarding areas in this connection is that broadly known as 'cultural factors in perception', including stereotyping.

Bartlett (1932), in his classical studies of remembering, demonstrated the influence of cultural factors by showing that the recall of exotic folk tales became distorted towards more familiar forms. The same process, but synchronous, is vividly manifest in Laura Bohannan's (1976) delightful account of her attempt to tell the story of Hamlet to the Tiv (in Nigeria) elders with whom she was working. The concluding part of this is cited below:

> We had emptied one pot of beer, and the old man argued the point with slightly tipsy interest. Finally one of them demanded of me, "What did the servant of Polonius say on his return?"
>
> With difficulty I recollected Reynaldo and his mission. "I don't think he did return before Polonius was killed."

"Listen," said the elder, "and I will tell you how it was and how your story will go, then you may tell me if I am right. Polonius knew his son would get into trouble, and so he did. He had many fines to pay for fighting, and debts from gambling. But he had only two ways of getting money quickly. One was to marry off his sister at once, but it is difficult to find a man who will marry a woman desired by the son of a chief. For if the chief's heir commits adultery with your wife, what can you do? Only a fool calls a case against a man who will someday be his judge. Therefore Laertes had to take the second way: he killed his sister by witchcraft, drowning her so he could secretly sell her body to the witches."

I raised an objection. "They found her body and buried it. Indeed Laertes jumped into the grave to see his sister once more—so, you see, the body was truly there. Hamlet, who had just come back, jumped in after him."

"What did I tell you?" The elder appealed to the others. "Laertes was up to no good with his sister's body. Hamlet prevented him, because the chief's heir, like a chief, does not wish any other man to grow rich and powerful. Laertes would be angry, because he would have killed his sister without benefit to himself. In our country he would try to kill Hamlet for that reason. Is this not what happened?"

"More or less," I admitted. "When the great chief found Hamlet was still alive, he encouraged Laertes to try to kill Hamlet and arranged a fight with machetes between them. In the fight both the young men were wounded to death. Hamlet's mother drank the poisoned beer that the chief meant for Hamlet in case he won the fight. When he saw his mother die of poison, Hamlet, dying, managed to kill his father's brother with his machete."

"You see, I was right!" exclaimed the elder.

"That was a very good story," added the old man, "and you told it with very few mistakes. There was just one more error, at the very end. The poison Hamlet's mother drank was obviously meant for the survivor of the fight, whichever it was. If Laertes had won, the great chief would have poisoned him, for no one would know that he arranged Hamlet's death. Then, too, he need not fear Laertes' witchcraft; it takes a strong heart to kill one's only sister by witchcraft.

"Sometime," concluded the old man, gathering his ragged toga about him, "you must tell us some more stories of your country. We, who are elders, will instruct you in their true meaning, so that when you return to your own land your elders will see that you have not been sitting in the bush, but among those who know things and who have taught you wisdom."

p. 257

While this is readily intelligible even without any knowledge of Tiv culture, my next example is rather different. It comes from a study of the so-called 'cargo' movement in New Guinea during the post-war period by Lawrence (1964). The cargo cult involved the belief that European goods (cargo) are not man-made but obtained supernaturally. One of the important threads in the highly complex story concerns some interesting misperceptions on the part of the (originally christianized) leaders of the cult. On a visit to Australia they were taken to the zoo, where they noted the great care with which Europeans treat animals. In a museum they remained unimpressed by the technological exhibits, but were bemused by the skeletons of pre-historic animals, puzzled by New Guinean artefacts such as bows and arrows, and shocked by the displays of face masks and statues of the old gods. Together with other influences, especially a version of evolutionary doctrine, they eventually came to the conclusion that the animals were the European's totems; moreover, contrary to the teachings of the missionaries, Europeans held the old gods in high regard—why keep them in museums, otherwise?—and the object on the part of missionaries and other Europeans in thus systematically deceiving them was in order to preserve the secret of the ritual which produces 'cargo', thereby keeping the New Guineans in perpetual subjection.

The notion of such a ritual which automatically yields cargo was in accordance with traditional cosmological ideas whereby the gods can be coerced to make the crops ripen and generally sustain life. Another perceptual-type factor was that the people saw only the arrival of ships and aircraft discharging masses of cargo, but never Europeans themselves producing any of these things. It may be that the Australians might have saved themselves a lot of trouble if they had taken their visitors around a factory instead of the museum and the zoo! This is, of course, a grossly oversimplified account of a very complicated series of events, but there is no doubt that culturally determined perceptual distortions played an important part.

Some anthropologists conduct investigations in areas virtually identical with those of social psychology. Brief mention might be made here of a study by Beattie (1977) of the perceptions of white Americans regarding American Indians, and the perceptions of the latter regarding themselves, that is, their self-images. He showed that the whites' perceptions have always been stereotyped, treating 'Indians' as a homogenous population, while Indians themselves have come to adopt the image created by Hollywood; for instance, the beaded headband— far from being traditional—was used by the actors to fix the wigs that concealed their short hair! Anthropological analysis is also usually informed by a historical perspective, often lacking in similar psychological research. Thus, Beattie pointed out that the contemporary

American Indians' self-perception of "hunting buffalo on horseback" as characteristic of 'real' Indians ignores the fact that prior to the horse being introduced by the Spaniards, the Indians had a long history without horses.[13]

One of the dangers of attempting to provide a variety of examples, unavoidably in the form of mere snippets, is that this might confirm the prejudices of some psychologists that anthropology, while dealing with interesting topics, tends to deal with them in a vague impressionistic manner. Obviously this may sometimes be true, but it is certainly not the rule. In fact, one of the special skills of anthropologists in the sphere of social behaviour is that of singling out some seemingly trivial aspect and demonstrating by detailed analysis its wider significance. In order to show this, I shall end with a more detailed discussion of greetings, an area chosen because a few social psychologists have also been interested in it.

At the outset it should be noted that greetings have also been considered from a biological standpoint by Eibl-Eibesfeld (1973), who regarded them as bond-establishing rites. Surveying such behaviour among different species of animals and in a variety of human cultures, he concluded that there are probably several significant pre-programmed elements in such behaviour that are shared by animals and men. Thus he suggested, for instance, that the bow is probably a ritualized form of invitation to social grooming; bodily contact, of which hand-shaking is one particular form, commonly occurs among chimpanzees. The biological function of a greeting was said to be "to establish or maintain a bond and to appease aggressive feelings" (p. 166). The main thrust of the biological perspective is to seek continuities in animal and human behaviour and to demonstrate their adaptive value, which may either persist or merely account for the origin of the behaviour.

The social psychologist Argyle (1975) referred to this biological aspect, but his distinctive contribution was to treat greetings as sequences of social interaction which he analysed in terms of his social skills model. Mentioning the fact that greetings are largely ritualized and the wide range of cultural variations, he commented: "Variations in greetings *within* a culture can be extremely informative and may communicate attitudes towards the person greeted." (p. 80.) Argyle's work generally aims at the understanding of ordinary social behaviour, and is thus in line with the anthropological approach. A more typical social psychological study is that of Brown (1965), who surveyed modes of address and greetings in numerous languages, covering both European and non-European cultures. He also questioned a group of young business executives as to how they habitually greeted their superiors, subordinates, and equals. From all this material Brown extracted what he regarded as a likely universal norm: for persons with unequal status, it is the superior only who is allowed to initiate advances in solidarity and intimacy. Brown found this a surprising norm since, as he said, the lesser person has more to gain and will wish to promote more intimacy, yet the norm forbids him to do it. One might interject here that it is really Brown's surprise that is odd, for if the inferior always had the option of reducing the distance between the superior and himself, the superiority would soon be eroded; and the norm, in stratified societies, presumably has the function of maintaining it. At any rate, Brown went on to devise a model of dyadic relations between persons of unequal status, based on consistency theory in attitude change. Its details do not matter, but the conclusion to which it points does, and was stated by Brown thus:

> In general, acts of intimate association between persons of unequal status will exert forces towards the equalization of status. This means that a member of the dyad who has less status should be motivated to increase the intimacy of interaction since he stands to gain, while the person of higher status should be motivated to resist such intimacy.
>
> p. 97

It is not necessary, for my purpose, to discuss this formulation critically, though I might just mention that the notion of low-status people invariably wishing to improve their status is an ethnocentric one and far from universal in other periods and cultures. What is important is that both Argyle and Brown were concerned to make *general* statements, presumably intended to be pan-human in range, and did so in terms of psychological characteristics. By contrast, anthropologists working in this field have generally confined themselves to intra-cultural studies, devoting a great deal of attention to the structure of the behaviour itself and its social implications.

This will be illustrated with a study by Irvine (1974) of greeting behaviour among the Wolof of Senegal. Greetings were related to status differences that are a fundamental aspect of Wolof social life, where, for instance, *griots* (a kind of wandering minstrel) are of relatively low status, and there is a high-ranking nobility. The methods used were field observation, the questioning of informants, and—very importantly—a quasi-experimental procedure whereby the ethnographer modified her own modes of greeting systematically and noted the effects.

Greetings play an exceptionally salient part in Wolof social behaviour and characterize every encounter:

In principle a greeting must occur between any two persons who are visible to each other. Out on the road, in the fields, or if someone is entering a compound yard, a greeting must occur even if one party must make a wide detour (perhaps hundreds of yards outside the village) to accomplish it. In the village center, a large open plaza which usually has many people sitting about, one must greet all those whom one passes within a distance of about a hundred feet.

p. 168

However, the rule about physical distance is secondary to that relating to rank: one must greet those ranking higher first, and if there are many important people assembled, one might never get around to those of lower status. Ranks within the community depend on age, sex, caste, and prestige achieved through wealth or exceptional moral character. Normally, the lower-ranking person initiates the greeting, but where relative status is uncertain, there is liable to be some manoeuvering and the strategies involved were carefully analysed. In any case, every dyadic encounter faces the parties with an unavoidable decision about their relative ranks, which do not always correspond to those of their membership groups. "e.g., the relationship between a particular noble and a particular *griot* may be the reverse of the relation between nobles and *griots* in general" (p. 170).

The structure of Wolof greetings is asymmetrical and consists of two distinct roles: the Initiator-Questioner and the Respondent, the former being the more active as well as the one of lower status. The underlying notion is that the low-status person is expected to do the work; it is he or she who makes the approach, extends the hand, and opens the exchange. The initial stages of this are rigidly stereotyped: "If asked about a kinsman's health, the respondent will say that he is well even if the kinsman is on his deathbed; the true information about him will only emerge later in the conversation, after the greeting is over." (p. 171.) A typical greeting pattern is shown in Table 6.1, where person A has, of course, the lower status. It will be seen that the higher-ranking party has an essentially passive role, merely responding in the prescribed manner. If the relative ranking is mutually agreed, the lower-status partner retains control of the initial exchanges. However, the most interesting aspect of this behaviour is that the parties do not always reach such tacit consent on their relative status, as when a younger man greets an older woman. In such cases, strategies are brought into play that form the major focus of Irvine's discussion.

Two main ones are distinguished, namely, attempting to take the low (I) or high (R) role, which she calls 'Self-Lowering' and 'Self-Elevating'. It is important to realize that this is quite distinct from being polite or rude, which constitutes a broader dimension of social behaviour that is independent. Moreover, as noted above, it must not be thought that people will always strive to capture the high-status role, since that role may entail certain obligations (e.g. financial help for the

TABLE 6.1
Wolof greeting structure (adapted from Irvine, 1974)

Salutation		*Notes*
1(a)	Peace be with you	
(b)	With you be peace	
2(a)	(A gives own name)	Stages 2 and 3 occur only if the parties have not previously met one another
(b)	(B gives own name)	
3(a)	(A gives B's name)	
(b)	(B gives A's name: yes, A's name)	

Questions and praising God			*Notes*
Q₁	1(a)	"How do you do?"	
	(b)	"I am here only"	At least one of these two questions must be asked
	2(a)	"Don't you have peace?"	
	(b)	"Peace only, yes"	

Q₂(a)	1(a)	"Where/how are the people of the household?"	
	(b)	"They are there"	These are optional, but A is free to ask about as many members of B's household as he can think of.
(b)	1(a)	"Isn't it that you aren't sick?"	
	(b)	"I am praising God"	
	2(a)	"Isn't it that anyone isn't sick?"	
	(b)	"They are praising God"	

P	1(a)	"Thanks be to God"	
	(b)	"Thanks be to God" "Blessed be God"	This set of phrases can be repeated several times, and if A remembers some other member of B's household, he has the option to re-cycle back to stage Q₂
	2(a)	"Thanks to God" "Blessed be God"	
	(b)	"Thanks be to God" "Blessed be God"	

End of preliminaries and move to main conversation

inferior) which one might be anxious to avoid. In fact, attempts to achieve 'Self-Elevation' appear to be less common than the opposite, perhaps partly because it is difficult to make sure that one does not initiate a greeting if the other person tries to do the same in a situation where there *has* to be a greeting. There are further strategies open when the greeting is under way, and part of the whole process will be exemplified in relation to Self-Lowering, as in the following example:

The most important is, of course, initiating the greeting, an act which not only positions the speaker as lower-ranking, but guarantees that he will have this position for at least four exchanges, during the questioning. If both persons are trying to be the Initiator, it may require some effort for a person to assure himself of the role: he must move quickly toward the other, and speak loudly and rapidly, the instant he has caught the other's eye or even before the other has noticed him. Once he has initiated the greeting, he can continue to show deference by making the exchange as long and as elaborate as possible. To do this the Initiator will increase the number of different questions (Q_1 and Q_2) and the number of repetitions: any question may be repeated almost indefinitely, or a set of questions recycled, and the same is true for naming. The Initiator should try to postpone Step P, certainly avoiding P_2, where the other would finally have the option of asking questions in his own right . . . A determined Initiator can keep up the questioning for many minutes, and then after P_1 proceed directly to some new topic of conversation, thereby preventing the other from ever reversing the roles and asking his own questions.

pp. 176–7

In summary, there are two types of strategy, namely, Self-Lowering versus Self-Elevation and Politeness–Rudeness. Together with the two paralinguistic features of stress and tempo, and taking into account the option of partial switching, Irvine shows that there are eight possible combinations corresponding to separate 'meanings' or ways of interpreting greetings. Furthermore, social behaviour *must* take place within the constraints of these permissible variants. The precise reasons depend on the fine details of the structural analysis, which cannot be given here in full. However, Irvine's gloss will provide some indication of what is involved:

It is structurally impossible, for instance, for a *griot* talking to a noble to be really polite (as opposed to just not being rude) and still claim dependency. For if he takes option (2), he signals that his self-image is not consistent with the expected image of his caste, that he does not consider himself to be in a true *griot*–noble relationship, and that therefore the noble is not obliged to give him anything. Likewise, if a noble talking to a *griot* chooses options (3) or (4), he will have violated the expectations of demeanor proper to his rank, shown a self-image which is unfitting, and will therefore jeopardize his following (who may suspect that he lacks 'self-control').

pp. 187–8

This penetrating study thus linked the hierarchical nature of Wolof social organization to the microstructure of social behaviour, showing how it revealed the social motives of the participants in an encounter. The picture that does emerge is particularly clear-cut, since among the Wolof greeting is obligatory and the rules and constraints governing it must perforce enter into any social relationship. Although the author made no claims to any generalizations beyond the Wolof, it is likely that lessons applying to other cultures, and of considerable interest to social psychologists, could be learned by following up her work. In fact, there is already some evidence of the wider relevance of the findings: E. Goody (1972) conducted a comparative study of 'greeting' in two other West African societies, Gonja and LoDagaa. Although neighbours with many similar cultural and economic features, they differ radically in social and political structure. Gonja is large and heterogeneous in population, ruled by a hierarchy of chiefs. LoDagaa is a relatively small, homogeneous and acephalous society where formal hierarchies are absent. Goody showed that the Gonja had most elaborate greeting rituals and that both modes of address and accompanying physical gestures (from removing one's hand to prostrating oneself on the ground) varied according to relative status. Moreover, greeting in Gonja is associated with 'begging', i.e. the seeking of favours of various kinds. While Goody did not undertake the kind of formal analysis done by Irvine, the parallel between Gonja and Wolof is obviously rather close. By contrast, LoDagaa use only kin terms in their modes of address, and abasement gestures are completely absent. There is, thus, here the germ of a general hypothesis relating greeting behaviour to degree of hierarchical social differentiation that might be tested by the hologeistic method!

This chapter has presented a somewhat kaleidoscopic view illustrating the variety of anthropological approaches to various aspects of social behaviour. In spite of that variety, there are certain common threads distinguishing the anthropological style from the social psychological one. For anthropologists interested in social behaviour, the primary focus is interaction within a specific socio-cultural context, and the aim is the understanding of particular processes rather than generalization. Thus, Turner analysed the processes governing succession to headship in Ndmebu villages, but these were clearly seen as a function of a particular social structure. When, and only when, such detailed processes have been studied in a variety of cultural settings, some anthropologists like Bailey will take the next step and show that certain patterns of interaction have a basic similarity in different cultures. As far as the role of individuals is concerned, anthropologists take *differences* of personality and life history into account, but usually treat these either as sources of variation (as in the case of Sandombu), or seek to show how even the exceptional individual's role is shaped by historical and cultural factors (as in the case of the leaders of the cargo cult). The general aim is mostly that of explanation in terms of socio-cultural process models, and some (like Geertz) would say understanding, but seldom if ever prediction.

Social psychologists concentrate in the main on intra-individual processes or disposition conceived as determining social behaviour: dissonance, attribution, helping behaviour and so on are all of this type. The kinds of social behaviour most commonly studied tend to be small-scale and inter-personal, mainly within spheres not subject to societal norms and sanctions, at least in modern industrial cultures where practically all social psychological work is conducted.[14] The ambitious aim is that of arriving at universal generalizations or 'laws' and also to make predictions; the latter is rarely accomplished, and then only in severely restricted settings. Another consequence of such an orientation is the fact that personality differences are treated as extraneous variables to be controlled.

There is thus a fundamental divergence not merely in aims and methods, but also in the modes of conceptualizing social behaviour. Nowhere is this more evident than in the social psychological study of 'group behaviour', which has really no equivalent in anthropology. While there are certain shared interests as, for instance, in problems of 'identity' (Tajfel, 1978; Epstein, 1978), anthropologists do not seek to discover any special properties as 'groups' in opposition to 'individuals' as recommended by Zander in the passage previously cited (p. 141); they merely view groups as loci of different kinds of interaction processes. Personally, I think they are right, and that the search for any unique qualities of groups stems from reification and is bound to remain fruitless.

Given the considerable gulf separating the perspectives of the two disciplines on issues of social behaviour, are there any reasons why social psychologists should try and get better acquainted with the anthropological literature—apart from the fact that it is fascinating in its own right? I believe there are several reasons why the answer should be affirmative. First of all, there is, as I have tried to show, a good deal of common ground in terms of the *content* of anthropological work. This may be used to illustrate the social psychological principles operating in real-life settings, which is valuable at least in teaching. More importantly, anthropological material could constitute a useful check on the cross-cultural validity of social psychological hypotheses (that are sometimes notoriously culture-bound) and perhaps also serve as a source for new ones. Lastly, there has been, over the past decade or so, a considerable amount of discontent concerning methods, theories, and applications within social psychology itself. The debate concerning such issues might well benefit from exposure to ideas and to practices prevalent in a neighbouring discipline.

Notes

1. Any findings relating to age and sex are likely to vary according to culture and are therefore bound to be of limited generality.
2. Turner checked to see if these rules applied in practice and confirmed that they did: out of 43 cases of succession sampled, the relationship of successor to previous incumbent were as follows:

Brother	20
Sister's son	15
Sister's daughter's son (Jumping one generation)	4
Son	3
Sister	1

3. Although Turner did not go beyond 'eyeballing', I worked out chi-square on the basis of equal chance expectations for 'brother', 'sister's son', and 'other'; for $df = 2$, $X = 7 \cdot 82$, $P < 0 \cdot 02$.
4. Since the account will consist of a mixture of quotation and paraphrase, quotation marks will be omitted. The passages concerned are on pages 95–115 of Turner (1957).
5. Generations between lineages had moved out of phase, as is apt to happen, so that G5.2 was already a middle-aged man.
6. This was due to gonorrhoea that had another consequence: his semen was not white, a colour associated with purity, health, and strength, but yellow; now yellow is categorized with red by the Ndembu, a colour associated with witchcraft and other evil power. When he had beaten his wives they gossiped about his semen, so that its discolouration was well known all over the village.
7. In this connection Bailey (1969, p. 101) wrote:

    > If we chose to look at the fall of Asquith . . . making use of the concepts of Freudian psychology, then the rules and regularities of politics would be the 'accidents' while the states of mind of the protagonists, which in this account are pushed aside as accidents, would constitute the essence. What is accident and what is essence depends on the discipline concerned.

    From this it will be evident that Bailey shared a misconception about psychology widespread among anthropologists, as discussed in Chapter 2, the sharp dichotomy between the spheres of individual psychology and anthropology indicates a lack of awareness that social psychology might serve as a bridge between the two spheres.
8. In order not to be misleading, I ought to mention that the idea of networks came from London, not Africa (Bott, 1957); and some of the quantitative measures were originally developed by social psychologists (e.g. Flament, 1963) and later taken over by anthropologists. Social psychologists appear to have lost interest in the method, which proved most valuable in the real-life settings described.
9. The concept of 'honour' which relates both to a person's self-image and

his or her estimation in the eyes of others is neglected in social psychology, which perhaps reflects the culture-boundedness of the discipline. While 'honour' has ceased to matter (or perhaps has undergone transformation) in Anglo-Saxon countries, it remains very much alive in some others (see Pitt-Rivers, 1977).

10. The fact that people can recognize their friends by movement alone has been demonstrated experimentally by Cutting and Kozlowski (1977).

11. Schildkrout (1978), who studied another Islamic culture, wrote that "Hausa children enjoy a freedom that no other group in the society commands—the right to wander in and out of people's houses" (p. 24).

12. Actually the de-individuation hypothesis was not even robust enough for a crossing of the Atlantic, as it did not work with Belgian soldiers; cf. the useful critical discussion by Eiser (1980).

13. In all the above cases, the term 'perception' is admittedly used in a rather broad sense. However, this in conformity with current social-psychological usage as an inspection of most texts will confirm.

14. This resulted in a cultural parochialism, discussed by Jahoda (1979).

PART 3

Mainly Cognitive

7 | A Classical Fallacy: 'Magical' Thinking and 'Magical' Thought

An African indigenous healer with whom I had worked (Jahoda, 1961) and found to have an acute and profound insight into his cases, once recounted to me how he had walked on the sea bed to America, where he had some strange adventures. This was no joke—the man was perfectly serious and utterly convinced of the validity of his experiences. Now in a European cultural setting, such behaviour might well be taken as evidence of a delusional system indicative of psychosis and the need for psychiatric treatment.[1] It is, thus, not surprising that early observers of 'primitive' peoples returned with reports suggesting that their modes of thinking were totally unlike those of Europeans:

> The whole mental furniture of the Kaffir's mind differs from that of a European. His outlook upon life is different; his conception of nature is cast in another mold . . . he is a complete stranger to Western conceptions of clear thinking and is as ignorant of logic as he is of the moons of Jupiter. His conceptions of cause and effect are hopelessly at sea . . .
> Kidd, 1905

It is important to realize that most early observers picked up only isolated bits and pieces which, of course, failed to make sense—the investigation of ideas and beliefs as part of a coherent world view lay far ahead in the future. The aspect of traditional cultures that perhaps made the greatest impression on travellers, missionaries, administrators, and the early anthropologists alike, was the wide prevalence of seemingly bizarre and fantastic beliefs and practices that may broadly be called 'magical'. It will be useful to give some examples of these,

167

and for reasons that will become apparent later, I draw these from the Bambara.[2]

The Bambara are a Sudanese people and constitute the largest ethnic group in what is now the Republic of Mali. Several other ethnic groups, especially the Malinke, are closely related to them culturally. Predominantly agricultural, they lived (and still live, in the villages) in houses constructed from mud bricks. They are polygamous, and their society is hierarchically structured into freemen, artisan guilds, and slaves (the last category now officially abolished). In spite of a long history of Islamic influence, their traditional religious and magical beliefs remained virtually unaffected and have only recently begun to disintegrate. The brief account that follows relates mainly to the period between the world wars. Quite deliberately, it is not a systematic survey, but a fairly random collection of some of the more weird and spectacular features of the kind with which readers of the old reports used to be regaled. Also, in order to avoid cumbersome phrasing, the historic present will be employed.

The Bambara believe in witchcraft, which they regard as inherited. Witches can change into animal forms, and as such they are man-eaters: they can either assume the form of a large predator like a leopard, and then consume their victim just as a real leopard would; or they can assume other forms, like snakes, birds, or bats. In the latter case, they visit their victim regularly at night, attacking their soul,[3] and gradually eat their internal organs. There is also sorcery, a magical technique that anybody can use. One such device is the *kolo*, which consists of a powder one inserts into a chicken bone. Armed with this, one creeps into the courtyard of the intended victim and gently knocks the bone against the wall of the hut. The magical poison will then penetrate through the wall and kill the intended victim. Other methods involve obtaining some body material of the victim, such as hair or nail parings, and then performing magical rites or burying magical substances under his house, and so on.

Obviously such activities are felt as threatening, and a secret society, the *Nama* cult, has as its major objective the protection of the community from such dangers. At a special ceremony animals are sacrificed and their blood is mixed with ashes and smeared over the cult objects and the upper part of the bodies of the officiants; this is followed by a ritual meal, and a procession through the village in order to cleanse it of witchcraft and sorcery.

Apart from evil magic there are numerous other magical techniques for achieving particular ends. A multi-purpose device of this type called *sirikou* (from siri = attach or tie + kou = tail) consists of the tail of an animal. If one wishes to silence somebody ('tie up' his mouth)—perhaps a potential accuser or a rival who extends his songs excessively and prevents an adequate display of one's own talents—then one proceeds as follows: a red, a black, and a white string are used to tie as many straws as there are mouths to silence onto the tail. A magical formula is recited that says, in effect, 'I tie up the mouth of so-and-so etc.' The device works better if the *sirikou* is strengthened with certain parts of a recently buried corpse. There is, of course, also a great deal of medicinal magic, including many procedures to ensure fertility. One of these makes use of elephant sperm, which is believed to ensure incredibly powerful procreative capacity. One could easily go on filling many more pages with illustrations of Bambara magical beliefs and practices; but this brief sketch, fairly typical of many traditional cultures, will be enough to convey a general picture.

The earlier observers attributed these Bambara beliefs to childishness[4] or to general dullness and lack of understanding and curiosity. The classical anthropologists were more specific, regarding such beliefs and practices as manifestations of modes of thinking in the main peculiar to 'primitives', hence the early theories of magic and religion were essentially theories of 'primitive mentality'. In fact such a view still lingers on to some extent, as when the writer of a relatively recent and authoritative article on magic argued that:

> The attempt to understand fully the inner workings of the mind of even the most primitive peoples is an obvious prerequisite to the analysis of their supernatural beliefs, behavior, and rituals. Without such penetration into what appears to be irrational and alien mentalities, all observations are bound to be superficial, rash, or wrong.
>
> Yalman, 1968, pp. 524–5

My contention is that such pronouncements are symptomatic of a confusion that has bedevilled anthropological discussions of so-called 'magical thinking' from Tylor and Frazer onwards. The present chapter will seek to show that this is the case by examining some of the ways in which the topic has been treated.

There is a plethora of theories of magic—no self-respecting anthropological theory-builder is without one—and it is neither necessary nor desirable to provide a comprehensive summary. In particular, theories emphasizing the emotional aspects of magic, such as those of Malinowski (see p. 24) will not be considered; rather, I shall look at two main types of theories: first, the so-called 'English School' of Tylor and Frazer and some of their more or less remote descendants, originally focusing chiefly on the thinking of individuals; in opposition to them, Lévy-Bruhl and his followers, who emphasized the social matrix of thought, will be considered. Nowadays these two once rival traditions have become largely fused with the addition of novel elements, especially symbolism, but it is still possible to discern the main strands.

The approaches of Tylor and Frazer, being rather similar in certain respects, may be considered together. Both subscribed to the notion of an evolutionary development whereby 'savages' are seen as being less advanced mentally and—as has already been said more than once—are in some ways akin to European children in their thinking.[5] Tylor described numerous magical ideas and practices to illustrate what he regarded as the crucial error, namely, resorting to false analogies in reasoning—taking a connection in thought to be one in real life also. For instance, he cited reports about Australian Aborigines who follow the track of an insect from a man's grave because they believe it will lead them to the sorcerer responsible for his death, or the Zulus, who chew a piece of wood to soften the heart of the woman from whom they want a favour. Both Tylor and Frazer appealed to the then-popular psychological theory of associationism in order to account for magical thinking. Frazer especially conceived magic in intellectual terms as a kind of false science; in other words, the magician wishes to account for the regularities of the universe, but applies mistaken principles. He distinguished two major types of magic, namely, homeopathic (based on similarity: like produces like and an effect resembles its cause) and contagious (based on the notion that things in contact once continue to be related in such a way that something done to one will affect the other even if they have been separated). Frazer listed numerous examples of both kinds, and the reader might wish to try his hand at categorizing the Bambara material in this way: most likely it will be found that it is not always easy to do so! It is worth mentioning in passing that Frazer's own massive documentation was not always drawn from 'primitive' peoples for, as he explained, the same confusion of ideas could be found among what he called "the ignorant classes" of Europe. From this it is evident that Frazer was not a 'racialist', but merely judged other people's modes of thinking by an implicit standard derived from the Victorian intelligentsia.

How did Frazer conceive of the manner in which psychological principles of association were related to magical thinking? This is set out in a crucial passage, cited below:

> The fatal flaw of magic lies not in its general assumption of a sequence of events determined by law, but in its total misconception of the nature of the particular laws which govern that sequence. If we analyse the various cases of magic we shall find . . . that they are all mistaken

applications of one or other of two great fundamental laws of thought, namely, the association of ideas by similarity and the association of ideas by contiguity in space and time.

Frazer, 1922, p. 49

The phrasing of the passage is rather curious—it is hard to see how psychological laws could be 'misapplied'—but the general meaning is clear enough: 'primitives' reason about the world, but their reasoning goes astray because they confuse psychological relationships with physical ones. It will be useful to consider the two parts of Frazer's statement separately, beginning with the first concerning the postulated assumption on the part of the 'primitives' of regularity of the universe. There has been little dispute about this, and anthropologists of all persuasions have concurred. For Lévi-Strauss (1966), who, it will be recalled, is a rationalist–structuralist, magic results from an all-embracing desire for ordering phenomena that is characteristic of people in traditional cultures. He refers to magic as "that gigantic variation on the theme of causality . . . it can be distinguished from science not so much by any ignorance or contempt of determination, but by a more imperious and uncompromising demand for it" (p. 11). There is no evidence of any people who regard the world as chaotic, and I have tried to show elsewhere (Jahoda, 1969) that a tendency to seek for order, meaning, and, if possible, control (or at least the illusion of such control) is probably a fundamental human attribute, performing an adaptive function.

The second part of Frazer's statement, which concerns the errors of reasoning, has given rise to much debate; but its ground has shifted over time. Modern descendants of the intellectualist school of Tylor and Frazer tend to play down the supposed errors and argue that they are equally common among the 'civilized'. It has even been suggested (Cooper, 1975) that the apparent contradictions in 'primitive' thought arise from the fact that people in tribal societies operate with a three-value logic of a type that has been employed to resolve some anomalies of quantum physics—hence 'primitives' cannot be charged with illogicality! This rather extravagant claim has, of course, been challenged (Salmon, 1978), but the exchange can be read with profit as it brings out some of the fundamental issues very clearly.

The contribution of Horton (1970), who stressed the essential rationality of traditional thought, has been very influential. He criticized those who are apt to contrast the Western scientist to the unschooled member of a traditional culture:

. . . the layman's ground for accepting the models propounded by the scientist is often no different from the young African villager's ground for accepting the models propounded by one of his elders. In both cases the propounders are deferred to as the accredited agents of tradition. As for the rules which guide scientists themselves in the acceptance or rejection of models, these seldom become part of the intellectual equipment of members of the wider population.

p. 171

It will be noted that Horton's arguments are pitched at the general level of the sociology of knowledge, remote from the behaviour of actual individuals. I therefore select for more detailed discussion a recent interpretation of magical thinking in the classical tradition of Tylor and Frazer. The thesis put forward by Shweder (1977), who is actually a psychologist, is that magical thinking results basically from human cognitive-processing limitations, coupled with a universal need to understand one's environment. He rehearsed the well-known (to psychologists) fact that correlational thinking is difficult, even most normal Euramerican adults never fully achieving it. For instance, nurses presented with information in a contingency table about the frequency with which a (hypothetical) symptom did or did not go together with a (hypothetical) disease were mostly unable to make an accurate judgement about the probability of any connection. Thus, correlation is a non-intuitive concept that has to be more or less painfully acquired, as many students know very well.

The next step in the argument relates to some interesting studies of personality judgements conducted by Schweder himself. These involved three distinct variables:

a. beliefs about *resemblances* between behaviour categories, e.g. his subjects believed that 'uttering aloud expressions of delight or disapproval' resembled, conceptually, 'talking more than ones share';
b. information about the *actual* extent to which such behaviour categories went together; and
c. *ratings* by observers as to how far they went together.

Shweder was able to show that reports about one's experiences with other persons (c) correlated more highly with pre-existing beliefs about resemblances (a) than with independently kept records of what actually happened (b). He concluded that people faced with a task of estimating co-occurrence likelihood tend to fall back on the intuitive concept of resemblance, making their judgements on that basis.

From this springboard Shweder took a considerable intellectual leap to the magical practices of people like the Azande who, it is said, rely in their healing magic substantially on resemblances between the presenting symptoms and the purported magical remedy. Thus, for curing epilepsy the burnt skull of a bush monkey was eaten; cases of ringworm were treated by the application of fowl excrement. Now the movements of the bush monkey are somewhat similar to epileptic seizures, and ringworm looks rather like fowl excrement.

From this Shweder argued as follows:

> Magical thinking seems to be no more a feature of Zande beliefs that ringworm and fowl excrement go together than of our own beliefs that self-esteem and leadership do . . . My study suggests that anthropologists interested in thought may have mistaken a difference in the content of thought for a difference in mode of thought. Magical thinking does not distinguish one culture from another. Resemblance, not co-occurrence likelihood, is a fundamental conceptual tool of the everyday ('savage?') mind.
>
> p. 638

Thus, according to Shweder, Frazer was right in regarding magic as an intellectual error, but wrong in confining it chiefly to 'primitives'. For reasons to be explained more fully later, I would agree that there is no real evidence that magic entails some special form of thinking. Some other aspects of Shweder's thesis, however, are more questionable. By his formulation, the term 'magical' is extended to cover practically the whole range of cases of faulty reasoning in ordinary life. One would, of course, not wish to deny that such faulty reasoning is common—it has been extensively documented by Nisbett and Ross (1980)—nor that magical beliefs and practices can be found in all cultures; the trouble is that Shweder's usage robs the term 'magical' of all distinctive meaning.

It is also somewhat doubtful whether one can extrapolate from personality judgements, which present special problems of their own (Jackson and Paunonen, 1980) to all other kinds of everyday reasoning. Lastly, it is certainly not justifiable to explain such false reasoning by the catch-all term 'resemblance', which harks back to Frazer's "Law of Similarity".[6] One can show this in relation to the examples of Azande magic, which were interpreted by Tambiah (1973) as entailing more elaborate forms of analogical reasoning. Take the ringworm case set out below:

$$\frac{\text{excrement}}{\text{fowl}} : \frac{\text{scabby skin}}{\text{child}}$$

Tambiah pointed out that in addition to the similarity between the two elements left and right of the colon, there are also relationships within each element:

While the 'like attracts like' argument would say the fowl's excrement is (falsely) used to attract the scabs on the skin which it (falsely) resembles, I am tempted to say that the analogy is interesting and is capable of being acted upon creatively because . . . of the positive and negative features it exhibits. The relation of fowl to excrement is one of *elimination* of (unwanted) waste products, while that of scabby skin on child is one of (unwanted) adherence to body. Hence it is that the fowl's excrement can convey the desired idea of eliminating the scabs when applied to the body, because while in one sense similar to it, it is also essentially different.

Tambiah, 1973, p. 216

There is no empirical evidence that would help to decide whose view is correct; my purpose was simply to demonstrate that, on the basis of the identical ethnographic data, it is possible to attribute to the Azande a more subtle mode of analogical reasoning. It may have been noted that Tambiah not merely wanted to go beyond the Frazerian 'like attracts like' argument, but was not really concerned at all with the empirical truth or falsity of the magical analogy. This is because his approach to magic stems from a different tradition, to which I now turn. Before doing so, it will perhaps be useful to restate the position of Tylor and Frazer briefly in its original robust form: 'primitives' seek to explain the world around them in an essentially rational manner; their intellectual functioning is of the same type as that of the 'civilized', but is less developed; hence they reason in what Tylor in particular characterized as a childish way and therefore make gross errors.

This intellectualist thesis was subjected shortly after the turn of the century to a powerful attack by Lévy-Bruhl, widely known and often misunderstood for his catch-phrase 'pre-logical mentality'. He challenged the basic assumptions of the 'English School' of Tylor and Frazer that 'primitive thought' is concerned with explanation and that it is both rational and of the same character as more advanced thought; nor, according to Lévy-Bruhl, can it be regarded as a kind of infantile form of the latter. He viewed 'primitive thought' as being influenced by what he called 'mystic participation'—meaning that it was pervaded by an emotional ambience which leads 'primitives' to experience relationships as mystical rather than as causal. Such mystic participation is an aspect of the *collective representations* which dominate the primitive world view. Now it will be recalled that Durkheim had viewed collective representations as constituting the matrix of socially imposed ideas and beliefs which the individual absorbs during the process of becoming an adult member of society. In primitive cultures, therefore, where such representations are 'mystical', such mystical notions colour all thinking, making it impervious to logical considerations like the need to avoid contradictions. Moreover, the simpler the society, the more complete the dominance of collective representations and the less the exercise of any individual reasoning. It is in this sense that Lévy-Bruhl described 'primitives' as 'pre-logical'—it is not that they are illogical, but that logic as such is simply irelevant to thought governed by what he called the 'law of mystic participation'.

It will perhaps be instructive to give an example of the way in which Lévy-Bruhl sought to provide proof of his thesis. The passage cited below is supposed to show how magico-mystical 'participations' determine food habits and avoidances:

> The Abipones [South American Indians] abhor the idea of eating hens, eggs, mutton, fish, tortoise; they imagine that such soft food produces laziness and lassitude in their body, and cowardice in their soul. On the other hand, they devour avidly the meat of the tiger, the bull, deer, and boar with the idea that nourishing themselves continuously on these animals they will increase their strength, toughness and courage. In the provinces of north-east India the owl is the emblem of wisdom, and eating the eyes of an owl gives the ability to see clearly at night. In New Zealand a good orator was compared to the *korimako*, the most melodious of the song-birds of the country. In order to help a young chief to become eloquent, he was fed on that bird. The Cherokees thought the same. He who eats venison is a faster runner and more clever than the man who lives on the meat of the clumsy bear or stupid fowls . . . an Indian who ate during a certain time like a white man would acquire the nature of the white man, so much so that neither the remedies nor the charms of the Indian doctor will have any more effect on him.
>
> Lévy-Bruhl, 1910–51, p. 346; my translation

First of all, it may be noted that this is much the same kind of evidence as that put forward by Tylor and Frazer, only the theoretical interpretation is different—mystic participation instead of sympathetic magic. The treatment is also that characteristic of the old style, being thematic rather than focused on a particular people: within a single page, the illustrations jump around four continents! A variety of beliefs and practices are thus lifted out of their context and presented jointly as exemplifying a particular mode of pre-logical thinking.

Lévy-Bruhl was attacked by several prominent anthropologists with field experience, such as Boas, Rivers, and Malinowski, because the image of the 'savage' that he painted was not one they could recognize. Among psychologists Bartlett (1923) attributed to Lévy-Bruhl the view that "the psychology of primitive peoples represents a kind of mystical, pre-logical, lawless phase of mental development which sets the early man at a very far distance indeed from ourselves'' (pp. 281–2).

It is interesting that Lévy-Bruhl was far more bitterly criticized than Frazer, which is probably due to the unfortunate label of 'pre-logical'. In fact, Bartlett had it wrong when referring to ''a lawless phase of mental development'', for it was precisely the notion of a lower evolutionary stage of intellectual development which Lévy-Bruhl opposed; in fact, it could be shown that Frazer's position implies a poorer view of the mental capacities of 'primitives' than Lévy-Bruhl's. Thus he stated clearly that 'primitives have the same senses that we have and, ''in spite of the prejudice to the contrary'', also the same cerebral structure (Lévy-Bruhl, 1910–51, p. 37). Moreover, he said that every individual in modern society is the recipient of a heritage of logical thinking transmitted from an early age through the social milieu, while 'primitives' acquire in the same way a totally different heritage.

By no means all contemporary reaction was hostile, and it is worth recording that in a debate held before the French Philosophical Society in 1923 Pièron defended Lévy-Bruhl vigorously. On that occasion Pièron raised an important issue not directly faced by Lévy-Bruhl, and attempted an answer:

> Does logical thinking originate in specific social structures, or is it the natural result of how the human body functions? . . . From the moment human society is formed, we can assume in it two features both necessary for society's existence: (1) a certain balance in the behaviour of its members toward one another that prevents the group from disintegrating; and (2) the adaptation of these members to a victorious struggle with the environment. 'Pre-logical thought' may have been necessary for maintaining this balance; it may have been the specific feature of society. But vital need would have kept prelogical thought open to experience, especially through technical, practical activity.
>
> Quoted in Nikol'skii, 1976, p. 35

This penetrating comment by an eminent biologically oriented psychologist on the one hand anticipates one of the key problems with which anthropological theories have had to come to terms, and on the other foreshadows some of the fundamental questions to which Piaget later came to address himself. Incidentally, Piaget himself was a supporter of Lévy-Bruhl, and his early work (especially on childish 'animism') was strongly influenced by the latter's ideas.

No doubt Lévy-Bruhl must share the blame for having been frequently misunderstood, since he was not always consistent in his writings, in places (e.g. 1922, Chapter XIV), seeming to deny that even the technical skills of 'primitives' involve any kind of reflection or reasoning. In his last published works (Lévy-Bruhl, 1938 and 1949), he somewhat changed and clarified his position, conceding both that the term 'pre-logical' may be misleading and that 'primitives' are not always in a mystical frame of mind, and are quite capable of functioning at the ordinary common sense level familiar to us.[7]

Lévy-Bruhl was certainly a profound and influential thinker, and those—including the occasional writer of psychological texts—who direct patronizing gibes at him are ill informed. I should like to illustrate briefly how he touched upon some problems critical for cross-cultural psychology. When discussing the transmission of collective representations through the generations, he pointed out that these included language and concepts: "but these concepts differ from our own, and, consequently, the mental operations are also different" (1910–51, p. 114). Extend the notion of what is transmitted, taking in also Lévy-Bruhl's own point that the effects of education are hard to disentangle from 'natural' developmental trends; add the subtle influence of environmental factors, and one has a problem that is as yet far from being satisfactorily resolved. Cross-cultural psychologists studying people in traditional cultures usually find that their performance differs from that of people in industrial cultures. The question then arises whether such performance differences reflect differences in the underlying mental operations, or merely in relatively superficial strategies. Most psychologists would take the latter view,[8] but the evidence so far is by no means conclusive.

Lévy-Bruhl's position, it must be admitted, suffered from two major weaknesses. The first is that, in his earlier work at any rate, he postulated far too radical a disjunction between the thinking of people in 'primitive' and modern societies. Secondly, his evidence consisting of old ethnographic reports about collective representations in 'primitive' societies was neither strong and reliable enough to sustain his thesis, nor even entirely appropriate. Studies specifically designed to test his interpretations would be needed, and the closest approximation is Evans-Pritchard's classical work on *Witchcraft, Oracles and Magic among the Azande* (1937). Evans-Pritchard himself was considerably influenced by Lévy-Bruhl and his study of the Azande may be considered a test of the latter's theory, which did not emerge unscathed. Rather than discussing this in the abstract, I shall summarize certain aspects of this famous work. Anthropologists of all persuasions, and even some psychologists and philosophers, have used the Azande for arguing their cases. While some have questioned Evans-Pritchard's interpretations, the field material itself has never been challenged.

The Azande, like many African peoples, were much preoccupied with witchcraft, and their thinking in this sphere is extensively dealt with. However, in conducting their lives witchcraft was secondary to their major concern with the verdicts of the poison oracle, which was consulted for all important decisions. In fact, when the oracle was consulted on the command of a prince, the outcome had the force of law. A brief general account will be useful to set the stage and further details will emerge progressively. The poison for the oracle was obtained from a creeper in the forests of what was then the Belgian Congo (now Zaire). The collection of the poison from such a distant source, and the fact that certain taboos had to be observed if the poison were not to be spoilt, meant that the Azande could never be sure whether the poison was genuine and of the right potency. The *modus operandi* of the oracle was the administration of poison to a fowl, followed by the asking of a question; the answer was provided by the fowl either dying or surviving.

The general background of ideas and beliefs against which the working of the oracle must be viewed is of a kind Evans-Pritchard called 'mystical'. He defined this term as relating to "patterns of thought that attribute to phenomena supra-sensible qualities" (p. 12) that can neither be based upon, nor logically inferred from, observation. However, it would be wrong to imagine that all behaviours related to the oracle were of this kind. On the contrary, some of its components were clearly empirical, if not experimental. In fact, it is possible to show that in certain respects the Azande thought about their oracles in much the same way as psychologists think about tests and questionnaires. The parallels will be highlighted below by the use of appropriate jargon, but applied to the *poison*.

1. *Is it discriminating?* When new poison was brought in, it had first of all to be tested in order to ensure that it was functioning properly. If all of a set of several fowls survived, the poison was said to be 'weak' or 'dead' and had to be thrown away; if all the fowl died, it was said to be 'foolish', but could become good after being kept for a time. A 'good' poison would kill some and spare others. Evans-Pritchard did not specify the usual number of test trials, but it seems to have been at least four.

2. *Is it reliable?* Unlike the first criterion, this one is not a general issue, but refers to specific questions and occasions. Questions were framed in pairs so that the same answer was signified in reply to one member of the pair by the death of the fowl and in reply to the other by its survival. An example from Evans-Pritchard (1937, p. 300),

which also illustrates the manner in which questions were formulated, is quoted below:

> *First test.* If X has committed adultery, poison oracle kills the fowl. If X is innocent, poison oracle spares the fowl. The fowl dies.
> *Second test.* The poison oracle has declared X guilty of adultery. If its declaration is true, let it spare this second fowl. The fowl survives.

From the cases described in more detail, it is clear that the order of positive and negative phrasing was random. If the answers were inconsistent—i.e. if both fowls suffer the same fate—the poison was regarded as unreliable on that occasion.

3. *Does it give false responses?* The test here consists of presenting the poison with impossible contingencies. For instance, "If I shall go up to the sky and spear the moon, or bring back the sun, poison oracle kill the fowl."

The aspects of the procedures relating to the poison oracle considered so far are basically similar to those employed by an empirical researcher. Hence, it follows that the Azande were perfectly capable of thinking in this mode. I have, of course, lifted these features out of the 'mystical' context in which they were firmly embedded, as will become apparent from the last example which cuts across the two domains of the logical-empirical and mystical.

4. *Is the response biased?* This is somewhat similar to (3), except that the contingency is unlikely rather than impossible. In this case, the poison oracle is expected to understand the real question to be whether perhaps some external factors influence its response. Hence, if the poison oracle responds in a manner indicating that the improbable event has happened or will happen, it is in fact acknowledging the operation of a biasing or distorting influence—namely, sorcery. In other words, someone is employing sorcery in order to prevent the oracle from revealing the truth.

The external observer might gain the impression that the verdict of the poison oracle is a matter of chance, and in fact all the information provided by Evans-Pritchard is consistent with such a view. Thus, he shows that neither the dosage of poison, nor the size of the fowl, appear to be systematically related to the outcome. Moreover, he provided a table of the patterns of outcomes of a series of seances; when one applies the One-Sample Runs Test to this material, one finds that there is no significant departure from randomness in the series.

Naturally, the Azande did not regard themselves as 'dice men' who deliberately allow their lives to be ruled by what we call 'chance', which is, in any case, an unfamiliar concept in traditional African cultures. But how did they actually view the poison oracle? The fact that they took great trouble to formulate the question clearly, so that it might be understood, might suggest that they regarded the poison in the same way as spiritualists regard the rapping table, namely, as the mere tool of a personal intellect. However, Evans-Pritchard quite clearly stated that they did not personify the poison. The very question whether the poison is in some sense a person cannot be framed in the vernacular without becoming nonsensical. The Zande language has four genders (masculine, feminine, animal, and neuter), and the oracles are, with one animal exception, definitely neuter.

Some 'symbolic' anthropologists interpret this as indicating that the Azande in some way draw a distinction between intelligent/rational and symbolic ritual, as in the example below:

> The fact that he addresses the poison oracle in words does not imply any *confusion in his mind between things and persons*. It merely means that he is not striving for intellectual consistency and that in this field symbolic action seems appropriate.
>
> Douglas, 1966, p. 89; my italics

The italicized phrase suggests that some kind of distinction is being drawn, but I believe this to reside in the mind of the anthropologist rather than the Azande. It seems more likely to me that the Azande were like an ordinary layman in our culture who interacts with a computer in a question-and-answer sequence in some context (e.g. an 'automated' medical diagnosis). The layman is asked or himself asks questions of the computer, without, however, imagining that it is alive. Without having any theory about it or understanding how it functions, the computer is merely taken for granted as one of the marvellous mysteries of science. In a similar way, the Azande have construed the world as being one where the poison oracle is a thing whose nature it is to respond to questions under certain carefully defined circumstances. There was thus no reason why they should have felt themselves to be in any way 'intellectually inconsistent', even if they had been given to that kind of reflection (which seems unlikely).

This standpoint is reinforced by Evans-Pritchard's convincing demonstration that Azande ideas about what he calls 'mythical' features of their world such as oracles or witchcraft constituted a coherent system without sharp discontinuities. The questions asked of the oracle mainly concern the operation of mystical forces so that they might be counteracted if they presented a threat. Since information about such forces cannot be gained in any other way, there can be no independent check on the validity of the oracles and concrete experience as such is incapable of contradicting them. For example, if a particular danger about which the oracle has been consulted is not avoided, this may be taken as evidence that the precautions taken have not been sufficiently effective, or that more powerful magic has overcome them. There may have been, and often was, scepticism about specific oracles or verdicts, but not easily about the system as a whole because it formed the overall framework within which Azande thinking about the world was largely confined. Moreover, as Evans-Pritchard (1937, p. 319) pointed out, the very language is such that it is difficult to use it to express scepticism or objections which do not occur to anyone within the culture.

In relation to Lévy-Bruhl's thesis, Evans-Pritchard confirmed the view that the misleadingly named 'pre-logical' mentality is simply a function of people adopting the beliefs prevalent in their social environment, which constrain their outlook upon the world. Within these constraints they behave sensibly according to Western standards of rationality. Evans-Pritchard also accepted, perhaps too wholeheartedly, Lévy-Bruhl's sharp division between the empirical and the mystical; but he showed that even the mystical was not as affect-laden as Lévy-Bruhl had supposed. This is because the occult, which for Europeans has overtones of mystery and awe, was for the Azande merely another sphere of life with its own rules and procedures. Lastly, Evans-Pritchard demonstrated that even with the mystical sphere Azande did not fail to take account of experience, as Lévy-Bruhl had claimed; but they had their own ways of handling this so as to leave the system as a whole intact.

There is no support at all in the Azande study for the view, shared by Frazer and Lévy-Bruhl alike, that there is a particular mode of cognition—'magical' or 'mystical'—that characterizes the thinking of people in traditional cultures. There are magical beliefs and practices, and one can talk about 'magical thought' in the same way as about 'religious thought' or 'communist thought'—that is to say, by referring to content rather than process.[10] People, be they Azande or Americans, can act under the influence of their magical beliefs in some contexts and in a rational–technical manner in others. When things go wrong in an uncontrollable and unforeseeable way, the Azande will attribute it to witchcraft, the Americans perhaps to bad luck. Since I started this chapter with a fantastic experience related by an African, it needs pointing out that such 'thinking' is by no means confined to Africa: after I published a book on superstition, a number of people who seemed to be able to function perfectly well in the scientific and technological environments of Europe and America (one was in fact an engineer) told me in all earnestness about such experiences as travel in space craft manned by 'aliens'!

There is thus a critical difference between the actual thinking processes of particular people who may be influenced by magical-type beliefs in one situation and by common or even scientific sense in another, and the *thought-systems* prevalent in a culture. Such systems must at one time have been the product of live thinking, but like a coral reef have become fossilized. Unfortunately the difference is often blurred, if not obliterated, in much anthropological writing. The classical heritage of Frazer and Lévy-Bruhl has been assimilated in a modified form, eliminating the connotations of Western superiority. This sometimes results in the paradoxical tendency for alleged magical thinkers to be credited with 'thinking' about their magic, as the following examples show:

> (i) Magic procedures are not constructed at random, without rhyme or reason. Rather, a definite intellectual effort does go into their construction, which means that we can legitimately speak of a pattern or mode of 'magic thinking'.
>
> Nadel, 1977, p. 4
>
> (ii) The significance of magical ingredients does not emerge from qualities thought of as intrinsic in the animals and plants of the environment, but from *man's deductive thought about them* [my italics]. So a ram, for example, does not itself symbolize virility or any other quality. The symbolic meaning of the hump on its neck follows from the observation that this knot of muscle is used by the animal in levelling blows with its horns against its sexual rivals.
>
> Willis, 1974, pp. 93–4

One is never told who does, or did, such thinking! It is a little unfair to single out particular instances, when examples abound in the literature; the excellent book on *Modes of Thought* edited by Horton and Finnegan (1973) contains many cases of arbitrary switching between the individual and collective levels—at the very least the language employed is frequently confusing in this respect.

The root of the trouble is, I believe, to be found in the manner in which the two grand traditions of Tylor and Frazer, on the one hand, and of Lévy-Bruhl, on the other, have become fused.[11] Collective representations, at least in traditional cultures, have no independent existence and are mediated through individual cognitive processes. This entails a fundamental ambiguity, since no one can tell where the influence of collective representations ends and truly 'individual' thinking begins. Unless this conceptual distinction is kept clearly in mind, which is rare in anthropological discussions, it is fatally easy to slip into the kinds of confusions that have been pointed out.

There is one type of anthropological theory of magic which escapes from that dilemma, though running into some difficulties of its own, and that is the rationalist/structuralist one. While also drawing upon the joint heritage of Frazer and Lévy-Bruhl, it manages to do so by transforming individual thinking and collective representations into the common denominator of culture, treated as a symbolic system and discerned through patterns of communication. Lévi-Straussians with that kind of orientation deal with cultural phenomena, including, of course, magic, in a quite distinctive manner, epitomized by Leach (1976) when he says that culture communicates and the job of the anthropologist is to decode the communication. Given the prominence of structuralist theory in modern anthropology, this account would be incomplete without indicating the manner in which it tackles the problem of magic; this will, at the same time, provide an opportunity of exemplifying this type of analysis. Hence, I shall conclude this chapter by outlining Leach's (1976) challenging interpretation. This cannot be done without going into some preliminary detail about the conceptual framework.

Leach distinguishes three main aspects of human behaviour, the first comprising expressive actions like greetings, prayers, or the giving of gifts "which either simply say something about the state of the world as it is, or else purport to alter it by metaphysical means" (1976, p. 9). These are contrasted with *technical actions*, like cutting wood, which change something in the physical world; then there are also *biological activities of the human body*, like digestion. All these are different but closely related aspects of human behaviour: in cutting wood my breathing accelerates, expressing the fact that I am working hard; and the particular tools I am using (stone axe or electric saw) convey information about my cultural background.

The notion of 'communication' is vastly extended from its usual narrow meaning to encompass not merely non-verbal forms of human behaviour, but such cultural products as clothing style, architecture, cooking and so on; all are regarded as patterned sets that may be decoded, and may thus be regarded as analogous to human communication by means of signals, signs, and symbols. Leach (1976, p. 12) put forward an elaborate terminology to characterize communication events, whereby an entity bearing message A conveys information about message B. From this large array, only those elements will be selected which are essential for the interpretation of magic and sorcery offered by Leach. I recognize that such a dismemberment of a complex and coherent scheme is bound to be somewhat misleading, and the interested reader is advised to consult the original source; at the same time, it does not seem to me that the distortion is such as to affect the main argument.

The relevant major distinctions, then, are as follows:

Signal. A causes B by trigger response; signals are mainly biological in nature, e.g. hunger pangs trigger eating.
Natural index. A is associated with B by nature, but selected as an index of B by human choice, e.g. smoke is an index of fire.
Metonymic sign. A stands for B as part for the whole, e.g. the crown as a sign for royalty.
Metaphoric symbol. A is a conventional but entirely arbitrary symbol for B, e.g. the serpent is a symbol for evil.

No sooner had Leach set forth these neat distinctions—one of a set of such schemes that have been elaborated by various writers—than he proceeded to undermine it by pointing out important slippages that occur. Since in his view the relationship between concepts "in the mind" and objects or events in the external world is an arbitrary one (a point to which I propose to return), there is an inherent ambiguity in meaning systems. Metaphor (symbolic) and metonymic (sign) relationships are normally kept apart so as to avoid ambiguity; but in certain contexts like poetic or religious utterances, the distinction is obliterated: "By code switching between symbols and signs we are able to persuade one another that metaphoric non-sense is really metonymic sense." (p. 22.)

Again, a signal is always part of a cause and effect sequence and in this respect resembles human technical action. The main difference is "that signals are 'automatic' in that they do *not* entail an *intentional response* on the part of the receiver, but they are *not fully mechanical* in that the effectiveness of the signal depends upon the sense response of the receiver, which is not fully predictable. Technical actions, on the other hand, are *fully mechanical*, and they entail an *intentional act* on the part of the sender (actor)." (p. 23.)[12]

The signal is causal in nature, while the index is not. Yet, Leach claimed, animals and humans respond to "habitually used" indices as though they were signals. In order to demonstrate this, Leach cited Pavlov's dogs, for which, he suggested, the smell of food was the real biological signal; but after conditioning the dogs treat the bell as a signal though it is really merely an index for the presence of food. Leach's human example is (to the psychologist) equally unconvincing: the printed letters on a page are said to be true indices, "but ordinarily you will treat the printed letterpress as a signalling apparatus which automatically generates information" (p. 24).

In this manner Leach established a base from which to consider Frazer's theory of magic, which implied that the magician's error was that of confusing expressive and technical acts. Leach stated (and this is agreed by all modern anthropologists) that anyone who observes the performance of magical acts is quite clear that the magician is *not* guilty of any such confusion—magical and technical acts are of quite different kinds. What then, according to Leach, is happening? It is true that the magician seeks to produce real effects in the world by action at a distance, but this occurs in a very complicated manner, and only Leach's summary statement in terms of a Frazerian prototype example can be quoted:

> A sorcerer gains possession of a specimen of hair from the head of his intended victim, X. The sorcerer destroys the hair to the accompaniment of spells and rituals. He predicts that, as a consequence, the victim, X, will suffer injury.
>
> What is the 'logic' of the sorcerer's fallacy? . . . the sorcerer makes a triple error. He first mistakes a metaphoric symbol (i.e., the verbal label 'this is the hair of X') for a metonymic sign. He then goes on to treat the imputed sign as if it were a natural index, and finally he interprets the supposed natural index as a signal capable of triggering off automatic consequences at a distance.
>
> p. 31

At first sight this might look like a statement about the presumed psychological processes of the magician; but it is nothing of the kind, and not intended as such: it is a logical and not psychological analysis, and has to be evaluated as such. This will become obvious if one stops to consider how the propositions might be empirically tested.

On the other hand there is the fact that the analysis rests in part on psychological postulates whose validity is open to challenge. The first of these concerns the relationship between ''concepts in the mind'', sense images, and objects in the external world. According to Leach, sense images and concepts are two complementary aspects of the same phenomenon; by contrast, the relationship between a sense image and an external object is always to some extent arbitrary, constituting a 'symbolic' linkage. This implies that the way in which we slice up the world is also essentially arbitrary, an inference explicitly affirmed by Leach himself: ''When we use symbols . . . to distinguish one class of things or actions from another, we are creating artificial boundaries in a field which is 'naturally' continuous.'' (p. 33.)

Since this issue is later to be discussed more fully in connection with problems of categorization, I will here confine myself to the simple assertion that there is evidence indicating that this extreme form of statement is wrong.

The second point relates to the claim that Pavlov's dog 'treated' an index as a signal. Actually (using the same anthropomorphic formulation), it did nothing of the kind. In terms of Leach's own conceptual framework, the bell simply had *become* the signal. As regards the letter-press example, it is difficult to see even within that framework how printed letters, meaningless individually, could be regarded as indices in the context of reading.

In common with all contemporary anthropologists, Leach does not believe that magical thinking is confined to pre-literate cultures. This is indicated by some of the examples he gives of 'political sorcery' or 'techno-magic in the home'. However, in such modern instances the distinction between technical and expressive acts often becomes so blurred that it ceases to be useful. This may be illustrated with a case cited by Langer (1977) of a Las Vegas gambler who blew a deep breath against the dice before every roll. The following conversation ensued:

> "Do you think that brings you luck?" the man standing next to him at the crap table asked. "I know it does," the shooter replied with conviction. "Las Vegas has a very dry climate, right?" "Right," his neighbour nodded. "So the dice are usually very dry. I have a very damp breath, and I always exhale against a six and an ace. That not only gives the six and ace a little extra weight but makes them adhere to the table when they roll across it. The opposite sides come up—and the opposite sides of a six and ace are an ace and six." "Does it really work?" his neighbouring player asked. "Well, not all the time," the shooter admitted. "The load of condensation is not quite heavy enough. But I've been on a hot liquid diet all day, and tonight ought to be the time I break the bank."
>
> p. 186

While an outside observer would probably regard the blowing on dice as an expressive action, the actor himself put forward an elaborate justification purporting to show its technical nature. Who is right, the actor or the observer?

The issue is pertinent to Leach's argument, since he contended that the operation of the light switch "is technical in intention and *may* be technical in its consequences, but the actual form of the action is expressive" (p. 32).[13] Hence it follows, according to Leach, that Frazer ought to have regarded the operation of the light switch as a magical act! We seem to have arrived at the curious conclusion that while people in traditional cultures clearly distinguish between technical and magical acts, those in modern cultures—presumably because the linkage between act and effect is often indirect and complex—do not!

In sum, the kind of analysis put forward by Leach is subtle and ingenious, looking at the familiar from an unusual perspective that reveals some unexpected relationships. While somewhat flawed by untenable psychological assumptions, these could probably be eliminated: it is hard to judge how serious the resulting damage would be to the edifice as a whole. With regard to magic in particular, the analysis yields two valuable lessons: first, it is not as easy as is usually supposed to distinguish magical from other kinds of actions; secondly, it points towards, without fully clarifying, the important symbolic elements in magic.

Much of the remaining chapters will be devoted to elaborating the problem areas adumbrated here, especially the relationship between individual thinking and collective representations, including their symbolic aspects. This contentious issue lies at the core of anthropological approaches to cognition. At the same time it will also be shown that thought systems, forming part of collective representations, can be of considerable interest to psychologists in their own right. In order to convey more concretely the nature of such collective representations, the next chapter will largely consist of a detailed illustration.

Notes

1. In fact, before the variations in cultural belief systems had become more widely recognized, it was not unusual for European psychiatrists to arrive at false diagnoses on the basis of such evidence: several such cases, mostly concerning students, came to my knowledge.
2. My main sources for this are Tauxier (1927), Dieterlen (1951), Paques (1954), and Imperato (1977).
3. Actually, the so-called *dya*, to be explained in the next chapter. A number of detailed case histories of man-eating witches are provided by Sidibé (1929). Such beliefs used to be common in West Africa, and I have myself been shown a crudely faked photograph of a leopard with a human head claimed as undeniable proof of lycanthropy.
4. "Une croyance imaginaire de ces grands enfants que sont les noirs." (Tauxier, 1927, p. 252.)
5. This equation of 'savage' adults with European children is a hoary myth that persisted for a considerable time. Thus the famous American educationist Stanley Hall regarded non-whites as the 'children' of the human race (Muschinske, 1977). Even among relatively recent psychologists Werner (1957) drew many parallels of this kind; although he specifically dissociated himself from Hall's position, the resemblances seem closer than the differences. In fact, the ideas espoused by Hall and, to a lesser

   extent, Werner, rest on a misinterpretation of evolutionary theory as it is
   understood today.

6. In fact, the concept of similarity is an exceedingly complex one; see
   Tversky (1977).

7. For a more extensive discussion of Lévy-Bruhl and his contemporaries,
   see Horton (1973); a good account from a more psychological perspective
   is provided by Warren (1980), whose views on some issues differ from my
   own.

8. See the excellent discussion by Cole *et al.* (1971) and Cole and Scribner
   (1974).

9. It should be noted that the questions addressed to the poison oracle were
   not usually about *what* should be done, which followed custom, but about
   the *best or least risky ways* of doing what was going to be done anyway. See
   Evans-Pritchard (1937, pp. 344–5).

10. This distinction has been lucidly examined by Colby and Cole (1973).

11. The fact that this has happened is really not surprising, as there was far
    more in common between them than the original protagonists supposed.
    Thus Frazer (1922, p. 11) wrote:

   > It is to be borne in mind that the primitive magician knows magic only on
   > its practical side; he never analyses the mental processes on which his
   > practice is based, never reflects on the abstract principles involved in his
   > actions.

    This is surely not far short of admitting that individual thinking is not
    an important part of magical practice. Similarly Lévy-Bruhl, especially in
    his later writings, allowed that there are spheres where 'primitives' rely on
    individual thinking.

12. Italics in original.

13. It is not very obvious from this abbreviated account why the action should
    be regarded as expressive, and I must admit that I did not even find the
    full explanation altogether convincing.

8 | Bambara Notions of Personality and Symbolism

Since the concept of 'collective representations' is relatively unfamiliar for psychologists, a brief reminder is perhaps useful that Durkheim defined the term as the entire complex of beliefs and sentiments common to average citizens of the same society. He was emphatic that this constituted a system independent of individuals and impinging upon them from the outside, though also mediated through them. Durkheim's ideas have had a powerful impact on both anthropological theory and practice.[1]

Accordingly, anthropological fieldworkers usually regard it as one of their main tasks to provide an account of the system of ideas, beliefs, and symbols of the culture with which they are concerned. While it is possible to draw important inferences from observations of behaviour, especially in communal settings such as political disputes, court cases and especially various forms of rituals, the chief method is inevitably the questioning of informants. The informants will usually consist of a mixture of ordinary people, knowledgeable elders and ritual specialists steeped in the traditions. What kinds of questions are asked will depend to some extent on the theoretical orientation of the field worker, and the same applies to the manner in which the data come to be pooled and eventually interpreted. It will be evident, therefore, that the final product, viewed as an attribute of the society at large (its collective representations), is always bound to embody at least some element of construction on the part of the anthropologist. When several different anthropologists independently study a given culture and arrive at congruent descriptions of collective representations, one may have considerable confidence in their validity.

The Bambara have been selected partly because there exists a great deal of ethnographic material about them from different sources, and partly because a relatively brief and yet thorough report by Cissé (1973) is available on their ideas and beliefs related to psychology.[2] Some basic information about the Bambara has already been given in the preceding chapter, in connection with the sketch of some of their magical beliefs. The description was deliberately cast in an old-fashioned style that is likely to have given the impression not merely that the Bambara were a technologically simple agricultural society, which is correct, but also that their ideas and beliefs were simple and crude 'superstitions', which is entirely wrong. The purpose of this mode of presentation was to illustrate the fact that partial information focusing on the more exotic and seemingly bizarre, typical of early reports, is liable to create a totally misleading image of a culture.

When the opposition between 'primitive' and 'civilized' ceased to be acceptable terminology, the dichotomy of literate versus pre-literate cultures took its place. When this criterion is applied, the Bambara, who had no written language, must be regarded as pre-literate. However, they did have locally restricted sets of pictographs that made simple forms of quasi-written communication possible (Zahan, 1950). Moreover, they had a highly developed graphic number system, illustrated in Fig. 8.1, which enabled them to carry out quite complex

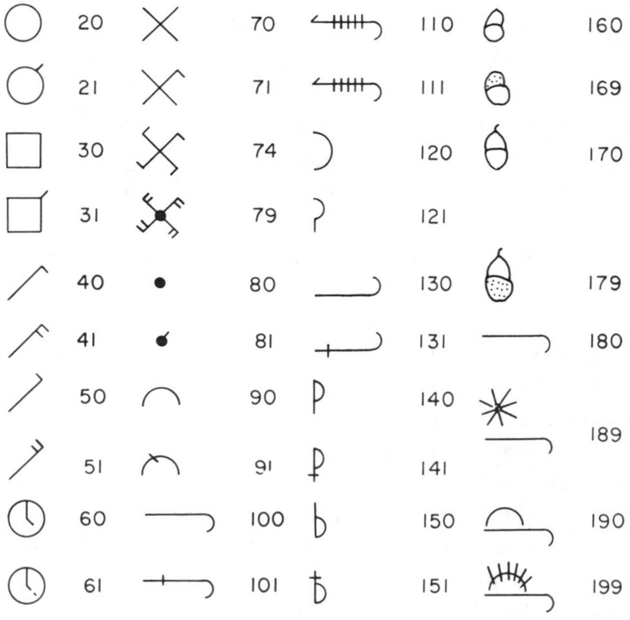

FIG. 8.1.   The graphic number system of the Bambara (from Ganay, 1950).

mathematical operations. As will become apparent later, their number system was closely connected with divination and an elaborate symbolism (Ganay, 1949) relating man to the cosmos, whose centre was for them the earth. They were interested in astronomy and measured the revolutions of the sun around the earth by means of a cylindrical granary with a conical roof, which they used as a gnomon. It was built on a carefully prepared square mount, with four heavy stones oriented east–west, one south, another north, and one in the centre; wooden beams were placed on the stones. By means of such gnomons they were able, by observing the projected shadow, to determine the dates of solstices and equinoxes. They represented the movements of the sun graphically by a zigzag line, whose variations corresponded to variations in the length of the day; such lines also figured prominently in the ornamentation of artefacts like pottery, in agricultural rites, and also the pattern of movement of their dances (Zahan, 1951). Even this cursory sketch should suffice to convey something of the richness and coherence of Bambara traditional culture, whose transmission through the socialization process has been studied by Fellous (1976). Against this background, the nature of Bambara 'psychology', to which I now turn, can be better appreciated.[3]

Since Bambara ideas about human personality do not constitute a more or less independent sphere, as in modern psychology, but are embedded within traditional cosmology, it will be essential to begin by conveying at least some aspects of this wider world view. The Bambara creation myth holds that the universe arose out of primordial unchanging nothingness, which ultimately is also the origin of the person. An initial spark set off vibration, animation, and illumination, and matter came into existence; a person is made of the same stuff—namely, water, earth, fire, and air. The principle of life, *ni*, has the same origin as (and may be identical with) the 'vibrations' which animate the universe. The Bambara say that without 'vibration' there is no movement, without movement no heat, and without heat neither life nor death. It is perhaps not merely coincidental that the word for 'vibration' also means 'oneself'. The symbol for the first movement is *kara*, 'the perfect circle', shown below:

It is heavily charged with multiple significations, including the creator, but here I shall single out merely those relating to personality. They are related pair-wise to the circumference and centre of the circle, respectively: 'thought and reflection',[4] 'destiny and future', 'will and desire'. These are regarded as the main elements of personality, and the circle as a whole is essentially a symbol of life and destiny.

A more concrete representation related to the person is the sign called 'placenta and umbilical cord', shown below. It consists of four parts, described as follows:

1. top vertical segment: 'attachment'—umbilical cord;
2. central circle: 'in front of the chest'—sternum and solar plexus;
3–4. two bottom hooks: respectively, 'call of the father' and 'call of the mother'.

This sign indicates in a concise manner what we would call the biological foundation of the personality. The 'calls' approximate what we conceptualize as the genetic 'message', which will in due course affect all parts of the body. The embryo has a 'core' of life, located in the solar plexus. The equal contribution of both parents to the new life is manifest, at the level of the placenta, by 'pulsations' of the umbilical cord which anticipate what the Bambara know as 'the call of the soul', i.e. respiration. Here again, one has a double mode of representation since, on a more functional plane, the four parts of the figure stand for the windpipe, heart, and lungs.

The placenta as the receptacle of life and destiny is the subject of special attention. It is always buried in the court of the family house, and one 'refreshes' it by watering until either the naming ceremony held seven or eight days after birth, or until the fortieth day when the mother resumes her normal cycle of fecundity. There is a saying 'where your afterbirth is, there is your fatherland', and the rituals may account for the powerful attachment to 'the father's house'.

The symbol for the stage where the embryo becomes a foetus is set out below. At that stage it is regarded as a miniature person already

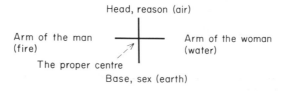

subject to the influences impinging upon the mother. It also anticipates the upright position appropriate for a human. It will be noted that the four arms of the cross represent at the same time body parts and what are believed to be the fundamental components of the person. The conjunction of the four parts creates the vital centre.

The complete person is said to consist of six essences:

> a brain to create,
> a sex organ to procreate,
> two arms to work,
> two legs to move about.

These are symbolized by the pair of signs below:

moko − man   komo − woman

The six parts of the person are considered as pair wise opposites: right/left arm and leg, head/genitals. Anything affecting one member of the pair influences the other, implying a notion of physiological and psychic harmony or equilibrium. Such correspondences are among the bases of traditional healing and divining; hence the signs are often used in this context.

Banāngolo—childbirth

This is a very complex symbol, crucial in traditional thought. Its name is derived from *ba* = mother, *na* = coming, being born, and *ngolō* = the first man. The symbol given below represents most directly a woman lying on her back in the throes of childbirth.

This symbol is traced on the ground, the heavy lines being done with the index finger. The nine levels correspond to the nine lunar months of alternatively 30 and 29 days, totalling 266 days, which is regarded as the duration of gestation. The 33 segments linked to each other represent the 33 vertebrae, while the isolated one stands for the pubic bone. The topmost level represents the head, the bottom one the vagina. The three and four vertical segments between these represent, respectively, the male side of the person on the right and the female side on the left.[5] Moreover, the number 3 symbolizes the penis and the two testicles, and 4 the 'four lips' of the woman.

As the left side (male) of the figure exceeds the right, it is asymmetrical and thereby considered dynamic; this corresponds to the idea that there can be no life without movement. It should be mentioned that in addition to this particular aspect of the *banāngolo*, it also constitutes a model of human anatomy which, as perceived by the Bambara, consists of 266 distinct elements. Clearly, one has here a central organizing principle of cosmological thought, as shown by the following quotation: "In order to create the universe God made use of his 266 names which, mediated by his word, became the 266 signs of creation. And man, created in 266 days in the image of God, naturally received 266 signs that constitute his bodily and spiritual nature."

The *banāngolo* is also related to the signs used in geomantic divination, widespread in West Africa. The 18 vertical segments are combined to obtain three geomantic signs of the person, and the operation whereby this is done is called 'taking out the *dya*'; and, as will shortly be indicated, the *dya* is one of the key concepts of personality.

The sixty dynamic elements of the person

These sixty elements or principles might be regarded as forming the core of Bambara psychology. They are linked pair-wise, one being masculine (M) and the other feminine (F). It will, of course, only be possible to present a summary of the salient aspects, using more familiar language.

Thought (M) and reflection (F). This constitutes a crucial pair of principles, whose significance is enshrined in many proverbs (e.g. "Where a person's thought ends is the limit of his universe").[6] Thought is related to the greatest and the smallest in the world, and it is no accident that the symbol ⊙ refers to both the person and the universe. In everyday speech the two terms are sometimes replaced by a single one of Arab origin which connotes not merely thought and reflection, but also intelligence, attention, memory—in brief, cognitive functions in general.

The seat of thought and reflection, as well as of many other principles, is the brain. For the whole, conscious person, the brain is the meeting point of two important activities called "the things up high" (the will) and "the things from down below" (impulse, desire). Through the seven openings in the head (2 eyes, 2 ears, 2 nostrils, mouth) there arrive in the brain four sensations from the outside world: light, sound, odour, and taste. Such sense impressions are conveyed to all parts of the body via the spinal cord. Other sensations coming from the outside follow an opposite path: from the skin surface or from internal organs they pass through the spinal cord to the brain. The brain itself is likened to the flour of the monkey-bread fruit; it preserves in its innumerable 'grains' all the information reaching it from within or outside the body.

There are two 'flows' of the soul whereby thought and reflection proceed; for the brain is not just a passive receptacle of impressions, but above all a centre of permanent 'vibrations'. The first flow, of thought, starts in the centre of the brain and goes through the forehead. This follows the flow of life in the external world, taking in the objects perceived through the seven openings and proceeding along the reverse path back to the brain where the information received is deposited.

The second flow (reflection) also has its origin in the centre of the brain, but passes through the brain stem and spinal cord down into the depths of the person, whence it reverses and brings back to the brain the information collected. It is held that thought and reflection are mutually incompatible, like alternating currents, so that one must be at rest while the other is active.

The 'intelligence' of a person depends on the intensity of these rhythmic flows and the capacity of the brain to store for a long time the messages received, which make it possible for thought and reflection to apprehend the 'essence' of things and the underlying links between them. It is recognized that both 'thought' and 'reflection' depend upon perception, which yields 'the things known by the person'. There is, in this general conception, no sharp distinction between body, soul, and mind; and 'intelligence' is often spoken of as though it could reside anywhere in the living body.

Speech (F) and authority (M). The birth of speech is attributed to the activity of the brain—especially thought and reflection. At a certain stage these can no longer be conveyed by gestures. Speech appears from the inside of a person in the form of a 'tension' which, once in the 'house of life' (the thoracic cage), and notably the lungs, increases and gains strength. The specific account of the air being modulated by the vocal cords, and so forth, is close to the standard scientific one. It is said that speech is also a gesture and even an act that produces an effect. All speech is charged with 'vital force' emanating from inside the person. Carrier of human sentiments, speech is the most potent social instrument and an essential tool for domination: "Without speech there is no power nor authority."

Nya ni dya: vital (M) and bodily (F) flux. The first of these may be described as a kind of radiation which, starting from the soul, creates inside and outside the person an extremely rapid intermittent flux. Its activation may be gauged by the expression of the eyes, whereby one can judge its intensity; its manifestations become most lively in joy or thrills. The Bambara liken it to a fire, and it is conceived as a vital energy which becomes extinct at death.

More important psychologically is the *dya*, which is commonly called the person's 'double'. There are four different forms of it:

1. The 'stupid' *dya* is the shadow of the person, whose movements it simply imitates.
2. The 'true' or 'real' *dya* represents the bodily image as reflected in water or a mirror; latterly, photographs have been assimilated to this category as well as ciné films, popularly named *dya*.
3. The 'little intelligent *dya*' is a kind of miniature replica of the person esconced in the body ('ghost in the machine'!)—some say in the brain, others mention the pancreas. It is this 'intelligent *dya*' which largely determines the behaviour of the person. It is closely associated with thought and reflection, which can only function when the *dya* is 'sitting down', i.e. inactive. There are numerous expressions describing the various states of the *dya*, which correspond to specific psychological states of the person. It can temporarily leave the body, and in such cases is totally identical with the person. It is this *dya* which sorcerers attack and 'eat', acting through their own 'intelligent *dya*'.
4. The last is the *dya* of the deceased, which joins the sacred pool of the village.

All except the last are carriers of part of the 'flux' of the person; hence, to possess any of them (e.g. a picture) by magic or sorcery is to attain the person herself.

ba ni fa: foundation (F) and fullness/fulfilment (M). Each person has a 'foundation'—biological, cultural and spiritual—and within a given social context tends towards his or her fulfilment. A saying has it that everyone has three *ba*: one that bears him, another that raises and trains him, and a third that maintains him. Any attitude or behaviour is in part the outcome of two things: the place and manner of his upbringing. If there is a shortcoming in any of these three *ba*, the person will be 'incomplete'; and in fact, it is recognized that everyone is in some ways incomplete, in failing to realize his or her potential. These principles thus embody what we would call the environmental factors.

Support (F) and axis (M). The spinal column is the key framework around which all other body parts are grouped. It is the axis and the support, biological and ontological. Where the spinal column is deformed, it is the whole being which is damaged in its most profound essence. Any abnormality of the spinal column involves a corresponding psychological and sexual abnormality; vice-versa, sexual problems or psychological traumas lead to back aches. Hence, there is the expression 'cutting of support' or 'cutting of the axis' to denote disappointments of any sort. Accordingly, a poor view is also taken of hunchbacks or other deformed people, and a person without an axis is a vagabond, a vile creature.

The 'Underneath' (M) and intimate essence (F). These notions relate to the faculties and dispositions of a person, revealed by their modes of behaving. There are expressions which, literally translated, mean 'bringing out the underneath of a person', i.e. to put them to the test, assess their potential talents and abilities. Similarly, other phrases concern the critique of a person's behaviour or the recital of their virtues and vices.

First name (F) and family name (M). These are important aspects of the person with which many beliefs and rites are associated. The first name is linked with the personality as such,[7] the family name with the *dyu* or 'intelligent double'.

Future (F) and destiny (M). It has already been indicated in connection with the earlier comments on graphic symbols that destiny is believed to be at least to some extent laid down at birth. However, there is a phrase used at initiation ceremonies showing that it is not a question of a fixed and ineluctable fate: ''What we have ourselves acquired and that which has happened to us, these constitute our destiny and our future.''

Character (F) and vital energy (M). The term *tere* designates simultaneously the totality of a person's character, each of the traits taken in isolation and the principles determining character. The latter manifests itself in physical signs as well as psychological features: gestures, tone of voice, brilliance of eyes, colour and abundance of hair, shape of the teeth, and so forth. Most oft the signs are concentrated on the head, hence the expression ''*tere* of the head''. Here are some:

Large forehead—intelligent and thoughtful;
Convex forehead—lively intelligence;
High forehead—man of action;

Squat jaws—talkative and quarrelsome;
Squint—tenacity and often intrigue;
Head held high on rigid neck—inflexible;
Head twitching—usually intelligent, but inclined to be authoritarian.

Tere is particularly carefully studied in women whom one is considering marrying. The ideal woman's *tere* has 4 × 3 things:

3 roundnesses—large enough head, breasts nicely curved, buttocks well rounded;
3 'links' (?)—good neck and waist, fine wrists and ankles;
3 blacknesses—abundant black hair, big black eyes, black gums and lips;
3 whitenesses—pure white of the eyes, brilliant white teeth, and a spotless interior life.

It will be noted here that the physical desiderata greatly outweigh the psychological ones! Several different features—e.g. narrow hips (making for difficult childbirth) are taken as signs of bad *tere*. In general, *tere* is considered as being carried by the blood, and physical contact or even proximity to someone with bad *tere* can bring misfortune.

Waãzo (M/F) and kaãzo(M/F). *Waãzo* is an 'interior vital force', obscure and disordered, which agitates children and adolescents and yet charges them with extraordinary vitality. It resides both in the brain and the genitals (foreskin of boys and clitoris of girls). It represents a kind of principle of disorder and anarchy within the individual: "Its result is that he/she cannot live with anybody, cannot get on with anyone else, not even themselves." It is also opposed to fecundity.

In order to become a stable, mature person who marries, procreates, makes sacrifices, and so on, the young person must be relieved of his *waãzo*. This is done by circumcision (boys) or excision (girls). Such an operation stabilizes the 'substratum' and the place of *waãzo* is taken by another force, *kaãzo*, which allows the individual to take up his or her status as a member of the community who fulfils his obligations.

Similar positive changes occur at 7 × 7 = 49 years, the blossoming of mature life, when yet another force takes over, and again at 60 when 'spirituality' appears. The last stage at 76 + brings a person close to the ranks of the ancestors, and they become free to transcend ordinary rules and taboos.

Inner (F) and outer (M) voices. The person acquires *yo*, the inner voice, at the time of his conception. Regarded as the voice of the Creator, it is close to our concept of 'conscience'. There is a second voice, *yaa*, man's own, whereby he asks himself about his proper destiny and the sense of his life. The ideal is that these two voices should be in harmony, but how is this to be achieved? The proverbial answer is "Know thyself; know how to control yourself; learn to know your fellows and be patient with them."

Weaving as the 'model' of human personality
The Bambara regard the occupation of weaver as the perfect symbol not merely of the various facets of personality, but also of creation and life: "It conceals the voice which presided over the creation of the universe." Note that the word *dali* means both 'to weave' and 'to create'. The weaver is shown in Fig. 8.2, and the correspondences between various aspects of the activity of weaving and the principles of personality will be illustrated rather than exhaustively treated. The numbers mentioned refer to those in the figure, where some others are also indicated.

> *The counterweight* (1), together with its attachment, indicates, by analogy, the 'underneath' of the person:
> *the two lines of thread* (2) called 'mother' and 'father' cord, respectively, are a material representation of the links between a person and his/her genitors;
> *the two parts of the warp* (3) with their opposing movements (up/down and down/up) stand for 'thought and reflection';
> *the pulley* (4) known as 'the little parrot' suggests, by its name as well as its squeaking, a person's speech;
> *the two pedals* (5) stand for the power and authority of the person;
> *the comb* (6) evokes the motion of 'force' involved in many of the principles of personality.

In addition to these and other correspondences, six movements are singled out as being basic, representing our spatial orientation in the world:

> foot movements—forward and backward;
> arm movements—right and left;
> the opposing movements of the warp—up and down.

Although brief, this summary will perhaps convey something of the richness and flavour of the densely packed symbolism of weaving.

Mɔkɔ dyogo dyira—the revelation of the 'essence' of a person
The Bambara have at their disposal techniques for the study of aspects of the personality, and they are very clear about their value in

educational and other contexts. They employ what we would call tests, two of which are fairly widespread in similar forms in some parts of West Africa; they will be presented in some detail.

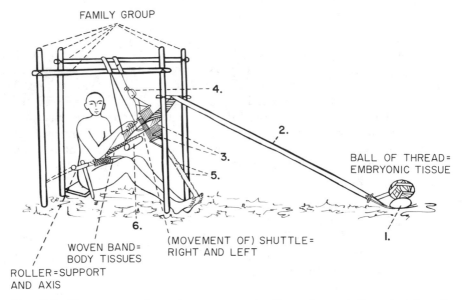

FIG. 8.2. The correspondence between aspects of weaving and the principles of personality.

1. *The Banāngolo.* This has already been described as representing certain important components of the person. It was at one time extensively used as a kind of psychological test since "it shows the inner character of the person". The task testees were given was that of tracing the figure properly in the sand, at the same time keeping count of the levels and correctly reciting a text appropriate to the level reached. The interpretation of the performance would take account of speed, regularity of the tracing, and the absence of errors in the recital of the text.

2. *The sumāngolo.* This is the name of the mythical first man who travelled throughout the world in the search for the source of know-ledge. The test this time is based on a rather complicated pattern (shown in Fig. 8.3) already drawn by the tester in the sand. The circles represent holes in the ground and the numbers indicate the sequences followed. As will be illustrated, it starts very simply but becomes increasingly demanding, as a test should.

Stage 1:

Tester: The little man has entered the dance!
The nasty little man has entered the dance!
Another man apart from this one has not danced!
Is it this one? (points to the first hole)

Subject: Yes! Sumãngolo!

Stage 4 (following preliminary recital of the appropriate text):

Tester: Is it this one? (points to first hole)

Subject: No! Sumãngolo! (This will be omitted hereafter)

Tester: Is it this one? (points to the second hole)

Subject: No!

Tester: Is it this one? (points to third hole)

Subject: No!

Tester: Is it this one? (points to first line)

Subject: Cross the river!

Tester: Is it this one? (points to second line)

Subject: Cross the swamp!

Tester: Is it this one? (points to first square)

Subject: Go down!

Tester: Is it this one? (points to fourth hole)

Subject: Yes!

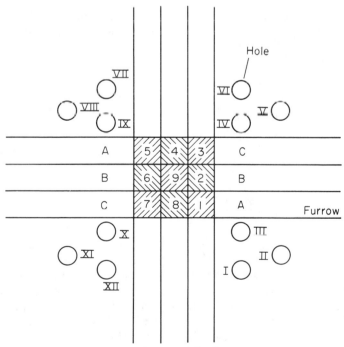

FIG. 8.3. The test of the *Sumangolo*.

At the conclusion of each stage, the sequence begins afresh and each time goes further until the 12th and last hole is reached. Throughout the procedure the subject is not supposed to make any gesture and, above all, is not allowed to count on his fingers. He must, as the saying goes, "let his *dya* be seated and make his thought work"; the *dya*, it will be recalled, is the small intelligent 'double' of the person. The Bambara very clearly regard it as a kind of intelligence test. In fact, it seems that in the old days, the 'people of knowledge' were selected by means of these tests, and both were supposed to have invariably given the same result—very high reliability!

The ability primarily tapped by *Sumāngolo* is, of course, memory: subjects have to remember in proper sequence the answer to no fewer than 132 questions! But it is not merely verbal memory, since the subject requires a clear mental image of the patterns in order to be able to give the correct responses.

Underlying both 'tests' are certain numerical correspondences to which the Bambara attach considerable importance. The *sumāngolo* consists of 132 questions and answers; add to this two of their fundamental units ('reason' and 'the foundation of all things'), and it makes up the sacred number 266, also yielded by *banāngolo*.

If one takes the 12 stages of *sumāngolo* and tabulates the questions (leaving out repeat ones), one gets the following table:

1											
2	3										
4	5	6									
7	8	9	10								
11	12	13	14	15							
16	17	18	19	20	21						
22	23	24	25	26	27	28					
29	30	31	32	33	34	35	36				
37	38	39	40	41	42	43	44	45			
46	47	48	49	50	51	52	53	54	55		
56	57	58	59	60	61	62	63	64	65	66	
67	68	69	70	71	72	73	74	76	76	77	78

This table constitutes the basis of philosophy, mathematics, and geomancy and therefore has several names such as 'the first creation', 'the mystery of numeration', and so on. There are also sayings like "the mystery of creation is to be found in numeration". As might be expected, there is an extensive lore elaborating this theme. For instance, 33 is said to be at the centre of gravity of the table, 'the just middle'; this is linked with the 33 vertebrae which provide the support and central axis of the person. It also corresponds to the number of lunar years in terms of which lunar and solar years periodically coincide. Such a cycle is called 'a return' or 'a revolution', the same expression being used for a human generation. The Bambara also believe that humans undergo substantial changes every 33 years; this 'revolution' is symbolized by the 33 numbers which form the circumference of the *sumãngolo* triangle.

Another key number is 78, the terminal in the 'table of number'. It corresponds to the cycle of Halley's comet, which appears every 78 lunar years (76 solar years). Called 'star of the heavens with the big tail', it is the symbol of the old people of more than 76 (solar) years who have, as explained previously, come close to the ancestors.

This concludes the sketch of aspects of Bambara collective representations, but before commenting on them a word of caution is indicated. Cissé (1973) did not describe in detail how he obtained his data, but there is internal evidence that a variety of informants were used: there was occasional mention of several alternative versions (mainly as regards details), and these I have omitted. While I tried, when condensing, to avoid distorting the general picture, it is bound to be a partial one. More serious is the fact that the material has been subjected to two translations: first from the vernacular into French, and then from French into English. At both stages some loss and/or partial change of meaning is likely to have occurred. While there is no doubt that in the present case extra noise was introduced in the course of transmission, such problems are, to some extent, ever-present in attempts to capture collective representations.

While it is worth keeping these reservations in mind, the general character of the set of ideas and beliefs is clear enough. There are certain family resemblances between the Bambara image of man and that of modern psychology, but the differences are rather more striking. They arise first from the fact, noted at the outset, that Bambara 'psychology' cannot be dissociated from a comprehensive cosmo-biological scheme linking the heavens, numbers, and human personality. Secondly, in contrast to a scientific description of the world, the linkages are mostly established through *symbolism*. Since much of the discussion in the following chapters relates directly or indirectly to symbols, it will be useful at this stage to make some further observations about the nature of symbols, a topic already touched upon in connection with Leach's interpretation of magic (p. 184).

It will be best to start with some common ground, namely, the distinction between symbols and conventional signs like the words in a language, where the relationship between the sound of a word and its referent is generally arbitrary. In the case of a symbol there is a connection, often metaphorical in character, whereby one thing stands for or represents another; the relationship is usually such that an abstract, general property is represented by a concrete, particular thing. This preliminary specification conforms to the psychological views put forward, for instance, by Werner and Kaplan (1963) in their volume on *Symbol Formation*, and corresponds very closely to the formulation by Firth (1973) in his excellent exposition of anthropological aspects of symbolism.[8] As soon as one goes beyond this base, however, one runs into disagreements. Thus Lewis (1977), in a perceptive essay which covers psychological aspects, wrote as follows about symbols:

> They both reveal and conceal, pointing towards, if not fully disclosing, a different order of reality and experience. Symbols thus are by definition mysterious.
>
> p. 1

This mystery suggests an echo of the psychoanalytical conception of symbolism, which tends to regard the symbol as typically the disguised manifestation of something (usually sexual) that has been repressed into the unconscious. These apparent disagreements can be reconciled by viewing symbols as complex and multidimensional in character, in the manner depicted in Fig. 8.4. One can then clarify the problem by introducing a number of relational distinctions. (The term 'relational' is used advisedly to indicate that the figure cannot be taken as a framework for the categorization of particular symbols—they are far too elusive to be pinned down in such a way. Anthropologists are primarily concerned with socially shared symbols, i.e. the right half of the figure space. The level of awareness, from fully conscious to entirely unconscious, also constitutes a continuum, varying both between individuals and according to context; and the same applies to the emotional loading of symbols.

Thus one might guess that Lewis's 'mystery' is probably located somewhere near the plane formed by the social/affective dimensions, being neither fully conscious nor totally unconscious. The bread and wine will be located in that region during communion, as contrasted with a convivial meal. The dependence of the affective loading of a symbol upon context may be illustrated by a Union Jack printed on a carrier bag: in a London street it is hardly likely to arouse patriotic sentiments, but the same bag perceived by an expatriate Briton in some remote corner of the world may well do so. In sum, any given symbol may evoke different meanings and emotions depending on cultures, individuals within cultures, situations and associated levels of awareness. This is an extension of the property called the 'polysemy' of symbols.

All the examples offered so far are, I hope, readily intelligible because they are drawn from within our own culture. For the anthropologist, matters are not so simple. Take, for instance, the Bambara symbol of the weaver, where two cords are known as 'father-' and 'mother-cord', respectively. It is by no means obvious, until one is told, that these stand for the indissoluble links between a person and the ancestors; when one *is* told, it makes good sense. Thus, anthropologists must ask the experts, who are the people concerned, and attempt a systematic exploration. Here is an example given by Schwimmer (1978, p. viii) intended to show that even theoretically divergent fieldworkers share common methods:

> . . . whatever the approach, each school would be interested in rather similar kinds of data. When a Maori says, for instance, ''This land is my backbone'', there would be wide agreement that each of the following

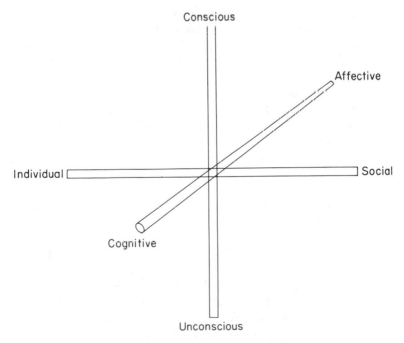

FIG. 8.4. Dimensions of symbolism.

questions would be a 'good' follow-up in a field investigation: do you
have other land that you would compare to other parts of your body?
Would you apply that remark to any land you inherited, or only to a
certain mode of inheritance . . .

It is therefore not a question of eliciting isolated symbols, but to discern
their patterning and varying manifestations. Thus in Bambara culture,
dyigi (the backbone) is simultaneously the biological and ontological
support of the person. It is symbolized concretely by roller of the loom, and
in a highly abstract manner as part of the key symbol, *banãngolo,* through
the number of vertebrae. The ontological meaning differs from that in our
own culture, where 'backbone' denotes strength of will; it stands for
mental and physical (especially sexual) well-being. Sexual problems and
psychological traumas are experienced (psychosomatically?) as back-
aches and called 'loss of support'; in a more extended sense, this phrase is
also applied to all kinds of disappointments. Linguistic aspects must also
be considered: *dyigi,* the term for support associated with the backbone,
also means 'hope'; hence, to be devoid of hope is an unhealthy state.
Thus, it can be seen how symbolism radiates outward in widening circles,
with subtle connections whose grasp demands a profound knowledge of
the culture. Another illustration from the weaver as master symbol would
be the up-and-down motion of the warp which symbolizes the process of
thinking; unless one is already familiar with the way thinking is
conceptualized in the culture, the basis of this symbolism cannot be
understood.

Although the discussion in this part is concerned primarily with
cognitive issues, it should be made clear that the affective aspects of
symbolism are extremely important. Durkheim regarded symbols as
essential for enhancing the kinds of values on which the functioning of
a society depends. Symbols also help to create and maintain the appropriate emotions and sentiments, and ensure conformity to social
norms. In Western cultures the national flag and the cross are obvious
examples, but their power to arouse has become considerably attenu-
ated. In traditional cultures symbols may still fulfil this function more
effectively, especially in the context of ritual.

This will be illustrated for the Bambara, who, according to Dieterlen
(1951), have rituals that are symbolic down to their smallest details of
time, place, forms of objects used, modes of dress, and gestures.
Circumcision rites, for instance, are packed with symbolism. The
blacksmith, who is also the circumciser, uses a knife decorated with
symbolic drawings he has forged himself. The knife itself symbolizes
the person of the boy and its metal sheath the foreskin. The date of the

operation is fixed for the day when Sirius, the star symbolizing one of the divine ancestors, rises in the evening at a certain point in the east. The circumcised boy wear a cap (shown in Fig. 8.5) that has been made from white cloth previously blessed, which serves as a protection during the period of retreat when the initiate is in a state of ritual impurity. The vertical line of seven black dots represents, on the one hand, the boy (3) and his *dya* (4), and on the other, the man (3) he will be in future and his wife (4). They also ensure his protection from east to weat, the remaining two dots performing the same function in the north–south direction. The cross formed by small dots relates to the *sumãngolo* and also the loss of the *waãzo* (see p. 198). Similarly, the ornamental tufts, spun by a grandmother, represent the creator. Even this brief and partial sketch will be sufficient to show that practically everything pertaining to the ritual is spun into a delicate web of signification. The ceremony itself links the initiates with the creator, the ancestors and with each other, symbolized by the fact that they sit in a circle and all bleed into the same earth. It is thus unquestionable that it must have a powerful emotional impact on the participants.[9]

Merely referring to emotional effects is not enough—one would like

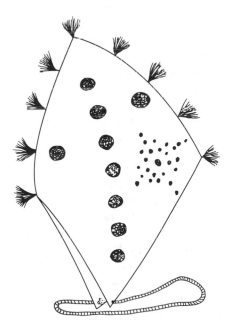

FIG. 8.5. Cap worn by circumcised Bambara.

to know in more detail about the processes involved. Among various anthropological accounts, those of Victor Turner (1967, 1968) prob-ably throw most light on the psychological aspects of rituals. A brief outline of his approach will therefore be useful.

One of the rituals that Victor Turner analysed most thoroughly is *Nkang'a*, the girl's puberty ritual of the Ndembu. The novice, wrapped in a blanket, is laid at the foot of a sapling of a tree which exudes milky latex when the bark is damaged, hence the term 'milk tree'. The adult women, excluding the novice's own mother, dance in a ring around the tree. At one stage the mother cooks a large meal and while the women walk around the tree, the mother carries a large spoon of cassava and beans. Suddenly she shouts an invitation and all the women run and try to be the first to eat from the spoon.

These are, of course, merely a few episodes culled from a lengthy ritual.[10] They all appear on the surface rather commonplace, yet Turner extracted a wealth of meaning from them, though it must be remembered that this was done against the background of a mass of information about the culture and social structure in general, and what Turner called the 'action-field' in particular. How were the symbols interpreted? Here three levels or aspects of meaning are distinguished. The first, already mentioned, is that of asking both ritual specialists and laymen and women among the people; and some anthropologists —but not Turner—are content with that. He calls the second level 'the operational meaning', which is essentially based on inferences from observations: the types of people involved in different phases of the ritual (as contrasted with those specifically excluded), their non-verbal behaviour and especially the emotions expressed. Lastly, there is the 'positional meaning' derived from any one symbol's relationship to the total, patterned set of other symbols.

Let us now return to *Nkang'a* and see how some of this works out in more detail. The milk tree is one of a nucleus of dominant symbols for the Ndembu, being dominant by virtue of the multiplicity of its mean-ings and the key position it occupies in the ritual. The tree's property of exuding milk is its salient characteristic for the Ndembu, and most women say that the milk-tree represents human breast-milk and the breast itself (the ceremony is performed when the girl's breasts take shape, not after menstruation). This central meaning is complemented by a whole series of increasingly peripheral ones. Thus the milk-tree is also said to be the tree of 'the mother and her child', linked with the ancestress and thereby via matriliny (central to the functioning of the society, which governs succession to office and inheritance of property —see Chapter 6) to Ndembu society as a whole. One educated man also conveyed this by likening the milk-tree to a national flag, and all the interpretations by ordinary people as well as ritual specialists spoke of the milk-tree as a symbol of harmony and unity.

However, such purely positive ascriptions were inconsistent with some important aspects of the behaviour observed in the course of the ritual. For instance, the women dancing around the milk-tree sang songs taunting the men, and the mother was excluded from this circle, symbolizing (according to Turner) a double opposition between female solidarity and the male world, and between the novice's mother and the rest of the women. Moreover, the spoon contest in its more indirect symbolism was said to represent the separation of the novice from her mother, since she will live in her husband's village after marriage; and each village competes for her child-bearing and working capacity.[11] It would seem, therefore, that certain important features of the ritual symbolism were ignored by the participants. The ambiguous word 'ignored' is used advisedly, since it is clear that the people themselves did not lack a general recognition of conflicts between various social categories, be it mothers and daughters or men and women. But while they implicitly enacted such conflicts as part of the rituals, it would seem that they were not aware of doing it.

Such a condensed version does not begin to convey the richness and subtlety of the symbolic meanings associated with the milk-tree for the Ndembu, but it suffices to show clearly that symbols have multiple meanings at different levels—it is not possible here to elaborate on the 'positional' ones. Instead, I go directly to Turner's more general theory of 'polarization', whereby at one extreme symbols may have a gross *sensory* meaning (e.g. breast milk), and at the other extreme what he called an ideological one (e.g. the unity of the tribe). One of the major functions of ritual, according to Victor Turner, is to establish a tie between the two poles:

> Within its framework of meanings, the dominant symbol brings the ethical and jural norms of society into close contact with strong emotional stimuli. In the action situation of ritual, with its social excitement and directly physiological stimuli, such as music, singing, dancing, alcohol, incense, and bizarre modes of dress, the ritual symbol, we may perhaps say, effects an interchange of qualities between its poles of meaning. Norms and values, on the one hand, become saturated with emotion, while the gross and basic emotions become ennobled through contact with social values. The irksomeness of moral constraint is transformed into the 'love of virtue'.
>
> 1967, p. 30

Turner went on to discuss the possible division of labour between social anthropologists, on the one hand, and psychologists and psychoanalysts, on the other, in the study of symbols as 'units of action'. He suggested that the latter would be better equipped to throw further light on the 'sensory pole', displaying thereby the common anthropological bias previously discussed. His general analysis is a powerful one, that has served as a model for subsequent work. It is certainly most persuasive, but is it valid? There is no simple answer to this question, and it is difficult to see how this model could be tested. There is one aspect, common to most interpretations of initiation ceremonies, where psychologists might perhaps make a contribution. This concerns the notion implicit in most theories about initiation rites that they result in certain psychological changes in the individuals taking part. As far as I know this has rarely been tested, and one attempt by Herzog (1973) has not been encouraging. The reason is probably that while such testing ought to be feasible in principle, the difficulty is that in practice any changes that might occur are probably of a subtle kind not readily identifiable by the relatively crude tools at our disposal, especially as the most important of the changes might be below the conscious level of the individual's awareness.

As he himself made clear, Victor Turner (1978) was influenced by psychoanalysis in the shaping of his theory, but it is certainly not the pure milk of Freudianism; in some respects he was highly critical of psychoanalysts, as when he reproached them with treating indigenous interpretations of symbolism as mostly irrelevant.[12] Yet while charging psychoanalysts with cultural bias, Victor Turner seems to have taken the objectivity of the anthropologist–observer for granted.

More recently such confidence has become somewhat undermined, symbolic anthropologists in particular having become aware of culturally conditioned subjectivity as a factor to be reckoned with. A dramatic impetus was given to such views by Castaneda's remarkable dialogues with Don Juan, a Yaqui Indian from Northern Mexico. An anthropology student intending to write a thesis on hallucinogenic plants, Castaneda underwent some 'mind-blowing' experiences that led in time to his becoming completely absorbed in the symbolic world of Don Juan. There was a good deal of controversy over these writings (perhaps at least in part because they became best-sellers!), their authenticity being questioned by some; the reviewer in *Man* expressed the opinion that "it is not a serious anthropological study at all" (1973, vol. 8: p. 136).

Other anthropologists, such as Mary Douglas (1975), took it very seriously as raising some fundamental problems about the relationship between the anthropologist and the people being studied. Willis (1975), in his introduction to a book on symbolism edited by him, drew some far-reaching conclusions:

> The current upsurge of anthropological concern with symbolism reflects a tendency . . . to shift from the fixed and unitary perspective of classical anthropology to a dual and dialectical perspective which addresses itself as much to the subjectivity of the anthropologist–observer, and of his cultural stance, as to the observed society and culture. The archetypal hero of this new and precarious self-awareness in social anthropology is of course Carlos Castaneda, who out of his perilous confrontation with the 'separate reality' of the world of a Yaqui Indian sorcerer comes to recognize the cultural specificity of what he had taken to be the safe and solid ground of fact.
> The dual perspective epitomized in Castaneda's extraordinary dialogue with Don Juan necessarily entails the abandonment of the comforting assumption implicit in classical anthropology that all non-Western cultures can be accounted for within the conceptual resources of Western natural and social science.
>
> pp xi–xii

This is slippery ground, indeed, reminiscent of the view increasingly voiced in some quarters that 'Western psychology' is culturally biased, and that each culture ought to develop its own psychology (Pedersen, 1979), or of the psychological subjectivism of Merleau-Ponty (1962). Intriguing as these issues are, their discussion would lead us too far afield into philosophical realms.

Let us retrace our steps, therefore, and return briefly to the Bambara: in presenting an outline of their 'psychology', the main object was to convey in concrete terms what is understood by 'collective representations'. The heavy symbolic loading of Bambara conceptions led on to a general consideration of the nature of symbolism, followed by some discussion of its affective aspects. It is perhaps worth emphasizing once more that the choice of an illustration was an arbitrary one —collective representations may consist of *any* kind of shared ideas, beliefs, symbols or myths enshrined in tradition. As such, they form, of course, an important part of a people's culture, and in some anthropological usage, terms like 'cosmology' or even 'culture' are treated as more or less co-extensive. However, I shall (at least for the present) continue to refer to collective representations as defined above, and explore some of their psychological implications.

Notes

1. For an excellent discussion of Durkheim's notion of 'collective representations' as well as other aspects of his thinking see Lukes (1973).
2. The original is in French and the translation is my own. The presentation is greatly condensed, with linking passages inserted, and in order to make for easier reading, quotation marks and detailed page references are omitted. It should perhaps be added that the Bambara are not exceptional in having a kind of theory about personality—there is evidence that most peoples have something of the kind, and it is probably a universal human characteristic to be self-reflective. The Bambara version is somewhat exceptional only in being rather sophisticated. For a useful survey see Heelas and Lock (1981).
3. The literature on the Bambara and related peoples is extensive, but mostly in French. A useful general survey is provided by Paques (1954); of particular psychological interest are the articles by Dieterlen (1947) and Ganay (1949).
4. The term 'reflection' may not be the optimal one, and Cissé, in the original French, also refers to the untranslatable *ésprit*; the manner in which these concepts appear in Bambara thought and the distinction between them will be considered in due course.
5. Since the view is a facing one, the left side of this and other figures is male.
6. Compare Wittgenstein: "the limits of my language mean the limits of my world" (1961, 5.62).
7. Cf. the Ashanti view, discussed on pp. 115–17.
8. However, insofar as Firth was willing to consider symbols in isolation, his views would be unacceptable to structuralists such as Leach.
9. Circumcision is, of course, merely one of many important rituals, among which that concerning refuse is particularly interesting. The notion is that household and public refuge is charged with forces transmitted by men (e.g. the *waãzo* of the uncircumcised or unexcised). The object of the rites is to offer these forces to the creator, who returns them to men purified and regenerated in such forms as rainwater, so that they are redistributed and used again for the communal good. The general conception is that of an ecological cycle, expressed in mythical terms.
10. Audrey Richards (1956) devoted a whole volume to a single initiation ceremony, which will convey some notion of the richness of such rituals.
11. In the absence of the full evidence adduced, some of this may seem rather far-fetched, but it should not be judged without examining that evidence.
12. Other anthropologists have adopted Freudian symbolism much more directly. An example of the absurd lengths to which this can be taken in what can only be described as speculative flights of fancy is Paul's (1976) interpretation of a Sherpa temple. The ground floor is wild and chaotic in appearance, while the upper floor is calm and serene; hence, the lower

part represents the ID and the upper the EGO, their spatial relationship symbolizing "the triumph of reason over passion"! In complete contrast, a study by Tuzin (1972) of the yam as a penis symbol among a Sepik group of New Guinea is based on a careful and critical marshalling of detailed evidence, which to me appears convincing.

9 | Collective Representations and Individual Thinking

From the classical works of Tylor, Frazer, and Lévy-Bruhl, who sought to explain 'primitive mentality', to quite recent discussions of 'modes of thought', most anthropologists have based their interpretations on evidence from collective representations. In other words, systems of ideas and beliefs have been scrutinized in order to determine what they reveal about the thought of the people from whom they have been obtained. Some of the ways in which this was done has already been described in Chapter 7, where a survey of theories and findings led to the conclusion that there is no support for the existence of a special kind of cognitive process that could be called 'magical thinking'. However, that was merely one aspect of a much wider problem area to which the remaining chapters will be devoted. In the present one, I shall consider the question of the extent to which it may be possible to draw inferences about 'thinking' from collective representations. The discussion will focus on two writers, both of whom rely on this type of data, although for entirely different purposes.

The first is Lévy-Strauss, whose role in modern anthropology may be compared with that of Piaget in psychology—both men are also structuralists in their different ways. It has already been said (see Chapter 2) that Lévi-Strauss conceives of anthropology as being rooted in an important sense in psychology. While he works at the collective level, the structures he discerns are located in the individual mind. These structures are said to be the outcome of biologically determined binary and combinatory processes, which organize all biological, mental, and cultural phenomena. How did he arrive at this position?[1]

There is a rather simple way of answering this question, but to give this answer immediately would be grossly misleading because it would

214

make Lévi-Strauss appear to be a simple-minded man, and nothing would be further from the truth. Originally trained as a philosopher, he was influenced by Rousseau, Freud, Marx, and the Prague school of linguistics, and all these strands are woven into his thinking. Early in his career he spent several years with Brazilian Indians, an experience that had a lasting impact and resulted in the captivating but rather strange book, *Tristes Tropiques* (1955). From Freud he adopted the notion of unconscious mental functioning but he confined this to the intellect, holding that emotion explains nothing. From Marx he accepted the primacy of the technical and economic infrastructure, yet he refused to regard the mind as merely reflecting that; the dialectical process, he would contend, consists of the interaction between mode of production and social relations, on the one hand, and structured as well as structuring mental activity, on the other. Lévi-Strauss was also influenced by modern structural linguistics, especially by Roman Jakobson, who postulated that all the differences between phonemes are capable of being analysed into irreducible *binary* oppositions. These and no doubt other influences led Lévi-Strauss to a conceptualization of the relationship between social and mental structures that has been condensed by one of his expositors into a series of (rather simplified) propositions, which I will paraphrase from Rossi (1974, pp. 108–9):

1. The nature and origin of social phenomena can only be understood in terms of their internal determinants;
2. One can discover these determinants only by reducing complex data to more elementary structures;
3. These elementary structures are mental, because social phenomena are nothing but 'objectivated systems of ideas' (which is Lévi-Strauss's way of referring to collective representations);
4. Such objectivated ideas have an unconscious basis, so that unconscious psychic structures underlie social phenomena and make them possible;
5. Because of their structural nature, social phenomena can be explained both empirically and dialectically.

In his efforts to explain social phenomena, Lévi-Strauss made extensive use of myths and folk tales as raw materials. As Price-Williams (1980) rightly said, few academic psychologists have taken mythical thought as a subject for investigation;[2] but it is entirely justified from the Lévi-Straussian point of view, since myths represent readily accessible samples of a universe of thought products that shares an identical underlying structure. The method applied for analysis is the 'oppositional' one of Jakobson; it has been outlined by Leach (1970) and David Turner (1979) and here only certain critical features will be mentioned. The story is divided into sentences in such a way that each unit refers to a given subject performing a particular function, which is known as a 'relation'; sets of relations resembling each other are called 'bundles of relations'. All units are ordered into a kind of matrix according to thematic similarity and temporal sequence.

On scrutinizing the patterning of numerous myths dissected in this manner, Lévi-Strauss saw each 'bundle' as referring to oppositions within a specific sphere (e.g. political, economic), pointing to a contradiction in the social fabric; at later stages in the myths there occurs a reordering such that the contradiction appears to be resolved. Hence he regards myths as logical models capable of overcoming a contradiction; thus the myth is not intended to portray reality, but merely to justify its shortcomings. This is done by showing imaginatively that the extreme positions implied by the two poles of the contradiction are untenable, so that the *status quo* is the best that can be had.[3]

An example of how the method works in practice will be instructive, but rather than selecting an exotic myth whose context would be unfamiliar, David Turner's (1979) demonstration of how the procedure can be applied to a modern story will be cited. The material consists of the very popular American film, *Jaws*:

> The plot is well known. The inhabitants of a small New England resort town are plagued by a great white shark at the beginning of the tourist season. The first attack is made on a woman swimming alone at night after making love on the beach. After an investigation by the local two-man police force, the chief, Brody, decides to close the beaches until the danger passes. But local businessmen put pressure on the mayor and newspaper editor to keep them open as they fear the publicity will keep people away during the Fourth of July national holiday period. Persuasion gives way to threats and the chief yields to the pressure. The shark, however, strikes again, killing a young boy and an old man the same day. Brody now closes the beaches and sends a fisherman out to hunt the shark. His boat is later found abandoned with gaping holes in its sides—evidence of a shark attack. A young technocrat now arrives on the scene from the Oceanographic Institute to investigate the shark incident and offer his services to the community. With no further attacks and under pressure once more from business, the beaches are once again opened for the Fourth of July holiday, this time patrolled by the police and the Oceanographer, Hooper. Hooper is not able to spot the shark in his technologically advanced boat and it, in fact, tracks with him to reach a swimmer but does not attack. Brody is now convinced the shark must be killed and hires Quint, a local and very traditionally-oriented charter fisherman, to do the job. He and Hooper go along as crew, the shark is eventually encountered and the battle is on. After a number of

skirmishes and failures, Hooper is killed in his shark cage when he neglects his weapon in favour of his camera. The shark attacks the boat and begins to dismantle it, killing Quint in the process. Armed with only a rifle and a few rounds of ammunition, Brody is reduced to occupying the end of the mast as the boat sinks beneath him. As the shark makes its final attack he takes one last, futile shot at the fish and by chance hits an oxygen tank which had become lodged in its jaws when it was demolishing the boat. The shark is blown to bits and Brody survives.

This tale can be organized into a series of oppositions with each expressing a separate but related theme. First is the major opposition between land animals (people) and sea animals (shark) which is mediated by swimming land animals. This 'anomaly' is at once removed by a sea animal through the process of incorporation (eating). But this reverses the relationship of man to animals within the Judeo-Christian tradition. It has been ordained that man will dominate (incorporate) animals (here, fish). What follows in *Jaws* after this initial reversal has been established is really an attempt at re-reversal to re-establish people's domination over nature. The First step in the process is to deny the original opposition and its mediation altogether. An attempt is made to prevent land animals from swimming, but it fails because it is opposed to the business interest—the tourists will not come to spend their money in the area if swimming is prohibited. A new opposition is thus raised in the story, namely the private versus the public interest. The next attempt involves trying to prevent the sea animal's existence, but this also fails because of poor technology (a conventional fisherman with conventional equipment). Ultimately this 'solution' cannot succeed within the framework of the tale because the original major opposition is misphrased—people (species) are opposed to shark (individual). No matter what happens to *this* shark there is the possibility that others will take its place.

With these initial failures, four factors are introduced to solve the problem, paired into two opposition-couples; first is folk knowledge versus scientific knowledge, and second, an older experienced sea captain versus a young college graduate. Scientific knowledge and youth at first fail to locate the shark but cannot kill it, while folk knowledge and experience find the shark but cannot kill it—in fact the shark kills the sea captain, removing the alternative he represents as an ultimate solution to the problem of the tale. Scientific knowledge, but in a traditional form (rifle and bullet) and in the hands of a nonscientist (a middle-aged policeman), then reappears to kill the shark, but does so by chance—chance consequent on the prior destruction of modern technology (shark cage, scuba equipment) by the shark. Left unresolved, then, is the ultimate status of folk versus scientific knowledge, youth versus experience, the public versus the private interest (the policeman is at the same time responsible for the deaths of the tourists as well as for their eventual protection by killing the shark), and man versus nature (people have achieved dominance over the individual not the species).

Other oppositions can be located within the extended plot and developed further, such as man/woman, natural/supernatural, but they seem to fall within the major themes outlined above. The significant thing about these themes together with their constituent oppositions, mediations, and attempted solutions is that they all remain within the frame of reference of mainstream American capitalist society. In *Jaws* there is nothing which transcends already thought solutions to already experienced contradictions. And perhaps this is the point of all 'soap opera'. It is intrinsically entertaining precisely because it locates problems that can be grasped by most people and offers and rationalizes those solutions already in practice in the society. In short, *Jaws* is a-critical, being neither educative nor illuminating. Like the Asdiwal myth, it reassures the audience that the present system, while imperfect, works well enough. The conservative–liberal, capitalist–competitive system balances stability with progress and deals adequately with problems as they arise even if the odd disaster must be tolerated.

pp. 133–5

All the analyses of myths carried out by Lévi-Strauss yielded essentially the type of structure illustrated by Turner's neat decomposition of *Jaws*. At this point it seems defensible to give the simple answer to the question previously raised: since Lévi-Strauss invariably found it possible to discern in myths—which, of course, are products of human thinking—patterns of binary oppositions, he concluded that binary coding must be the fundamental characteristic of human cognition, which governs our logic and all forms of social classification. Subsequently he cited findings of neurology and psychology in support of his conclusion. Thus he moved from structural features he claims to have detected in the contents of collective representations, to inferences about the nature of cognitive processes. In short, the human image of the world reflects the built-in structure of mental processes.

There is, of course, a very general sense in which this must be true, but Lévi-Strauss means more than that. Thus he referred to the Gestalt view supported by neuropsychological research, that we perceive not so much objects as relationships (1969, p. 100), which is undeniable; but he goes on to attribute an 'oppositional' character to such relationships, which seems little more than a verbal formula unless one postulates that all relationships concern oppositions. The fallacies involved in this kind of argumentation can be shown most readily when Lévi-Strauss states that what the eye transmits to the brain are not pictures, but systems of binary oppositions (1971, p. 605). While this is again correct, the result *is* a picture, from which it follows that a binary mechanism does not dictate a binary output! So far it has been tacitly taken for granted that all the binary oppositions Lévi-Strauss and his followers find in collective representation were actually (albeit unconsciously) in the minds of those who participated in the creation of the myths, and not largely in the minds of those who unpick the fabric of the myths and put the pieces together again in their own fashion. For it must be remembered that the oppisitional structure of the collective representations is not as such visible to the naked eye. The procedure requires a search for oppositions and their transformations, which are then reduced to a standard structural form. Both initial search and subsequent grouping into 'similar' relations involve a great deal of subjective judgement, as many critics have pointed out.[4] Even adherents, such as David Turner, have deplored the fact that Lévi-Strauss has been quite happy to study the myths of cultures about whose social organization he knew little, thus not being in a position to assess whether the contradictions supposedly resolved by the myths did in fact correspond to social reality.

This is not to deny that many such analyses of myths appear to bring out new and frequently fascinating facets of meaning, while others seem laboured and far-fetched. I suspect that some of these variations in impact may be primarily a function of the writer's persuasiveness of style; the basic problem of verification remains unsolved.

With regard to the main issue addressed here, I would argue that collective representations such as myths cannot serve as the basis for inferences about the characteristics of cognitive processes. The relationship postulated is an unduly simplistic one,[5] which ignores the complexity of the nexus between a social product like a myth and the mental functioning of its creators and equally plausible alternative interpretations. One can admit the importance of binary oppositions in human thinking, but this may merely reflect the fact that they are also salient in our environment: such oppositions as those of day and night, male and female, right and left, and so on, are of a kind to impose themselves, irrespective of the nature of cognitive processes.

Another aspect of the Lévi-Straussian thesis that may be regarded as a psychological issue is his concept of unconscious intellectual activity. The fact that it exists is not in dispute—a number of creative scientists have described how they wrestled unsuccessfully with a problem, until after varying periods the solution suddenly came, often at a time when they had not been conscious of thinking about the problem. However, the claim by Lévi-Strauss goes well beyond this, as it seems to imply the unconscious *apprehension* of a problem (i.e. the presence of a contradiction within the culture) as well as its resolution in the form of a myth. An additional difficulty is the fact that a myth cannot be regarded as the product of the thinking of a particular individual, and in the process of transmission is presumably constantly subject to accretion and modification. Unfortunately, by its nature, we have little knowledge of the details of such a process.[6] Thus, on the fact of it, the theory looks highly implausible. There are certain considerations, however, that should make us pause. The notion that myths are merely quaint imaginative productions has long been dead. When Durkheim coined the expression 'collective representations'—which of course includes myths—he was concerned to show that these played an important role in the regulation and maintenance of social systems; and the work of Lévi-Strauss may be regarded as an elaboration of this tradition. More recently the view has gained ground that collective representations are also related to the ecological bases of societies. I have already mentioned Rappaport (1968), who studied a remote New Guinean tribe and showed that their belief in the ancestors' insatiable appetite for pigs, together with certain rituals and linked periodic outbreaks of warfare, constitutes an adaptive mechanism for ensuring a suitable ecological balance. One of the most explicit statements of this view is that of Reichel-Dolmatoff (1976), who worked with South American Indians:

> Until relatively recent times the cultural image of the Indian tribes of tropical America has been that of a group of rather primitive and hostile peoples whose contribution to human thought had been negligible . . . In the more recent past, this image has undergone a notable change. Ethnological research among the surviving tribes of the tropical rain forest has begun to reach a depth and breadth of inquiry that were formerly unthought of, and these newly gained insights are beginning to shed an entirely new light upon the intellectual achievements of the aboriginal peoples of the Amazon Basin . . . It seems that the old stereotypes are disappearing at last; and instead we are presented with a new image: the Indian, not only as a highly pragmatic thinker and an individual with a sound sense of reality, but also, the Indian as an abstract philosopher, a builder of intricate cosmic models, and a planner of sweeping moral designs.

pp. 307–8

From the detailed analysis of Tukano (the particular tribe studied) cosmology which follows the above general statement, certain salient features may be extracted. In the Tukano myth of origin there is a sun-father who created man, animals, and plants and not merely gave each species a set of rules to live by, but also placed animals and plants under the care of spirits whose function it is to protect them. The sun is at the centre of the cosmos, which constitutes a giant circuit through which a limited quantity of procreative energy flows. Man may take out of this what he needs only under specified conditions such that the transformed essence can be reincorporated into the circuit. This conception, derived most directly from a model of sexual physiology, extends beyond natural and physiological facts and consists of abstract symbols and images; eventually, "at a higher cognitive level, they come to constitute a systems theory of balanced, finite, energy flow" (p. 310). Reichel-Dolmatoff draws attention to the striking similarity between such conceptions and modern systems theory.

The question that springs to mind at once is how far this coherent world-picture might be a construct by the anthropologist himself, rather than in the minds of people in the tribe. Reichel-Dolmatoff is quite explicit about this:

> In Tukano culture, *the individual person is conscious that he forms part of a complex network of interactions* [my italics] which include not only society but the entire universe. Within this context of an essential interrelatedness of all things, a person has to fulfil many functions that go far beyond his or her social roles and that are extrasocietal extensions of a set of adaptive norms. These rules and norms, then, guide a person's relationships not only with other people . . . but also with animals, plants, as a matter of fact with all biotic and non-biotic components of the environment. The rules the individual has to follow refer, above all, to co-operative behaviour aimed at the conservation of ecological balance as the ultimately desirable quality.
>
> p. 311

The sanctions for the enforcement of these rules are closely related to the indigenous theory of disease, whereby a key role is allocated to the shamans. The shamans themselves in their healing activities focus not so much on the individual as on the social malfunctioning involved, which is a common pattern in traditional cultures. However, among the Tukano this seems to go further, to the extent that the shaman's task is to "apply his treatment to the disturbed part of the ecosystem" (p. 315). Thus the shaman also actively controls hunting, fishing, and gathering activities.

When it comes to the question to what extent the shamans themselves are aware of their role as 'ecological brokers', the answer is that younger and inexperienced shamans tend to express their notions in simplistic terms, e.g. over-hunting will annoy the spirits. On the other hand, some shamans state clearly that scarce food resources have to be preserved.

Lastly, in various rituals said to be mainly concerned with ecological balance, the recital of myths and genealogies plays a prominent part. These myths and tales "are not mere 'literature'; they represent a truly remarkable effort at intellectual interpretation, at providing a cognitive matrix for life. They are a guide for survival because they establish rules of conduct, not only for ritual occasions but for everyday life; a fact which sometimes goes unnoticed as long as one has not discovered the metaphorical code in which the myths are transmitted.'' (pp. 317–18.)

This challenging work makes a number of provocative claims (see also Ross, 1978): the Indians are abstract philosophers; individual members of the culture are aware of the ecosystemic implications of their behaviour; and many shamans have a rational understanding of ecological principles. In this connection one may note an apparent contradiction in the account: since it is admitted that not all shamans have such an understanding, it would seem unlikely that a majority of non-specialists within the culture have it. The author was, of course, not particularly concerned with the characteristics of individual thinking, so there must be some doubts about this. Nevertheless, he was obviously much impressed with the level of thinking of at least some individuals.

However, let us leave this open and concentrate instead on the collective representations resulting in such a remarkably efficient eco-system adaptation. One is led to ask who were these builders of intricate cosmic models and planners of moral designs? Ultimately, unless one shares their mythology, it must have been some individual thinkers. The further question then imposes itself whether they had in their minds a clear conscious image of their existential predicament and deliberately worked out (whether at one stroke or by successive approximations) a solution of the problem. While it is possible to imagine such an intellectual giant or giants whose thinking rivalled that of modern systems theorists, the idea is hard to swallow in view of the lack of environmental support for such rational–scientific thinking.

One is therefore forced back to the alternative suggested by Lévi-Strauss, namely, that over long spans of time particular individuals *unconsciously* grappled with the predicaments of their culture and arrived at solutions coded in the mythical idiom that was for them the natural medium. This line of reasoning indicates that it would be unwise to dismiss out of hand the views of Lévi-Strauss on this, unless one has a better solution. At the moment this is all largely speculative, and in order to throw further light on the problem much more intensive study of individual thinking as it is related to collective representations would be required.

The final part of the discussion prompted by Lévi-Strauss relates to his (not always entirely consistent) views about the equivalence of 'primitive' and modern scientific thinking or 'logic' as he terms it. In support of this he cites, among other examples, the by no means unique observation that indigenous people are able to explain the details of their complex kinship system, which students of anthropology some-times have difficulty in grasping, by means of diagrams drawn in the sand.[7] Sartre, unconvinced, characterized such a performance as mere manual labour controlled by what he called 'unexpressed synthetical knowledge', which seems to refer to collective representations. Lévi-Strauss retorted that one would have to say the same about a university professor demonstrating a proof on the blackboard. In this controversy Piaget (1971) sided with Sartre:

> If the concept of self-regulation or equilibrium has any sense at all, the logic or pre-logic of the members of a given society cannot be adequately gauged by already crystallized cultural products;[8] the real problem is to make out how the ensemble of these collective instruments is utilized in the everyday reasoning of each individual. It may very well be that these instruments are of a level visibly superior to that of Western logic. Lévi-Strauss reminds us that there are plenty of natives who can 'calculate' the implicit relations of a kinship system exactly. But the kinship systems are finished systems, already regulated, and of limited scope. What we want to know about is individual inventions.
>
> p. 117

It is likely that when Piaget referred to ''individual inventions'' he was referring to formal operations, and that would certainly be justi-fied. On the other hand, the objection would not apply to the concrete operational level. After all, arithmetic (for instance) is a ''finished system'', yet in achieving conservation of number the child must develop the idea of reversibility and thus in a sense construct some of the principles underlying the system. The Western child is aided in this by schooling, while a child in traditional culture is in the main merely exposed to exemplars of the kinship system, without any coherent teaching. Nonetheless, the child develops the relativistic mode of think-ing required by asymmetrical kinship relations as shown by LeVine and Price-Williams (1974).

Psychologists and anthropologists usually differ in the ways in which they arrive at judgements of the level of thinking prevalent in traditional cultures. Psychologists undertake studies of individual performance in test situations. This may take the form of either the conventional Piagetian methods partly modified and adapted to the culture, or of the more radically novel 'experimental anthropology' introduced by Cole et al. (1971), which seeks to embed the procedure more fully in the cultural background of subjects. Anthropologists, on the other hand, tend to

base their judgements on either collective representations in the manner of
Lévi-Strauss, or (probably more commonly) on their personal experience
of daily interaction with people in ordinary everyday life, or some
combination of both. In general the two sets of judgements —one based on
formal testing and the other on impressions from experience—remain
separate and independent. Many anthropologists, in fact, are inclined to
have some reservations about the outcome of psychological testing in this
sphere, and one can hardly blame them when one recalls that it was
anthropologists who first cast doubts on the findings of cross-cultural
comparisons of intelligence based on tests, at a time when psychologists
were by and large content to take these at their face value.

Recently, however, Hallpike (1979) wrote a book entitled *The
Foundations of Primitive Thought* in which he reproached his fellow
anthropologists for having ignored Piaget in their discussions of primitive[9] thought, and thus failed to understand it properly in relation to
our own thinking. Accordingly, he provided a concise and in some
ways admirable introduction to Piagetian theory in terms of which he
cast his whole presentation. The burden of the general thesis propounded is that individuals in primitive cultures function essentially at
the *pre-operational* level in their thinking; that is, at the level characteristic of European children between the ages of about four to seven.
Certain exceptions are granted, either as regards outstanding individuals, or certain spheres such as that of kinship previously mentioned
where it is conceded that people might function at an operatory level.
Apart from that, a majority of adults in such cultures are said to be
characterized by a pre-operational primitive mentality.

Thus baldly stated, the attribution of a childlike nature to primitive
adults may have been plausible to the Victorians, but tends to strike us
as absurd. Well aware of this, Hallpike turned to an attack, accusing
anthropologists of having made the mistake of failing to distinguish
"between cognitive processes, on the one hand, and knowledge and
experience, on the other . . . it is surely an extraordinarily narrow
assessment of human beings to say that wisdom, experience, and
emotional maturity count for nothing by comparison with the ability to
conserve quality or to grasp logical inclusion" (p. 39). In other words,
they may not be capable of doing our kind of thinking beyond the level
of young children, but "a man's a man for a' that". Thereby the impression gained by anthropologists in their personal encounters is
supposed to be reconciled with certain alleged shortcomings. Similarly,
collective representations may be rich and subtle in content, and
beyond anything an individual might create; yet a complex cosmology
might still arise from a pre-operatory level of thinking.

Such, in broad outline, is Hallpike's main thesis, which will now be critically examined. At the outset it should be noted that although his presentation of Piagetian theory is concise and lucid, he has misunderstood it in some crucial respects. The reason is probably that Piaget's own thinking underwent some considerable changes, partly as a result of cross-cultural studies. The two most damaging errors in Hallpike's formulation both relate to the notion of 'stages'. First, he assumed that stages are fixed and rigid, uniformly characterizing the thinking of a particular individual; the second error, which follows from the first, is the belief that the performance of an individual or set of individuals on a specific task is sufficient for confident assignment to a given stage. The consequences of these misinterpretations will become evident in the course of the discussion, but at the outset it will be shown that Hallpike's conceptions run counter to current understanding of Piagetian theory. Thus, Furth (1980) wrote of stages:

> One would do well to ascribe to them a mobile rather than a rigid or all-encompassing status which would militate against the very model of Piaget's structural development. Stages refer to charactertistic structural properties of behaviour in contrast to levels in the sense of observable performance criteria. They are simply cross-sections of a continuous developmental process, and like the divisions of the colour continuum, have something arbitrary about them, albeit only to a certain extent.
>
> p. 157

Similarly, Dasen and Heron (1980), dealing specifically with cross-cultural problems, emphasized that one cannot allocate an individual to a particular stage on the basis of a limited set of performances, since the type of reasoning used will vary with the content to which it is applied. Reasonable consistency across various domains, but no more than that, is to be expected. Since it is hazardous to determine even the stage reached by an individual unless his or her cognitive skills have been sampled over a wide range of tasks, it is difficult to see how it can make any sense to label entire societies as 'pre-operational' in the manner of Hallpike. However, let us suspend judgement until the evidence has been considered, of which there are three main types: collective representations, cross-cultural psychological studies, and anthropological descriptions of behaviour.

First and foremost is the question of whether it is legitimate to use collective representations as indicators of levels of cognitive functioning in a society. Hallpike contended that collective representations "are, in their most general characteristics, manifestations of the cognitive processes of the average adult member of the society" (1979, p. 58).

The arguments put forward in support of this claim are roughly as follows: while we do not know the way in which collective representations originated, they must inevitably be assimilated by individuals and passed on through the generations from one person to another. The contents of collective representations will be such as are capable of being understood by members of the society and therefore correspond to the cognitive levels of the transmitters; and the same applies to the changes introduced in the course of transmission.

> Collective representations, in short, are themselves rooted in certain basic assumptions about reality which are not specific to (particular peoples), but which are the result of the way in which human beings think when in a primitive milieu, as a result of interaction with their physical as well as their social environment.
>
>   1979, p. 55

Hallpike allowed for some degree of variability such that some individuals might rise above the limitations prevalent in the society as a whole, whilst others might understand collective representations only in a cruder way than the majority; but the essential part of the claim is that collective representations faithfully mirror average cognitive capacity.

In considering the validity of these arguments, the initial question that needs to be asked concerns the nature and logical status of collective representations. Since Chapter 8 has been largely devoted to one kind of collective representation, the reader will be broadly familiar with what is being discussed. It was pointed out then that the source of the account may range from one particularly knowledgeable individual within the society (whence unknown representativeness) to a multitude of piecemeal stories woven together into a pattern by the anthropologist. Thus in most cases the collective representation is 'filtered', not merely through the mind of the informant, as pointed out by Hallpike, but also through that of the anthropologist. The latter may impose upon the narrative a coherence greater than it really warranted; or alternatively, owing to deficient grasp of the language or erroneous belief about the cognitive inadequacies of the primitives, do it less than justice. There are thus reasons for doubt regarding the modes of recording collective representations.

Let us assume, though, that the process just described did not result in any significant distortions. One can then go on to ask how far it is true that collective representations must be geared to the *understanding* of the people holding them. They are certainly a collective product, modified over time by accretions and deletions whose implications I have considered more fully elsewhere (Jahoda, 1970). In short, it seems questionable whether such collective products need necessarily correspond to the cognitive level of the aggregate of individuals, since they may have distinctive characteristics of their own. In oral cultures, collective representations are not uncommonly transmitted in an archaic form such that some of the meaning has become obscure (Vansina, 1965).

Even more important is the fact that collective representations tend to be emotionally charged; Hallpike alluded to this, without much consideration of its consequences. As in the case of the Bambara, one finds a mix of myths, supernatural beliefs, and empirical knowledge which provides people with a satisfying account of their place in the universe. In Western culture, religion has long performed this function, and with the decline of its influence there has been a revival of various occult beliefs that flourish side by side with modern science. A third-world anthropologist who recorded such collective representations could make considerable play of their irrationality. In this connection one might refer to Hallpike's observation that the Christian beliefs of an Irish peasant and of a Jesuit theologian would, while fundamentally similar, "be understood and justified at quite different cognitive levels in each case" (p. 65). While no doubt true, such a judgement is based on knowledge of the behaviour of particular groups of people, and could not be inferred from Christianity viewed as a collective representation. Thus there is a considerable gulf between collective representations and people's actual behaviour in their everyday lives, which Hallpike chose to ignore; his theoretical case suffers from serious weaknesses, and it remains to be seen whether the empirical evidence presented is any stronger.

Beginning with cross-cultural psychological studies, Hallpike cited extensively from the work of Cole and Dasen; but from the way he presented their material the reader could hardly guess that both these writers would be radically opposed to the conclusions drawn by Hallpike. In other words, the presentation is selective and slanted, as some examples will show. Dasen (1977) contains a figure showing comparative levels of achievement of conservation of quantity by samples drawn from a variety of cultural groups, ranging from about 30 to 100 per cent. Hallpike regarded these findings as supporting his thesis, except that he questioned the results for the Tiv, who were shown as having outperformed whites! In connection with this data, Dasen (1977, p. 169) had the following footnote:

> It seems that the following interpretation of such curves may sometimes be made: 'Tribe X does not mature beyond the European 11-year stage if 50% of the members of tribe X conserve and 50% do not.' We personally know of no such silly statement in print.

However, this is precisely the position taken by Hallpike, who went even further by equating primitives not with European children aged eleven—but with those who were not more than about seven![10] Dasen's own interpretation of the overall pattern of the findings was that cultural groups develop those cognitive skills that are needed in their particular environments. He provided evidence for this contention by comparing cultural groups from contrasting ecologies, e.g. nomadic versus settled agriculturists, showing that the former more readily attained conservation on spatial tasks, while the latter did so in conservation of quantity. None of this was referred to by Hallpike, who either omitted inconvenient facts or at least played them down.[11] He also appears to overestimate (in common with Piaget, admittedly) the cognitive level characteristic of adults in modern industrial cultures, especially among older people and those with limited education but also among well-educated persons of middle age (Graves, 1972; Sinnott, 1975; Labouvie-Vief, 1977).

Generally the conclusions drawn by Hallpike from cross-cultural studies of cognitive development are totally at variance with those of the experimenters themselves and with other competent judges, and as such they are untenable. The essential features of the findings are that there appears to be developmental lag for the acquisition of conservation, and that varying proportions of subjects in different cultures do not seem to reach conservation at all *in the particular domains tested* (e.g. weight, volume, length). The italicized phrase is of critical importance, since the evidence is rather fragmentary and does not preclude conservation being attained in domains outside the usually limited range sampled. This is consistent both with Dasen's proposal of ecologically determined variations in cognitive development, and the rather similar idea of 'local constructivism' put forward by Harris and Heelas (1979), who critically examined an earlier brief version of Hallpike's thesis (Hallpike, 1976); their excellent discussion touches on several of the problems considered here, though from a somewhat different perspective.

It should also be kept in mind that the picture of cognitive development yielded by cross-cultural studies is likely to be a conservative one, in the sense of indicating merely minimum levels of achievement. The reason is that the technical difficulties of such studies are considerable, so that some of the apparent shortcomings of the subjects may be attributable to failure of proper assessment (Ashton, 1975).

Having shown that cross-cultural psychological studies cannot be regarded as providing much support for his case, there remains the anthropological evidence to be considered. Most of this concerns collective representations, and some general considerations have already been put forward showing that such evidence is in principle inappropriate. Some specific illustrations will nonetheless be useful in clarifying the nature of issues, beginning with one of Hallpike's theoretical arguments about the relationship between the prevalence of concrete operational thinking and collective representations. Hallpike asks us to assume that 50 per cent of a population are able to conserve quantity, the other half being unable to do so. Taking social interaction to be random with regard to conservation, he showed that only in one encounter out of every four will two conservers be talking to each other, and "it is therefore evident that mastery of a conceptual problem must be far above the 50-percent level in adults if such a notion is to be incorporated into the collective representations of the society" (1979, p. 61).

Such a static hypothetical model ignores the point made in theory by Piaget and demonstrated by Doise and his collaborators in an extensive series of studies,[12] namely that social interaction plays a key role in the elaboration of new cognitive coordinations. Thus, if the problem is relevant to everyday living in the society, the chances are that operational structures concerning it will become progressively diffused throughout the population; but that does not mean that collective representations will be affected, since these rarely contain much about practical problems of living.

In the present context Hallpike's comments on "primitive conceptions of the mind", as reflected in collective representations, are of particular interest. He suggested that while in modern industrial societies people analyse their own states of mind and those of others, primitives develop no awareness of their private experience and have no means of expressing it. Moreover, they cannot reach any understanding of the cognitive functions of mind, and they fail to draw a proper distinction between the physical and the psychical. While the last point may be valid, it should be noted that this relationship remains a problematic one in Western thinking.[13]

For the rest, the reader is in a position to judge on the basis of the collective representations of the Bambara whether such ideas are as crude as Hallpike made them out to be. He also singled out the West African belief in a depersonalized destiny, described earlier (see p. 116) in relation to an empirical study, as typifying primitive thinking. It would probably surprise him that a closely similar belief was held by Kepler, the discoverer of the elliptical motions of the planets, whose cognitive functioning could hardly have been confined to the preoperational level! This is a vitally important point: people can hold all kinds of 'irrational beliefs' and yet function in other spheres at the highest level of formal operations. There is usually no *logical* incomparibility between such beliefs and scientific or technological notions. People with schooling may know and accept the causal chain linking mosquitos with malaria; but since everybody gets bitten all the time, it is only witchcraft or sorcery that can explain why a *particular* individual succumbs while others do not. All this is rather hackneyed, but needs repeating precisely because Hallpike omitted it. As regards malaria, he referred to the Konso, who apparently discovered for themselves that it is caused by mosquitos; but instead of entering this on the positive side of the cognitive ledger, Hallpike laboured the fact that they were not fully scientific—i.e. they did not understand the exact mode of transmission! Several other cognitive achievements by various peoples were treated in the same manner. A particularly telling instance is that of the Eskimo, who were able to draw remarkably accurate maps of vast areas of thousands of square miles without any instrumental aids; yet what Hallpike chose to emphasize was that these maps were subject to some distortions.[14] One of the few peoples to whom Hallpike was willing to grant an operatory understanding of space were the navigators of the Pacific, who made journeys of hundreds of miles between tiny islands without a compass.

With these last examples we have moved to accounts of cognitive skills displayed by people in action, from which inferences about cognitive functions may be drawn. In order to seek additional evidence relevant to Hallpike's thesis, I went through a great many anthropological books and publications. Looking at all this material—some of it already familiar—from this particular angle, I was forcibly struck by the comparative scarcity of descriptions of *individual* behaviour relating to practical skills in anthropological studies (though there is a great deal about the social behaviour of individuals). No doubt material will have been there in the notebook, but individual behaviours of this kind come to be fused into very generalized statements in their published form. Exceptions to this tend to occur either in older work, or in some recent specialized studies, and it will be of interest to consider some of these.

Hallpike stated repeatedly that primitives are, on the whole, incapable of coherent arguments and generalized explanations, or of bringing out the logical order of a series of events rather than stringing them together chronologically. He claimed that they lack the skill to make deductive inferences, relying mainly on mere oratory or appeals to custom. Hallpike suggested that this was an experience shared by all ethnographers; but long ago Rivers (1906–67) had this to say about the Todas, a hill tribe of Southern India:

In all my work with the men, it seemed to me that they were extremely intelligent. They grasped readily the points of any inquiry upon which I entered, and often showed a marked appreciation of complicated questions. They were interested in the customs of other parts of the world and appeared to grasp readily the essential differences between their own ways and those of other peoples.

1967, p. 20

Admittedly Rivers recorded only his general conclusion without giving specific instances, but he was psychologically sophisticated and his judgement cannot be lightly dismissed. On the other hand, full details of legal argumentation among the Lozi of Barotseland (in what is now Zambia) were provided by Gluckman (1967), whose reasons for including a special chapter on "Judicial logic" in his book are worth citing:

> The logic that is present in Lozi judgements should be apparent from the judgements I have quoted. I shall here make this logic explicit, because it is unfortunately still necessary to demonstrate that Africans and other non-European peoples use processes of inductive and deductive reasoning which are in essence similar to those of the West, even if the premises be different.

p. 271

With regard to Hallpike's assertion that primitive thought is disinclined to accept arguments based on counterfactual hypotheses, this has been refuted in a most thorough manner by a recent study also based on litigation. Hutchins, a psychologist with anthropological field training, conducted his research in the Trobriands, where Malinowski had worked. His aim was specifically the systematic exploration of modes of reasoning in natural situations, and he concentrated on land disputes. For this purpose he constructed an elaborate model, with a family resemblance to artificial intelligence ones, that enabled him to analyse the logical processes underlying ordinary discourse. In this model an attempt was made to formalize the structure of cultural knowledge and premises implicit in such discourse, but seldom explicitly stated—hence the false impression sometimes gained by uninformed outsiders that there is no logical reasoning involved. A detailed account of the theoretical basis and methods adopted is given in Hutchins' (1980) book entitled *Culture and Inference*. It would not be possible here to expound this exciting and in some ways novel[15] approach, which is highly complex and technical. Instead, a passage will be quoted from an earlier abbreviated summary of the argument that will serve to make the critical point. Hutchins (1979) had presented a formal analysis of part of a land case and went on as follows:

> Understanding this brief fragment of discourse requires a total of twelve inferences. Six are weak plausible inferences, and six are strong deductive inferences. All of the inferences are based on the simplified major premises of land tenure defined earlier in terms of causal and temporal relations among abstract classes of events. The act of either understanding or producing this bit of discourse requires (1) the ability to treat concrete instances as members of abstract event classes, (2) a comprehension of the nature of causal and temporal relations between abstract event classes, and (3) the ability to determine the truth values of hypothetical concepts in accordance with their logical relations to other concepts whose truth values have already been established.
>
>   1979, p. 16

So much, then, for the alleged inability of primitives to engage in coherent and logical reasoning. Turning to another sphere, namely that of conservation, Hallpike argued that it could not be achieved in the absence of standardized units of measurement; he went so far as to suggest that "even so simple a problem as finding out how many cups of tea can be obtained from one pot does not present itself in the context of primitive life, since drinking vessels are seldom used" (Hallpike, 1979, p. 99). This is really quite absurd since primitives build houses, construct implements, and engage in trade, activities usually entailing some form of measurement, however crude; conservation does not depend on the precision of the measures, but merely on their consistent application coupled with an understanding of reversibility.

The literature contains sufficient accounts of such activities, which should have made Hallpike pause. Thus Richards (1939) wrote about the Bemba that they had no definite units of measurement, but had no difficulty in comparing the sizes of different objects by using a strip of bark fibre, which they used for such purposes as house-building or making furniture. Thus, they had clearly attained conservation of length. Hallpike said that quantitative analysis is required in situations where there is scarcity of resources and the need to plan in advance—with the implication that these circumstances do not obtain in primitive life. Now here is what Firth (1939) wrote about the factors governing the depths of nets used in lakes: ". . . there is variation according to the owner's estimate of its efficiency, the resultant weight, and the labour and materials he has at his command." (p. 99.) This book by Firth is particularly rich in detailed descriptions of various practical activities which provide strong indications of the achievement of several kinds of conservation. Corresponding accounts relating to trade and exchange can be found in Nadel's (1942) book about the Nupe.

While the Nupe were a relatively complex, hierarchically organized society, the !Kung are hunter–gatherers living in small bands in the Kalahari. They belong to an ethnic group that used to be known as 'Bushmen', long regarded as the very epitome of the 'primitive'. The !Kung were studied by Blurton Jones and Konner (1976), who conducted 'seminars' on animal behaviour with them and accompanied them on hunts. The 'seminars' revealed that the !Kung had observational knowledge of the fauna which the authors regarded as highly sophisticated, by no means confined to what was essential to them for practical purposes. The !Kung were capable of using a number of different classifications of animals, and of shifting readily from one to another. While on a hunt, they displayed an ability to make subtle inferences worthy of Sherlock Holmes. An example of this is given below, followed by the conclusion drawn by Blurton Jones and Konner on the basis of such evidence:

> Konner observed a zebra hunt in which the working hypothesis, that the zebra was wounded high on the body, had to be abandoned when a man showed that grass, which had been bloodied near its high tip, had first been bent to the ground by the passing animal, bloddied by its foot, and then returned to the upright position after the animal had passed. Thus the hypothesis of a wound in the foot was still sufficient to account for the data.
>
> Such an intellective process is familiar to us from detective stories and indeed also from science itself. Evidently it is a basic feature of human life. It would be surprising indeed if repeated activation of hypotheses, trying them out against new data, integrating them with previously known facts, and rejecting ones which do not stand up, were habits peculiar to western scientists and detectives. !Kung behavior indicates that, on the contrary, the very way of life for which the human brain evolved required them.
>
> p. 343

The more one reads Hallpike, the clearer it becomes that he not merely underestimated the cognitive abilities of what he calls primitives on the basis of unwarranted inferences from collective representations, but also that he grossly overestimated the cognitive skills of the average member of 'advanced' society. For example, he would expect such a person to be able to generalize in abstract terms about how society works and the purposes of its institutions (p. 57); and to understand the principle of correlation (p. 465), which as Shweder was at pains to show,[16] few are able to grasp, even in modern industrial cultures. Many of these cognitive skills posited are at the *formal operations* level, and as such are not reached by a substantial proportion of people in advanced societies.[17] These are some among the numerous pointers to the fact that Hallpike was insufficiently equipped with psychological knowledge for the task he set himself. One final example will be given, which also leads towards some interesting recent anthropological work.

Hallpike (1979, p. 62) cited a study of fish-marketing in Ghana that, according to him,

> shows that while the ability to make accurate probabilistic estimates of demand in various markets would be economically highly advantageous to the entrepreneurs, they do not have this ability and proceed by guess-work in a rough-and-ready manner. Merely because a society manages to get by with its existing repertoire of collective cognitive skills does not demonstrate that these are wholly adequate to its needs . . .

The clear implications of this passage is that people in advanced societies do have the ability to make probabilistic estimates. Now quite apart from the fact that the phrasing misrepresents Gladwin's findings, it also betrays total innocence of the large volume of psychological studies of the heuristics employed by individuals when they make decisions. Here is what Tversky (1972) wrote:

> It seems that people are reluctant to accept the principle that (even very important) decisions should depend on computations based on subjective estimates of likelihoods . . . When faced with an important decision, people appear to search for an analysis of the situation and a compelling principle of choice which will resolve the decision problem by offering a clear-cut choice without relying on estimation of relative weights, or on numerical computations.

p. 297

In a later elaborated version of his otherwise very effective model, Gladwin (1975) still made the error of assuming that the fish sellers used their accumulated knowledge to make conditional probability estimates, but were unable to verbalize this process. In an excellent paper based on intensive studies of the behaviour of the fish sellers, and taking full account of psychological decision theory, Quinn (1978) was able to show that the assumption was unwarranted and that in fact the fish sellers behaved very much as would be expected from the findings of experimental studies of decision-making conducted with Western subjects.[18]

There has been an encouraging trend, especially among economic anthropologists, to conduct studies of decision-making in real-life situations that are informed about relevant psychological theories. In this manner Ortiz (1979) examined the expectations and forecasts of a group of South American Indian peasant farmers and constructed a model of their perceptions of expected future prices and yields. It is to be hoped that such intensive work on individual behaviour in various cultures will be more widely undertaken, going beyond the purely economic spheres and dealing, for instance, with details of technological and household activities. This would require a considerable re-orientation on the part of the anthropologists, for as Bloch (1977) pointed out, they often tend to compare what he calls their "ritual communication view of the world" with *our* "everyday practical one", Hallpike being an outstanding example of just such a procedure. From such a perspective, cultural variations are enormous, but that has not much to do with such differences in cognitive skills as may in fact exist. In order to learn more about the cognitive skills of people in traditional cultures, and the factors influencing the development of such skills, psychologists need the help of anthropologists, but that should be a detailed picture of *their* everyday practical world, and not just their collective representations.

Before concluding this discussion two final points need to be made. First, it was evidently not Hallpike's intention to crudely denigrate 'primitives'. He stated this explicitly in several places, and near the end of the book claimed that it is possible "to use the resources of pre operatory thought to express important truths about life and society" (p. 494). Enough has been said already to refute such a claim, but here it is merely cited to indicate the author's sentiments. Unfortunately, it is likely that for the uninformed reader such worthy sentiments are likely to be overshadowed by the general message that 'primitives' are, after all, like children in their modes of thinking.

It should also be made clear that Hallpike's views are not shared by the vast majority of his professional colleagues. Although, as has been repeatedly demonstrated, anthropologists are rather apt to draw unwarranted inferences from collective representations, they very rarely make the mistake of underestimating the abilities and skills of the people with whom they have been working. It is therefore only right to give the last word to another anthropologist who commented on the implications of Piagetian theory for his discipline:

> Anthropologists will easily be able to accommodate their cultural perspective to the proposition that some cultures encourage the development and internalization of certain generalized abstract mental processes more than others. They will be likely to object only if mature, culturally well adapted adults in such cultures, with the relatively low level of development of formal operations their cultures demand, are directly compared or considered on the same footing with retarded individuals or children with a similarly 'low' rating from societies where such capacities

are culturally encouraged, in a way that could appear to give support to popular prejudices about the innate mental capacities of 'primitives'.

Terence Turner, 1973, p. 368

What about the questions posed at the outset concerning the possibility of drawing inferences about 'thinking' from collective representations? One answer is that it certainly cannot be done in the simple and direct manner attempted by Hallpike. Yet it would be foolish to deny any connection between ideas and beliefs held in common by a group of people and their thinking. One may not be persuaded by the theories of Lévi-Strauss, and psychologists especially would wish to see some evidence for the processes so casually implied in the majestic sweep of his arguments. Yet there is the evidence, of which only one example could be cited, of collective representations that appear to have been devised by a systems theorist for the purpose of ensuring optimal ecological adaptation! It is an intriguing question, to which no answer is in sight, what part individual thinkers may have played in the elaboration of such collective representations. On the other hand, there is a more restricted field, namely that of folk classifications, where it has proved feasible to establish links between the collective and the individual levels.

Notes

1. The best brief introduction to Lévi-Strauss is that of Leach (1970).
2. Myths, however, constituted a major theme for Jung; but for him the various elements of myths—be they the activities of people, natural or supernatural phenomena or whatever—had nothing to do with external reality. Jung regarded them as projective manifestations in symbolic form of unconscious dramas enacted within the psyche. According to him, it would therefore not be correct to say that 'primitives' *invent* their myths, since these are an involuntary reflection of inner experience: "they *are* the mental life of the primitive tribe, which immediately falls to pieces and decays when it loses its mythical heritage" (1953, p. 314).

   There could hardly be a greater contrast than that between such heavily mystical pronouncements and Lévi-Strauss's cool rationality, yet both are agreed on the importance of myths.
3. For a concise formulation of his position see Lévi-Strauss (1978).
4. I have discussed some of these issues in greater detail elsewhere (Jahoda, 1970); for a radical anthropological critique, see Thomas *et al.* (1976).
5. For a discussion of some of the difficulties entailed in discovering the connection between brain and behavioural processes, cf. Wilkes (1980).

6. One exception is to be found in the studies of Australian Aborigines by David Turner (1974). He came across a radical modification of a myth concerning the path of the spirits to the Land of the Dead. He traced this to one particular individual, then still living, who was able to give Turner an account of the reasons why he had changed the 'song'. Apparently it was due to the influence of the missionaries symbolically portraying the roads to heaven and hell. This led him to a recognition of the contradiction between the ancestral myth and the Biblical teachings. He resolved this by reasoning that both accounts were true, but that of the Whites more complete. Taking the picture literally and thus identifying its details with actual topographical features, he thereupon changed the 'song' in such a way that the ancestral path became defined as the road to hell, and the missionaries' path as leading to a specific hill upon which heaven was located. This version became adopted by the rest of his tribe.

It should be noted that it is not clear whether or not this would constitute a confirmation of Lévi-Strauss's contention, since the man was conscious of the contradiction and deliberately sought to resolve it. Lévi-Strauss generally worked with 'dead' material and was thus forced to postulate the operation of unconscious processes; but as far as I know he never explicitly denied that the process might sometimes be a conscious one. It is this kind of ambiguity that makes it hard to envisage rigorous empirical testing of his theoretical assertions.

7. Lévi-Strauss (1966, p. 251). Non-anthropologist readers who have troubled to cope with the relatively simple diagram on p. 143 will appreciate this point.

8. That is, what is here called 'collective representations'.

9. In accordance with Hallpike's usage the inverted commas will now be omitted.

10. It is quite evident that Hallpike has never studied any young children with Piagetian-type tasks, or the absurdity of his claim would have become obvious to him.

11. For instance, while data from Papua New Guinea and European children indicated that from a low level at the beginning of primary school, the former consistently improved until they were close to their European peers in secondary grade III. Hallpike (1979, p. 320) chose to emphasise that the European children "were greatly superior". As regards a conservation task, it is stated that *only* [my italics] 82 per cent of New Guinea pupils solved them correctly!

12. Recently summarized in a book by Doise and Mugny (1981).

13. Owing to the lack of a clear distinction, 'primitives' have practised psychosomatic medicine for a long time, which in Western culture developed only in recent times with the realization of the interdependence between psyche and soma.

14. American university students who have been taught geography introduce far greater distortions into their maps when drawn from memory (Gould and White, 1974).

15. The qualification refers to the fact that Gluckman has pursued a similar objective as described above; moreover, Epstein (1969) also studied land disputes in another, culturally similar New Guinea island. While they of course worked within the anthropological tradition and confined themselves to descriptive accounts, both brought out quite clearly the rational nature of the proceedings. It is therefore astonishing that Hutchins did not even mention either of these predecessors in the very same field.

16. See p. 172.

17. For a summary of studies, cf. Blasi and Hoeffel (1974).

18. A useful survey of the fallibility of cognitive judgements among 'advanced' people is provided by Nisbett and Ross (1980).

10 | Classifications: 'Natural' and Symbolic

The collective representations of all peoples invariably include a variety of 'folk' (as opposed to scientific) classifications, showing the manner in which they divide up the seen—and unseen—world. Anthropologists have long been interested in classifications, and what is new is not the problem itself, but the fact that it has become a specialization in its own right and thus the object of much intensive study, material being collected for the specific purpose. When Durkheim and Mauss (1903/63) wrote a famous essay on the topic, they had to extract from ethnographies then available the relevant features. It is easy to do the same for some aspects of the Bambara data, and as an illustration part of the Bambara taxonomy of the body is set out in Table 10.1.

While this indicates considerable empirical knowledge of anatomy, the groupings of body parts is very different from that found in anatomy texts. Moreover, as might be expected, the classification may be viewed from a symbolic standpoint. The Bambara example will serve to bring out the several different anthropological approaches to classification which have one element in common, namely, a reliance on language data. The major types of approach may be roughly summarized by the dichotomies of *emic* versus *etic* (see p. 55), and whether or not they are concerned with symbolic aspects. I have taken some liberty here in imposing a neat scheme which may not meet with universal agreement. Unfortunately, anthropological usage is so inconsistent and confusing[1] that it is not possible to follow it. It should be understood, therefore, that there may be a certain amount of overlap in the scheme as set out below.

	Non-symbolic	*Symbolic*
Emic	Cognitive anthropology	Symbolic anthropology in ⎫
Etic	Ethnoscience	rationalist/structural tradition ⎭

The example of Bambara body taxonomy will be used to illustrate these various approaches. Cognitive anthropologists would not be concerned with symbolism as such, except insofar as it throws light on

TABLE 10.1

Parts of the Bambara taxonomy of the body. Five major divisions, plus two special organs (50 + 2). Special organs: tongue—verbal creation and manifestation of intellect; glans/clitoris—procreation. (Based on Cissé, 1973, p. 143.)

1	2	3	4	5
24 ribs (12 male, on the right, and 12 female); these form the thoracic cage known as "the house of life" since it contains the heart and lungs (respiration = soul)	*12 essential organs* 2 lungs 1 heart 1 liver 1 gall bladder 1 pancreas 1 spleen 2 kidneys 1 bladder 2 testicles/ ovaries	*12 openings* 2 eyes 2 ears 2 nostrils 1 mouth 2 breasts 1 navel 1 urinary passage 1 anus	*1 alimentary canal*	*1 marrow* (This includes the brain or "marrow of the head", the spinal cord, and bone marrow)

the manner in which the Bambara construe the body. The particular taxonomy would be treated as just one sub-set of all types of Bambara classifications, noting the kinds of distinctions made or not made—as, for instance, the groupings of brain tissue with bone marrow. Generally, cognitive anthropologists would attempt to map classifications in such a way as to constitute a kind of blueprint for the linguistic structure of the Bambara cultural world. Ethnoscientists, by contrast, would compare body taxonomies across different cultures with a view to arriving at some general principles underlying such classifications. Symbolic anthropologists would, for instance, be interested in the number symbolism, which could be related to its numerous other manifestations within Bambara culture that have been previously described; or again, it could be compared with parallel forms of number symbolism associated with the body, as among the Dogon (Griaule, 1965).

It has already been said that the boundaries of inquiry are in practice not so well defined, and when a particular problem area is being discussed, such distinctions are often ignored, all relevant information being brought to bear on the issue. In the present context this may be seen in Ellen's (1977) review of anatomical classifications, which draws on all kinds of research traditions to show not merely communalities and variations in body taxonomy, but also that the symbolic and metaphoric use of the human form is probably universal. I propose to deal with each of the several approaches in turn, beginning with cognitive anthropology.

The term 'cognitive' is liable to be misleading for psychologists, since the orientation is essentially linguistic. For anthropologists the term 'cognitive' implies an opposition to 'symbolic', since cognitive anthropologists are completely unconcerned with symbolism as such. Thus the major text edited by Tyler (1969) has no entry for 'symbol' or 'symbolism' in its index. Tyler has epitomized the objectives of cognitive anthropology in the following manner: "What material phenomena are significant for the people of some culture; and how do they organize these phenomena?" (p. 3.) In other words, the aim is to produce cognitive maps of people in various cultures through the study of their language behaviour. The term 'cognitive' is justified by pointing to the fact that the data are mental phenomena, and it is claimed that they can be analysed by formal methods like those of mathematics and logic. In this way it was hoped to arrive at something like a grammar of culture, some cognitive anthropologists going so far as to equate 'culture' simply with the total set of folk classifications prevalent in a given society (Sturtevant, 1964). The possibility of ultimately arriving at a universal, etic theory of culture was looked upon as a distant prospect, the immediate task being that of obtaining "complete, accurate descriptions of particular cognitive systems" (Tyler, 1969, p. 14). Note that we encounter something analogous to, but rather more ambitious than, the collective representations previously discussed.

How are these so-called 'cognitive systems' to be studied? The procedures are more formal than is usual in anthropology, and modelled to some extent on psychology and linguistics. The first stage is to obtain, usually from specially trained informants, a corpus of terms by means of what are known as 'eliciting frames'. Within a chosen domain, a very general frame is first developed for class inclusions such as: *What are the names of the kinds of* ——*?* An example from a study of concepts related to law and justice, conducted in Tenejapa, Mexico (Black and Metzger, 1969) would be: "What are the names of each kind of crime?" Respondents differentiated major and minor crimes, and lists of these were generated; taking each item in the lists, further breakdowns into subclasses were elicited, e.g. "What is the name of each kind of killing?"—and so on. Subsequent steps have been concisely summarized by Johnson (1978), as follows:

(2) reduction of the groups to a set of stable, mutually contrasting terms;
(3) investigation of the semantic organization of the reduced set of terms, using the principles by which native speakers contrast terms and group them into larger categories; and

(4) development of a set of native 'rules of correspondence' by which informants relate their 'native concepts' to the world of practical experience.

p. 160

This is, of course, a greatly simplified outline of a highly elaborate procedure, which is followed by an even more complex application of componential analysis to lexical sets. A brief indication may be given by culling a few features from a study of English kin terms by Romney and D'Andrade (1964). They developed a coding scheme for various types of kin, of which two samples are given below:

$$Aunt \quad a + a \, (+ a)^{0,\,1} \, 0 \, (m =) \, f$$
$$Cousin \quad a + a \, (+ a)^{0,\,1,\,2} \, 0 \, (a -)^{0,\,1,\,2} \, a - a$$

All this was built into a structure which I shall not attempt to reproduce here, and the next problem to be dealt with is how far such a structure actually corresponds to people's cognitions. For this purpose further studies were conducted with individual subjects, using the semantic differential and other psychological techniques. This is indicative of the wish, during the early period of cognitive anthropology, to demonstrate what was called the 'psychological reality' of the findings. The initial aim, according to some of the more sanguine exponents such as Goodenough (1964) had been to provide a description of whatever knowledge and beliefs may be necessary to function as a member of the culture studied. The very stringent criteria of adequacy had been two-fold: the subjective reaction of informants indicating that the description had the right 'feel', and the ability of an outsider to use the terminology in a manner which 'natives' would regard as corresponding to their own (Goodenough, 1965). Such claims have been cruelly, and not altogether unfairly—when one thinks of the codes cited— lampooned by Harris (1968):

> Goodenough's componential definition of an American grandmother's second husband goes something like this: a kinsman at less than two degrees collateral distance; in lineal relationship; in a senior generation; of male sex; in the presence of a marital tie; senior party involved, senior party being the first person in the particular relationship to become known to the junior party . . . Goodenough appears unconcerned by the possibility that some natives might not share his convictions concerning the adequacy of the definition.

p. 573[2]

This example illustrates in exaggerated form how remote the products of componential analysis are from everyday language and behaviour. Moreover, the outcome of such an analysis is usually not clear-cut, since any one set of contrasting terms can be cast into several different structures, and it is not easy to decide which of these conforms most closely to the informants' meanings. These and other problems, discussed by Johnson (1978) in more detail, have led to the virtual abandonment of the ideal of 'psychological reality' as unattainable. One of the original pioneers of cognitive anthropology, Frake (1977) has critically examined the notion of 'frames'; while rightly stressing its continued importance as a methodological tool, he also surveyed its weaknesses—above all, the high degree of informant variability, a problem initially hidden by the use of trained informants. However, the major weakness has been diagnosed some time ago by Keesing (1972), namely, a reliance on taxonomic linguistics as a model at a time when linguists themselves had abandoned it. The debate about the merits of cognitive anthropology has raised many important issues about the relationships between language, culture, and behaviour, but these cannot be pursued here. What is certain is that componential analysis is not a royal road to either culture or cognition. On the other hand, the related approach which I have distinguished as ethnoscience has much more in common with psychology than with cognitive anthropology.

Ethnoscience is concerned with the comparative study of classificatory systems across cultures. In common with cognitive anthropology, it operates mainly, but not exclusively, with language data. On the other hand, ethnoscience does not purport to be a theory of culture, its aims being more restricted in one sense, and wider in another. They are more restricted inasmuch as ethnoscience confines its work to certain specific features of cultures, namely, the manner in which various peoples linguistically encode particular aspects of their material environment. This means that they are not interested in magical beliefs, spirits, demons or other immaterial entities. This still leaves an immensely rich area of study, so that several specializations have developed such as ethnobiology, ethnobotany, or ethnomedicine. The sense in which the aims are wider is that ethnoscientists are not merely seeking to discover how aspects of the environment come to be conceptually organized within a particular culture, but they search for general principles underlying modes of classification in all cultures. Since this involves issues of perceptual salience and selectivity, modes of categorization and semantic structure, and memory, it has meant that many ethnoscientists have looked across the fence to psychology for help in tackling their problems. Because the field is obviously an extensive one, and my own competence rather limited, the discussion will focus merely on some aspects of particular psychological interest.

Leach's theory of magic and sorcery, discussed in Chapter 7, is in part based on the assumption that the objective world constitutes an undifferentiated continuum, sliced into more or less arbitrary sections by a cultural process. If this were the case, one would have little reason to expect much congruence between the various classifications found in traditional cultures, and even less between these and a Linnaean type of scientific classification. Now while it is certainly the case that there are important variations—and even scientific taxonomies have their problems[3]—the broad divisions of fauna and flora in cultures from all parts of the world share certain important features. Not merely do people everywhere classify their environment, which serves an obvious adaptive function, but they do so in broadly similar ways. Before discussing these, it will be useful to indicate briefly how information on classifications is collected.

The procedure for eliciting taxonomic hierarchies is essentially similar to that described for cognitive anthropology. However, this is usually coupled with more objective methods, as may be illustrated from a study by Diamond (1966) of the zoological classification system of the Fore, a New Guinean people:

> (1) Upon arrival at Awande, I asked individual Fore men to describe and name all the animals with which they were acquainted. Many of the resulting descriptions were sufficiently detailed that a zoologist acquainted with the fauna of New Guinea could recognize the identity of the species in question.
> (2) After the collection of specimens had begun, individual men were brought to the collecting table and asked to name all the specimens and provide information about habits and voices.
> (3) While taking census of wild life and making field observations in the jungle, I took men with me and had them name species we encountered and the bird songs we heard.
>
> p. 1102

Diamond found the amount of detailed knowledge of their fauna by the Fore most impressive, and this is certainly not exceptional. Many a non-specialist anthropologist has had to suffer the disdain of his or her people for the inability to distinguish animals and plants which even quite small children in the culture are readily able to differentiate—I shall return to this later.

Such extensive knowledge of flora and fauna has in the past been attributed mainly to utilitarian reasons, but while these are certainly operative, they fail to account for the inclusion in indigenous classifications of species and subspecies that are of no economic value to the populations concerned. It is tempting to fall back on a generalized psychological need to impose order, structure, and meaning upon one's environment as suggested long ago by Bartlett, or the 'curiosity' postulated as a drive by Berlyne (1960). Nonetheless, pragmatic value is undoubtedly important, and it may have been noticed that Diamond questioned men rather than women—presumably because they were more likely to have detailed zoological knowledge in connection with hunting. By contrast, two ethnobotanists (Heinz and Maguire, n.d.) working among Bushmen found women, who do most of the gathering, to be best informed; their knowledge of the distribution of plants is in fact so accurate and detailed that it is the means whereby Bushmen are able to orient themselves in a monotonous and seemingly uniform environment.[4] Such exceptional specialized skills would be worthy of psychological investigation, which does not appear to have been undertaken.

Nothing has been said yet of the forms taken by what are usually known as 'folk biological' classifications, whose general principles have been discussed by Berlin, Breedlove, and Raven (1973); a condensed and more easily accessible version, on which the present account is largely based, is available in Berlin (1978). The hierarchy of folk biological ranks proposed by Berlin (1978, p. 12) is set out below:

1. Kingdom	Plant, animal	
2. Life form	Tree, fish	
3. (intermediate)	Evergreen, fresh water fish	
4. Generic	Pine, bass	
5. Specific	Whitepine, blass bass	
6. Varietal	Western whitepine, large-mouthed black bass	

The examples are, of course, drawn from English ethnobiology. Berlin suggests that there are usually not more than five levels in folk biological classifications that are mutually exclusive and related by class inclusion. Berlin discussed each taxon (i.e. taxonomic group) from the taxonomic, linguistic, biological, and psychological points of view; and I can here only touch upon two important issues. The first is the finding of several studies indicating that in many cultures there is no special terms for the most inclusive taxon such as 'plant'; cognitive anthropologists as here defined, and some ethnoscientists, would therefore not regard such general domains as starting points of classifications; Berlin, however, argued that if there are adequate indications of the cognitive recognition of such a general category, it should be accepted even in the absence of a name. Psychologists would certainly share this unwillingness to equate linguistic and cognitive categories. The other important generalization is the following:

> *Psychologically*, generic taxa are highly salient and are the first terms encountered in ethno-biological inquiry, presumably because they refer to the most commonly used, everyday categories of folk biological knowledge.

p. 17

Ethnobiological studies have thus established the existence of certain fundamental similarities in folk classifications; moreover, it is remarkable that several of these are closely similar to standard scientific ones. This is unlikely to be merely the accidental result of the manner in which certain folk classifications have developed, and are then just mechanically applied by the members of the culture. Thus, in the New Guinea study previously mentioned, informants were presented with species of animals not known to the Fore and asked to name them. In 90 per cent of such cases the name given was that of the Fore species regarded by professional zoologists as being its closest relative. This kind of evidence indicates that common cognitive processes are at work. Hence, it is not surprising that ethnoscientists have increasingly turned to cognitive psychology for help in understanding their results and interpreting them theoretically. Thus, Hunn (1976) proposed what he called a 'perceptual' model which is in fact largely based on classical concept attainment studies by Bruner *et al.* (1956). Similarly, Randall (1976) discussed the manner in which taxonomic trees are stored in memory with reference to the writings of Miller *et al.* (1960) and Tversky (1969). The most directly relevant work, however, and the only one that can be considered here in somewhat more detail, is the version of 'prototype' theory[5] put forward by Rosch (1977, 1978, and Rosch *et al.*, 1976).

The theory of categorization developed by Rosch and supported by a most thorough and ingenious experimental program will be sketched in the barest outline. Two general principles are postulated, the first being that classifications have the function of carrying a maximum of relevant information about the attributes of a category while at the same time imposing the minimum necessary cognitive load, there being a trade-off between these two requirements. The second principle states that real-world objects (in contrast to the stimuli used in laboratory concept formation studies) have attributes possessing a high correlational structure, and are perceived as such; for example, creatures with feathers are more likely to have wings than those with fur.

From these principles Rosch went on to consider two major dimensions of classifications, the horizontal and the vertical. The former refers to the internal structure of categories at any given level. While boundaries of categories tend to be fuzzy, their centre consists of clear cases in which cue validity and category resemblance are maximal. Now Rosch proposes that categories are coded in terms of *prototypes* which "appear to be just those members of a category that most reflect the redundancy structure of the category as a whole" (Rosch, 1978, p. 37). Not only has the importance of prototypicality been demonstrated in relation to a variety of psychological processes such as reaction time or speed of learning, but it also accounts neatly for the success of the Fore in dealing with previously unknown types of animals.

Taxonomies are, as already mentioned, nested sets of class inclusion varying in a gradient of abstraction. This constitutes the vertical dimension, about which Rosch made two assumptions:

> (1) In the perceived world, information-rich bundles of perceptual and functional attributes occur that form natural discontinuities and . . . (2) basic cuts in categorization are made at these discontinuities.
>
> 1978, p. 31

What is suggested is that there will be one basic level of abstraction at which both cue validity and category resemblance are maximal as compared with superordinate or subordinate categories. This is in concordance with the fact that ethnoscientists have found the generic level to be the salient one in most cultures, so that it may be regarded as the basic level. However, when Rosch conducted experiments with American subjects, she found the basic level, as defined by numbers of attributes in common, to be not the folk generic one as expected, but what Berlin called the *life form* (level 2, on page 245); thus, for Americans it was 'tree' rather than 'oak'.

This discrepancy was closely examined by an ethnoscientist, Dougherty (1978), who reviewed the evidence and looked particularly at developmental data. A study of the acquisition of botanical names among Tzeltal Mayan children is particularly illuminating:

> By age four the Tzeltal child typically knows more than one hundred botanical terms, the bulk of which are folk genera. The life-form terms are included in his repertoire at this age, but are not yet defined appropriately. Even so, some notion of the core concept of each life form category has developed, and flora of relatively low salience may be recognized as members of a particular life-form category or other suprageneric category before the appropriate generic designation is learned. By age six, the child's definition of the life-form categories closely approximate the adult model.
>
> p. 70

In contrast to this, a sample of American children had relatively few folk generic names among their earliest plant names; even these often referred to plant products like 'banana', the child being unable to identify the plant from which it came. One child named spinach, but knew only that it is eaten and comes out of a can! The differing developmental sequences for children from the two cultures are set out in Fig. 10.1, in which the linear order means that at least one item of any given taxonomic rank will be learned before any categories at a rank on its right.

Tzeltal

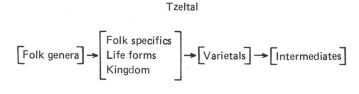

American

FIG. 10.1. The sequence for the acquisition of categories at distinct taxonomic ranks by Tzeltal Mayan and urban American children (adapted from Dougherty, 1978, pp. 70 and 75).

On the basis of this and a great deal of other evidence, Dougherty suggests that Rosch's results concerning basic level are likely to have been in part a function of the particular set of objects selected for testing categorization. More generally, he put forward a principle of the *relativity* of basic object level, which will be determined by the extent of an individual's or a culture's interaction with the particular domain. The botanical one has little significance for urban Americans, but is vitally important in subsistence cultures. Hence, "those classes that are seen as best reflecting objective structures vary according to the interests and attention of human groups and individuals" (p. 78).

Both interest and attention are powerfully affected by social change, so that one might expect substantial modifications of whole category systems. This has been documented for Tahiti, where new animals were introduced which changes the character of the indigenous classifications along the lines that would be expected from Berlin's (1973) theory; at the same time, the missionaries 'translating' the names of

Biblical animals created names which were incapable of evoking any images for the Tahitians (Lemaitre, 1977).

A particularly interesting case of historical change has been described by Fernandez (1972) for the Fang of Cameroun and neighbouring areas. The classification is that of 'people', and the successive modifications are displayed in Fig. 10.2. In stage 1, animals were contrasted with people and, as is commonly the case, sub-divided into domestic and wild; but gorilla and chimpanzee were classed as 'people'. The Fang grouped themselves, together with related clans, as being descended from a common ancestor. Those not sharing this ancestor were classed according to their unintelligible language, and only secondarily by pigmentation. During stage 2, the higher apes have become reclassified as wild animals and the Pygmy split off as a separate category straddling the boundary between animals and people; while not shown in the figure, some differentiation of 'speakers of gibberish' also began at that stage.[6] In stage 3, Pygmies have been promoted to people, though still constituting a distinct category. Language has been dropped as a criterion and, presumably by adopting European notions, the classification has become 'racist'; moreover, white men have now come to be differentiated in terms of both occupational role and nationality. Thus modes of categorization may be seen to reflect profound changes in the perception of the social environment.

In addition to such a 'natural' system of classification, Fernandez also discussed another kind propounded by the *Bwiti* reformist cult founded before the First World War. In this category of 'people' is subdivided into seen and unseen parts, with some aspects (such as witchcraft) straddling the divide. The body is composed of blood and sperm, but its 'capacity' comes from the unseen part transmitted through the lineage from the creator gods. White men are masterful and derive their capacity from a large share of the unseen. The full scheme is of course far more elaborate, but enough has been said to make it evident that this classification is predominantly a symbolic one, and meat for the symbolic anthropologist. The fairly sharp distinction in this case is exceptional, the Bambara body taxonomy cited earlier in this chapter being more typical. Needham (1979) suggested that any classification can take on a symbolic aspect, and as an example referred to the spatial groupings of occupations in towns; from one standpoint this may be regarded as being of practical convenience (e.g. butchers or cloth merchants all clustered in particular areas), and from another as a form of symbolic ranking which divides 'good' and 'bad' parts of a town. This prompts the question as to what renders a classification

symbolic as distinct from merely practical. Needham touches on this
question, only to set it aside: "Anthropological opinion is very divided

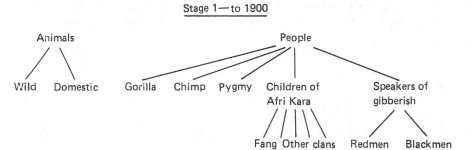

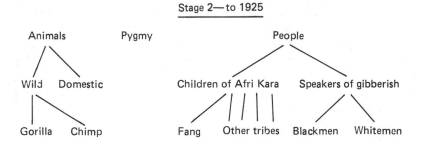

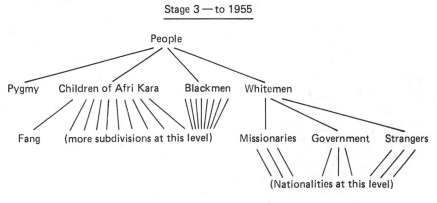

Fig. 10.2. Changes in Fang categorizations of 'people' (adapted from Fernandez,
1972, p. 42).

as to how this difference should be defined, and here is not the place to treat such a hard and contentious matter." (1979, p. 4.) While this is rather lame, it is not just Needham's fault: in order to be able to answer the question satisfactorily, one would require criteria for distinguishing the symbolic from the non-symbolic in collective representations. Since people themselves do not attach such labels as 'symbolic' and 'non-symbolic' to their classification, such a property has to be inferred or attributed. This means that anthropologists of differing persuasions look at their material through spectacles equipped with different filters: hence, a particular classification may be treated in its symbolic aspects by some, and its practical ones by others. This does not imply a denial that the aspect not considered exists, nor even that it may be important as well; it merely reflects a difference in focus of interest, which will now be examined.

It will be useful to concentrate at the outset on the simplest and at the same time most common type of symbolic classification, which is the dual one. Dual classifications can take two main forms, one consisting of two dominant categories such that everything belongs either to one or to the other (Needham, 1979). Perhaps the best known case of this is the Chinese classification into *Yin* and *Yang*, where *Yin* represents the feminine, dark, weak, night, moon, earth, and so on, while *Yang* stands for masculine, light, strong, sun, sky, and so on. Such comprehensive symbolic dichotomization, while found in some other cultures, are relatively infrequent.

Most widespread is the symbolic linking of categories into pairs of opposites, usually with different values attached to each member of the pair so that a kind of ranking is also involved. The categories are not necessarily absolutes: for instance, a given group may, according to context, be either wife-givers or its opposite (wife-takers). One crucial opposition on which I shall focus has been prominently displayed in the Bambara material of Chapter 8, and another statement is cited below:

> The limbs materialize the right and the left. 'Right' are rectitude, firmness, directed action. 'Left' means uncertainty, indecision, variability of behaviour. The right is male; it symbolizes the man's work; the other is female. All gestures, profane and religious, the representations of all kinds of objects, testify to this. During the first dressing applied to the fields before the rains, the farmer makes three strokes of the hoe with his left hand so as to absorb the impurities of the earth. Thereafter he works with his right hand until the harvest.
>
> Dieterlen, 1951, p. 69

Far from being confined to the Bambara, it is extremely common.

Thus, in the above-mentioned cult of Bwiti, rituals and ceremonies are explained by the leaders in terms of dichotomies of qualities or forms of conduct of the following kinds (see Fernandez, 1972, p. 39):

right hand	*left hand*
male	female
white	red
death	life
northeast	southwest
hot	cold
day	night
sky	earth
bone	flesh
sperm	blood
speech	silence
activity	tranquillity
dispersion	knitting together
paternity	fraternity

There is actually no need to go to anthropological sources in order to illustrate the importance of the right–left polarity, and the fact that by and large the right is more positively valued. In the Old Testament the Lord's right hand is said to be full of righteousness, and in the New Testament we are told that the sheep will be placed on the right of the Son of Man and the goats on his left, and the latter will be cursed.

The symbolic significance of right and left was first examined in a classical essay by Robert Hertz, first published in 1909 and contained in Needham (1973), a book entirely devoted to this opposition, with which numerous others are said to be associated. While it is only in recent years that psychologists have become actively interested in the lateral asymmetry of cerebral functioning, Hertz was well aware of its anatomical basis, quoting Broca as saying, "We are right-handed because we are left-brained". However, Hertz suggested that the reverse might well be true, arguing that social pressures favouring the right hand could have led to corresponding hemispheric specialization. Today this is probably a less revolutionary thought than when Hertz first put it forward, but it is characteristic of a pupil of Durkheim's that he emphasized possible social rather than physiological factors. In effect, he proposed that an originally slight difference might have become progressively accentuated because of the social significance attached to the right hand, which became embodied in custom and child training. Why did this happen? The hypothesis advanced was that 'primitive' man conceived the cosmos as divided into a masculine and a feminine half, one sacred and the other profane, one auspicious and the other inauspicious. Around this central core a variety of dichotomous symbols came to be clustered which, while differing somewhat across cultures, shared similar emotional loadings. With reference to the then available ethnographic literature, Hertz was able to document the consistent symbolic use of the left–right polarity over a wide range of human cultures.

In spite of its brilliance, which makes it well worth reading even now, Hertz's work was largely ignored for a generation. When rediscovered, it inspired anthropologists to explore right–left symbolism in depth, their studies confirming and considerably extending the empirical foundation of his thesis. In order to show this, the most common pairs claimed to be associated with the left–right opposition among the studies reported in Needham (1973), are listed in Table 10.2. In

TABLE 10.2
Concomitants of lateral symbolism

Right	Left
Man/male	Woman/female
Older/superior	Younger/inferior
Good/moral/auspicious	Evil/amoral/inauspicious
Strong/important	Weak/unimportant
Day/light/sun	Night/dark/moon
Above/in front	Below/behind
Settlement/home	Bush/wilderness
Domesticate/cooked/farmer	Wild/raw/hunter
Life/health/abundance	Death/sickness/poverty
East	West
South	North

each case, items associated with *right* tend to be more highly valued. The question is whether this is really a human universal and, if so, how one might account for it. It may have been noticed that Hertz's hypothesis fails to explain why, in the absence of much lateral asymmetry, the symbolism should have arisen. This may be the reason why some of the contributors to Needham's (1973) collection abandoned the ideas of the old master, putting forward instead their own interpretations, which are hardly an improvement. Thus Cheldhod and Littlejohn described pervasive left–right symbolism in an Arab culture and the Temne of West Africa, respectively. The parallels are striking: e.g. eating and drinking with right, touching genitals with left, setting out on journey with right foot lucky, left unlucky, and so on. Yet the explanations put forward for these similar forms of symbolism have nothing in common;

Cheldhod referred it to an ancient solar cult, while Littlejohn sought to show that it had something to do with the proper relationship to one's fellows. It would seem that both at least partly took for granted the very phenomenon that had to be explained.

There is a lesson here, worthy of brief mention. It is perhaps one of the main hazards of the interpretation of symbolism in specific socio-cultural terms that it can nearly always be done if one tries hard enough: cultures are so complex that by appropriate selection some kind of plausible fit can almost invariably be achieved. It is only when one looks at consistent patterns of symbolism *across* different cultures that the inadequacies of such interpretations become glaringly obvious. If an explanation in terms of social structure is to be valid, it must refer to common features in the cultures where the particular kind of symbolism occurs.

The neat arrays displayed in Table 10.2, which is an amalgam of several such lists in Needham's volumes, have not remained unchallenged. On the specific issue of a list attributed to the Banyoro, Beattie (1976), who had worked with these people, stated: "Not only is there no evidence that a number of the 'oppositions' he [Needham] tabulates are, or might even conveivably be, regarded as 'opposites' by Banyoro, but in some cases the very terms or concepts which he opposes do not exist in Nyoro language or thought." (p. 230.) The details of the somewhat acrimonious debate are not relevant here, but it involved also the general problem of the relationship between collective representations of this kind, which Needham characterized as 'supra-individual', and the conceptions held by individuals within the culture. Beattie maintained, in my view correctly, that collective representations of this kind should not be imputed unless it can be shown that the people themselves do in fact make the postulated distinctions. Note that Beattie did not question the existence of complementary dualism which, he agreed, is found in "most cultures".

A more radical critique has been put forward by J. Goody (1977) in an illuminating essay on the effects of literacy on cognition, from which psychologists can glean many stimulating ideas. In brief, Goody argued, on the basis of his own ethnographic experience, that while the left–right polarity and similar types of colour symbolism undoubtedly exist, the oppositions are not as sharp and absolute as might appear from their abstract presentation in an orderly scheme; such a scheme is a product of our own classificatory habits, which are a function of literacy. The critique is epitomized in the question whether Needham's interpretation could be "a result of *our* tables rather than *their* thoughts" (p. 65).

With regard to several of the empirical problems, such as the extent to which various other dichotomies are associated in different cultures with the left–right dichotomy, and the affective loading of members of these pairs, psychological studies of individuals within these cultures might help to provide firmer answers. Generally psychologists have shown little direct interest,[7] though a large-scale study by Osgood *et al.* (1975) concerned with affective meaning systems is at least remotely related. Employing the Semantic Differential, they produced an *Atlas* of affective meaning that actually included 'right hand' and 'left hand' as concepts to be rated. Unfortunately the material is not in a form permitting direct comparison with anthropological data,[8] and the subjects consisted of Westernized high school students. However, suitable methods are available and have in fact been used for a comparable purpose (Burton and Kirk, 1979).

Osgood (1979) has also written an article in which he referred to the Chinese Yin and Yang in order to illustrate his contention that the basic characteristic of human cognitive processes is their *bipolar organization* (Osgood's italics); there is no indication in the article of any awareness that Lévi-Strauss had said much the same before him. Since bipolarity is built into the Semantic Differential scales with which Osgood mainly operates, he may be inclined to overrate its salience in human thinking in general.

J. Goody (1977) at any rate took a different view of the origins of trans-culturally prevalent dichotomies of right versus left, coupled with associations like left–sinister–female. Questioning that these entail basic features of human cognition, he wrote:

> I suggest that some of the associations of right and left are less reflections of the structure of human thought than of the structure of the human body (mediated, of course, by the mind). It is hard to see how any linguistic system could avoid such an elementary opposition. Nor, given the structure of the brain, is it difficult to understand how left gets negatively valued and right positively. A similar argument applies to the second set of associations, i.e., similarities across cultures. It could be as well the structure of the situation as the structure of the mind that gives rise to such identifications.

p. 65

Some of this is perhaps a little sweeping, especially the jump from the structure of the brain to the nature of evaluations. Nonetheless, the contention that laterality underlies dual classifications is probably the most parsimonious explanation. It is supported by an analysis of handedness as depicted in graphic representations, which indicates that the incidence of 90 per cent right-handedness has remained roughly constant over a span of some fifty centuries (Coren and Porac, 1977).[9]

So far an important area of cross-cultural similarities in symbolism has been surveyed. Other studies have been concerned with intra-cultural patterns of symbolic classification, and the particular study used to exemplify this will be a well-known one by Tambiah (1969) entitled "Animals are good to think and good to prohibit". This may sound rather strange, but is in fact very much to the point. In order to elucidate its meaning, it is necessary to sketch at least briefly some further intellectual background of the whole symbolic approach. As usual, the starting point is Durkheim, who, it may be recalled, believed that practically all knowledge comes to the individual from the social group of which he is a member; it was therefore inconceivable for him that the elaborate systems of classification found in every society could have been built up as a product of individual thinking. Jointly with Mauss (Durkheim and Mauss, 1903/63) he wrote an essay on *Primitive Classification* in which it was suggested that society itself is the prototype model for all kinds of classifications. When the book was subsequently reissued Needham wrote an introduction in which he demonstrated the theory to be untenable by showing that Durkheim and Mauss tacitly assumed the existence of what they intended to prove. The general issue was also discussed by Lévi-Strauss, who turned the argument around: instead of denying, as Durkheim and Mauss had done, that the mind is incapable of arriving at classifications, he said that it is in the very nature of the mind to classify everything. In support of this he appealed to the fact that people everywhere and at all times classify and categorize their environment, which he had no difficulty in establishing. This argument in itself hardly constitutes a decisive refutation of Durkheim and Mauss, since they did not question the ubiquity of classifications; but there is no doubt that psychological evidence (which he did not cite) supports Lévi-Strauss. While classifications are ever-present, what varies according to him is how they come to be established. With regard to the 'primitive' Lévi-Strauss resorted to the famous analogy of the *bricoleur*, an untranslatable term referring to a person being able to make things from all kinds of bits and pieces. Now the 'primitive' is said to be such a *bricoleur* who constructs a logic from whatever materials are available in his environment. This includes what Leach (1970) called "observed sensory qualities of objects—e.g. the difference between raw and cooked, wet and dry, male and female"; but above all, animal and plant species; and thus it was that Lévi-Strauss coined the phrase, "animals are good to think" in the context of his discussion of totemism. Out of this raw material logical classifications are shaped with an extremely variable *content*, but with an essential *form* that is constant, since they result from the uniform mode of functioning of the human brain. It should be noted in passing that there is an implication, widely accepted by anthropologists, that classifications directly reveal something about modes of thinking.

The second part of Tambiah's title, namely, that animals are also "good to prohibit", can be dealt with more briefly since the issue has already been discussed (p. 209). It refers to the view that symbols are also carriers of social values, serving to maintain and enhance them.

In sum, the relationships between classifications systems within particular cultures are regarded by structuralists as critical for understanding the manner in which the collective representations of a people express their relationship to their environment. Moreover, particular styles of classification, according to Lévi-Strauss and his followers, ought not to be confined to any particular domain but remain consistent across different ones, being merely transformations of the same basic code.

Let us now return to Tambiah (1969), who provides one of the most compelling illustrations of this thesis. He worked in a Thai village, addressing himself to the problem of understanding the prevailing dictary rules relating to animals. Regrettably it will be necessary to omit all the ethnographic material and the details of the argument, leaving merely the bare bones! Making sense of dietary prohibitions clearly requires consideration of the scheme of animal classification. Less obvious is the reason why Tambiah included in the framework of his analysis the relationship between rules concerning the eating of animals and those dealing with sex and marriage. The symbolic connection between eating and sexual intercourse is not just a Freudian notion, but has been documented in widely different cultures; for instance, there is frequent correspondence between the norms regulating whom a person is permitted to marry and with whom that person is allowed to eat. There is yet a third domain overlapping with the two others, which consists of the spatial categories into which the house is divided. This may seem surprising, and a brief digression to explain it will be helpful.

The village houses are built on stilts, animals being kept in the space below the house. The orientation of the house and its component parts have symbolic values, the sleeping room on the north side being the most sacred place; the right side is east (when one faces north) and represents the male sex; west and the left hand represents death, impurity, and the female sex! The relationships of people within the house are closely connected with these values—e.g. the spaces that various types of outsiders are allowed to penetrate, who sleeps where (and even whether they sleep on the west or east side: father right and mother left, but this is reversed for the son-in-law, who sleeps to the left of his wife, symbolizing his inferior status in the house). These few examples of a very elaborate set of rules indicate how closely they are tied to symbolic values. Hence, one pragmatic reason for studying symbolic classifications is that they help to make sense of rule-governed behaviour. Also, it should not be imagined that the Thai house is unique in being redolent with symbolism; not merely are there many other studies of this kind, such as that of the Berber house by Bourdieu (1973), but such symbolic aspects can be discerned nearer home. Even though the days of symbolic status loading of 'upstairs' versus 'downstairs' are past, one has only to think of the 'parlour' as opposed to the kitchen as places for entertaining people!

It will therefore be apparent that it is logical to include the rules relating to the house with the two other sets. With regard to the animal classification, one point should be briefly noted since I shall shortly return to it: Tambiah was particularly interested in the relationship between dietary taboos and the position of the forbidden animals in the classification scheme, though it will not be possible to enter into its lengthy details. The culmination of the study is the juxtaposition of the three series, shown in Table 10.3. Examination of the table reveals a remarkable correspondence between the three sets of rules, which could not reasonably be regarded as fortuitous. Moreover, there are parallels elsewhere: Douglas (1966: 41–75) discussed the relationship between dietary prohibitions and animal classification systems in the Old Testament, and similar patterns have been found in Benin by Ben-Amos (1976). In commenting on the implications of his findings, Tambiah showed that they are in conformity with the theoretical position of Lévi-Strauss. On the other hand he dissociated himself to some extent from the latter's stark intellectualism, suggesting that the emotional aspects of such symbolic classifications should not be ignored.

Mention has been made of Tambiah's special concern with the relationship between taxonomic position and edibility, where he found that species problematic in their classification also tended to be doubtful as regards edibility. Another oddity to which he paid attention were the inedible members of a mostly edible class; an example is one sub-type of forest animals such as deer, squirrel, or hare, which were all edible, in contrast to the monkey that was not. He found that the avoidance of monkeys involved a belief in a kind of inverted Darwinian notion, namely, that the monkey is descended from man.

These are instances of what are known as *anomalies* of classification,

TABLE 10.3

Relationship between three series: marriage and sex rules, eating rules and etiquette concerning house categories. (Adapted from Tambiah, 1969, p. 442.)

	Blood siblings	First cousins	Classificatory siblings beyond second cousins	Other people	Outsiders
Human series	Blood siblings	First cousins	Classificatory siblings beyond second cousins	Other people	Outsiders
Marriage and sex rules	Incest taboo	Marriage taboo; sex not condoned	Recommended marriage (and sex)	Marriage and sex possible	No marriage
House categories	Separate parts of sleeping room	Sleeping room	Guest room	Platform	Compound fence
Rules relating to house space	Sleeping rules separating parents from son-in-law and married daughter	Rights of entry but not sleeping	Taboo to cross threshold into sleeping room	Visitors wash feet if invited in	Excludes outsiders
Animal series	Domestic animals that live inside the house	Domestic animals that live under the house (and have been reared there)	Domestic animals belonging to other households	Animals of the forest: counterparts (to domestic), deer, etc.	(1) Powerful animals of the forest (2) Monkeys
Eating rules	Inedible and taboo	Cannot be eaten at ceremonials	Eminently edible at ceremonials	Edible	Inedible and taboo

which have exerted a great fascination on anthropologists. Before glancing at the theoretical issues arising, another well-known case will be cited, the study by Bulmer (1967) of the zoological taxonomy of the Karam people of New Guinea. Bulmer concentrated his discussion on the marginal status of the cassowary, a bird not classified as such by the Karam. At first sight the reason for this might appear simple: it is virtually wingless and does not fly, has no feathers and is much larger than any other birds in the area. However, other New Guinea peoples *do* classify the cassowary as a bird in spite of its unbird-like attributes; moreover, bats, which lack feathers, are classified by the Karam as birds. Bulmer went on to show that in order to make sense of this classification it is necessary to consider the cassowary's relationship to man. He discovered that its hunting and eating were regulated much more strictly than other game (noting, incidentally, that this may have been of ecological value in ensuring its survival in Karam territory, where it was not common). One or at most two men were allowed to hunt it, and since it was forbidden to shed the blood of a cassowary it had to be killed with a blunt instrument. Cassowaries being powerful creatures, this meant a personal struggle quite unlike any other form of hunting. The eating of cassowaries was also forbidden during the period of planting and growing of taro, the most highly valued food crop featured prominently in rituals. Bulmer then went on to show that there seems to be an elaborate antithesis in Karam thought between forest and cultivation, linked also to kinship rights and roles, especially those of siblings and cross-cousins. It would appear that in some respects cassowaries were regarded as siblings and cross-cousins, whence their special taxonomic status.

A somewhat similar analysis concerning the central symbolic function of the pangolin (scaly ant-eater) among the Lele of Kasai had been undertaken by Douglas (1957, reprinted 1975). Subsequently Douglas (1966) put forward a broader theoretical statement widely acclaimed by anthropologists. She argued that culture provides people with a system of categories for the ordering of their ideas and values. Such categories, being public, are rigid and cannot be easily modified. Then she went on as follows:

> Yet they cannot neglect the challenge of aberrant forms. Any given system of classification must give rise to anomalies, and any given culture must confront events which seem to defy its assumptions. It cannot ignore the anomalies which its scheme produces . . .
>
> 1966, p. 39

Douglas then went on to list various ways in which anomalies could be dealt with, such as physical elimination (as used to be done with twins defined as anomalous in some West African cultures), labelling anomalies as dangerous, or utilizing anomalies as symbols in rituals.

The work of Douglas has been highly influential in anthropology, and her interpretations have been widely adopted. Moreover, psychological principles have been appealed to in support of her thesis. For instance, Lewis (1977) pointed out that Kelly's (1955) theory contains some striking parallels. Kelly defined anxiety as "the recognition that the events with which one is confronted lie outside the range of convenience of one's construct system" (p. 495). In explicating this seemingly curious definition, Kelly said that such an event could not be right outside one's construct system, or one could not even perceive it; but it fails to fit into the existing structure. If, as seems not unreasonable, one can regard construct systems as types of personal classification, then there may be continuity between anomalies in the personal sphere generating anxiety and, insofar as these feelings may be shared, collective representations giving rise to avoidances or propitiatory rituals as defences against anxiety.[10]

However, it is as well to pause before being carried away. For the psychologist there arises from Douglas's interpretation the same problem already previously encountered on several occasions: who are 'they' responding to the challenge of aberrant forms, how does 'a culture' confront events? If the concept of 'anomaly' is a valid one, there must be intra- and inter-individual processes mediating the development of such cultural phenomena. While these may mostly be inaccessible in the remote past, could some not be taking place in the present? Simply ignoring the problem means that nobody is trying to locate such processes that may well be traceable (if they exist) in a rapidly changing world that surely calls for many adjustments in thinking.

From within anthropology the thesis of Mary Douglas has been critically examined by Sperber (1975) in a penetrating essay that is, however, not easy to read. He charged Douglas with postulating, but not explaining, the relationship (which he accepts) between anomaly and 'symbolicity'. In order to establish the thesis one should not, as did Douglas, pick on symbolic animals to see if they are anomalous within the cultural taxonomy, but look at all the anomalies of the taxonomy to see if they are treated symbolically. Moreover, Douglas' thesis fails to account for the fact that ideal-type animals as well as monsters such as dragons are prominent in symbolism. Sperber also argues that it is not necessarily true that all empirical taxonomies must give rise to anomalies. He put forward an alternative hypothesis, based on an analysis of the general conditions of conceptual representations in zoology, which does not lend itself to a summary; his hypothesis is that the capacity of particular animals to evoke symbolism stems from their position within, or in relation to, a taxonomy (the latter being true of fantastic animals). Crudely put, animals are judged in relation to a norm[11] and any departure from that norm is liable to evoke symbolism.

I have devoted some space to Sperber's hypothesis, since it appears to be of considerable interest from the standpoint of cognitive psychology and might lend itself to empirical testing. This applies to the concept of anomaly generally, which has also been discussed by Ellen (1979). It is certainly not true that all taxonomic anomalies provoke symbolism and thereby a cultural response. Thus Morris (1976) reports of the Hill Pandaram of South India that the *pandan* or flying squirrel constitutes a clear anomaly in their taxonomic system, but is not the object of any rites and is in fact eaten! The whole problem is certainly an intriguing one, and one wishes to establish the conditions under which anomalies have the effects attributed to them by Douglas. For this purpose one would have to look at the patterns of anomalies across cultures, which does not seem to have been attempted systematically so far.

There has been at least one effort by an ethnoscientist to establish a bridge between his own tradition and symbolic anthropology. Hunn (1979) showed for some of the *Abominations of Leviticus* discussed by Douglas (1966) that one might account for them in terms of the fact that they constitute empirically infrequent trait complexes. Thus, in Table 10.4 the off-diagonal cells are all 'abominations', the single entry

TABLE 10.4

Distribution of character co-occurrences (from Hunn, 1979, p. 113).

	+ Chew cud	− Chew cud
+ Cloven hoof	10	1
− Cloven hoof	5	90

in the top right cell being the pig.[12] According to this view, the symbolic nature of anomalies arises from the perception of the correlational structure of the environment. Douglas might well retort that while the emphasis is different, the proposed interpretation does not really reach beyond her own; and Sperber (1975), as already mentioned, would reject a purely statistical criterion of normality. Obviously, there is a great deal more to be discovered here, especially as regards the psychological processes involved. Unfortunately, psychology is currently ill-equipped to handle such problems, as we do not yet understand much about symbolism.

Notes

1. Many writers treat the expressions 'cognitive anthropology' and 'ethnoscience' as more or less synonymous, grouping them together as part of the 'new ethnography'. My justification for separating them in the way I have done is that the major text by Tyler (1969) with the title *Cognitive Anthropology* is confined to a specific set of theoretical and methodological principles that are not usually shared by most of those who regard themselves as 'ethnoscientists'.
2. It should perhaps be made clear that Harris is not just opposed to cognitive anthropology as here defined; lumping it together with symbolic anthropology and ethnoscience, he would dismiss them all as being 'idealist'.
3. These and several other relevant issues are more fully discussed in the book edited by Ellen and Reason (1979).
4. Heinz and Maguire cite the following incident:

> In an area seventy miles north of Ghanzi, two-hundred miles from the home of his four *Iko* companions and while travelling in a northerly direction on a dark rainy night, the first author asked one of the Bushwomen to pick a suitable place to spend the night. (It is a woman's prerogative to choose a camp site.) This woman then led the vehicle through the trees and bushes in a large sweeping curve to stop two hundred yards away from the road at a clump of large trees, which, as seen from the road, formed a relatively inconspicuous landmark. On returning from another trip, a year later and on an equally dark night, he was driving southwards towards Ghanzi in the same company. The woman suggested that the party sleep at the camp of the previous year. It seemed to the author quite impossible for her to locate the place in country of such utter uniformity. Yet with very little hesitation she signalled the author to stop the car; she got out, and beckoned him to follow. At an angle to it, but in a straight line, she left the road and with determination led the way directly to the camp site of the previous year. On the present occasion she had left the road at least 300 yards to the north of the point from which she left it when choosing the camp site a year earlier and on which occasion the party had been travelling in a northward direction. It seemed quite clear that no single tree, bush, or other 'signpost' guided her, but rather the complete plant community, the peculiarities of which she had mentally absorbed in the minutest detail.
>
> p. 33

It should be added that this is by no means an isolated case, even more spectacular ones having been reported by D. Lewis (1976) about Australian Aborigines.

5. Prototype theory has recently been critically evaluated by Osheron and Smith (1981), who consider that it fails to explicate adequately the truth conditions of thoughts. However, they credit it with being able to satisfactorily account for the process of category identification, which is the only concern in the present context.

6. The nature of the change from Redmen to White men is probably only a linguistic one. In several African languages the European skin colour is described as red; so it is likely that only the European self-description came to be accepted.

7. For instance, a book by Corballis and Beale (1976) consists of a most thorough survey of laterality from a psychological standpoint. The authors were also familiar with Hertz and Needham, but confined themselves to the comment that the associations "no doubt . . . are largely a matter of superstition" (p. 177); this is hardly a satisfactory explanation for patterns recurrent in many parts of the world!

8. For curiosity's sake, numerical values corresponding to the concepts 'right hand' and 'left hand' are set out below (pp. 437 and 444):

	Evaluation	Potency	Activity
Right	$0 \cdot 7$	$0 \cdot 1$	$1 \cdot 1$
Left	$0 \cdot 1$	$-0 \cdot 7$	$-0 \cdot 2$

Although in the expected direction, both concepts cluster rather closely around the neutral point; there are no details how they relate to various qualifiers, which would be essential information.

9. The origin of handedness is an intriguing and as yet unsolved problem. Yerkes (1943) cited the work of Finch indicating that among chimpanzees right-handedness, left-handedness, and ambidexterity occur with about equal frequency. Yerkes' view was that an initial bias exists in both men and primates, which is socially reinforced in men: ". . . the fact seems clearly established that in respect to handedness . . . the chimpanzee is free to act according to its natural characteristics . . . while we humans, by contrast, are slaves to convention." (p. 114.)

Yerkes thought that this constituted a handicap for human psychobiological development, a view reminiscent of one prevalent two centuries ago that forced ambidexterity would radically increase human potential (see Herron, 1979); today this would certainly not be accepted, and there is considerable evidence for a genetic component in handedness (J. Levy, 1976). However, the disparity between men and other hominids remains puzzling, though speculative accounts have been put forward (Frost, 1980). The notion that handedness resulted from mothers holding their infant with the left against the heart, leaving the right free to carry out skilled activities, raises the question why this is not done by primates and makes them predominantly right-handed. According to the available evidence their preferred hand is randomly distributed; unfortunately this evidence is mainly based on primates in captivity, where infants are commonly removed from the mother and hand-reared, so that the mother had no opportunity of 'teaching' the offspring. What seems to be required is large-scale observation of behaviour in the wild.

10. It is easy to think of other seemingly supportive psychological findings. Thus a tendency has been demonstrated experimentally for 'atypical' stimuli to have a high saliency and obtrude themselves upon awareness (Benjafield and Adams-Webber, 1976; Shalit, 1980). Incongruity has been shown to arouse fear in young children, and the theory of dissonance suggests that it poduces tension and unease—but note how difficult it is to define objectively what is "dissonant"!

11. Sperber's concept of 'norm' is an unusual one, being related neither to ideal type nor statistical frequency; as far as I understand it, his norms relate to the necessary as opposed to the contingent features of a taxonomic definition.

12. Harris (1977), in a delightful popularization put forward the materialist explanation that "pig farming was a threat to the integrity of the basic cultural and natural ecosystems of the Middle East" (p. 35); unfortunately a substantial part of the argument rests on the dirtiness of the pig at high temperatures, about which nothing is said in the Old Testament.

Conclusion:
Towards Better Understanding

Someone knows something
that someone else does not know;
someone does not know something
that someone else knows (says the shuttle);
one is in front of the other;
the other is behind the first;
the other is in front of the first;
the first is behind the other (say the steps);
that one goes up,
the other goes down;
that one goes down,
the other goes up (repeat in turn the parts of the warp).
Understanding! Understanding!
Let us understand each other!

from the Bambara Song of the Weaver

The general message of these pages has been that there is a close kinship between psychology and anthropology, and that we have much to learn from each other. It is, however, one of the lessons from anthropology that kinship as such does not necessarily entail close and warm sentiments—they may well be distant and cold, depending upon the structure in which the relationships are embedded.[1] In this case the structure of academic departments has produced a distance that has reduced mutual understanding and cooperation. Fortunately, as has also been shown, there are hopeful signs of the trend being reversed, especially in certain areas of inquiry which constitute a natural meeting-ground. While welcoming such developments, I am not among those who envisage a "synthesis of anthropology and psychology" (Bock, 1980, p. 246), which in the foreseeable future is neither realistic nor even desirable. Differences can be instructive and used creatively, unless one chooses to ignore them. Many variations in approaches will have been apparent in the preceding pages, but two of them are particularly salient and have been like a thread running through the last few chapters: I am referring to collective representations and symbolism. It will be useful to examine these once more, not just in the abstract but in relation to a famous problem, that of *colour*.

Colour is a kind of arena in which a game of nature versus culture has been played for well over a century. In this game the teams are not lined up according to disciplines, but anthropologists and psychologists (as well as others) are to be found on either side. The story has often been told, though usually by dedicated supporters of one side or the other; a balanced account of the state of the game up to the mid-70s is given by Lloyd (1977). Here a brief sketch providing the essential background will be sufficient. It all began, improbably enough, with William Gladstone who in that more leisurely age was not only a statesman but also a distinguished Homeric scholar. Gladstone noticed that the Greek colour vocabulary was in some respects curiously restricted, and attributed this to a less developed visual system (nature). His view was opposed by a comparative psychologist and an ophthalmologist who suggested that what was insufficiently developed was merely the colour vocabulary (culture), shown to be widely variable across the globe. Rivers (anthropologist/psychologist) proposed on the basis of his data from the Torres Straits (see p. 19) that a physiological deficiency in sensitivity to blue was involved (nature). He was challenged by both Woodworth and Titchener (psychologists), who suggested that the solution of the problem must be sought in the evolution of abstract colour vocabularies (culture).

The game was then suspended for about half a century, until Ray (anthropologist) published a study concluding: "Each culture has taken the spectral continuum and has divided it into units on a quite arbitrary basis." (1952, p. 258) (culture). A few years later the Sapir/Whorf notion of linguistic relativity (culture) was tested with colours, the outcome being somewhat inconclusive. A major turning point in the game was the work of Berlin and Kay (anthropologist) who demonstrated a regular encoding sequence of 'focal' colours across languages, and some crucial aspects of their theory were tested by Rosch (psychologist) in New Guinea and confirmed (probably nature). The next step was the demonstration of the physiological basis of the observed linguistic regularities, accomplished by Bornstein (psychologist), who scored decisively by showing that the spectrum is divided into distinct hues even for pre-verbal infants. It might be imagined that the game was then concluded with a victory of nature over culture, but as with the heredity – environment game familiar in psychology there never can be a clear victory of one side over the other.[2] What happens is a shift sufficient to accommodate the new findings without abandoning the old position.[3] It is at this point that our real discussion starts, focusing on the views of Sahlins (1976), expressed in a well-known article entitled *Colors and Cultures*.

Sahlins starts by paying tribute to the work of Berlin and Kay, describing it as being "among the most remarkable discoveries of anthropological science" (p. 1), and reviews some of the physiological evidence. Having thus duly acknowledged the biological determination of perceived colours, Sahlins proceeds to relegate it to a secondary plane:

> I argue that these results are consequent on the social use of color not merely to signify objective differences of nature but *in the first place* to communicate significant distinctions of culture.
>
> p. 3; italics in original

In other words, what is primary is the cultural *meaning* of colours, which cannot be reduced to the simple act of pointing; indeed, Sahlins accuses some anthropologists of "conspiring" with cognitive psychologists in putting forward such a restrictive interpretation, by resorting to empirical testing of colour naming which, according to Sahlins, does not get at the "essential meaning" of colour. The question then arises where such essential meaning comes from, and Sahlins' answer is that "it would be the collective tradition, or *Völkergedanken*, which informs the subjective apperception by an historical conception" (p. 12). Thus we are back to collective representations. The general argument is epitomized in the following passage:

> How then to reconcile these two undeniable yet opposed understandings: that color distinctions are naturally based, albeit that natural distinctions are culturally constituted? The dilemma can be solved, it seems to me, by reading from cultural meaning of color to the empirical test of discrimination, rather than the other way around. We must give just due to this third term, culture, existing alongside subject and object, stimulus and response, and mediating between them by the construction of objectivity as significance. Moreover, a semiotic theory of color universals must take for 'significance' exactly what colors do mean in human societies. They do not mean Munsell chips. Is it necessary to document that colors signify the difference between life and death, noble and common, pure and impure? That they distinguish moieties and clans, directions of the compass,[4] and the exchange values of two otherwise similar strings of beads?
>
> 1976, p. 12

Sahlins' stand has the merit of uncompromising clarity: he asserts the primacy of collective symbolic meanings (culture) over physiologically based distinctions (nature); he says that human mental equipment is "the instrument of culture" rather than its determinant. The statement is one of principle, not confined to the particular domain of colour; and it is not just directed at psychologists, but also at anthropologists of a different persuasion.

For my purpose it is important to distinguish between collective representations, symbolic or non-symbolic on the one hand, and symbolic meanings on the other. Beginning with the former, it should be stated with equal bluntness that there is an unbridgeable gulf between psychologists (other than Jungians) and those anthropologists who, like Sahlins, reify (or almost deify) culture and collective representations by picturing them as hands reaching out from a nebulous past to shape the present irresistibly. The question whether collective representations themselves might not be rooted ultimately in man's biological nature is never even asked; they are not merely taken as given, but assigned absolute causal priority. More frequent than this kind of dogmatic absolutism is the rather more casual, though uncritical, acceptance of the Durkheimian tradition that has been repeatedly encountered in preceding chapters. The intellectual habit of treating collective representations as 'cognitive systems' detached from individuals, while deeply ingrained, is also beginning to be challenged from within anthropology. Thus Bloch (1980), in his *Munro Lectures*, contrasted the conceptions of developmental psychologists with traditional anthropological ones. Although making some entirely justified critical comments about the acultural character of much psychological research, one of his main aims was to suggest ways in which the contrasting approaches of anthropologists and psychologists might be harmonized.[5] There is thus a good prospect of closer understanding in future.

It is possible to reject Sahlins' notion of collective representations, with its special flavour of Teutonic mystique, and yet accept the priority of social meaning over biological determination, for which Bousfield (1979) has argued on rather different grounds. However, the present concern is not with issues of priority, which I am inclined to regard as a pseudo-problem. Rather, I wish to underline Sahlins' emphasis on the importance of the symbolic aspects of colour, which seems to have been entirely ignored by the psychologists involved in the debate. Generally there is a kind of blind spot as regards this aspect of human behaviour, which may perhaps be partly accounted for by the fact that Freud and Jung were among the few who took symbolism seriously. Some of the classical writers like Külpe and William James contrasted directed thinking with the free play of images, and their notions were taken up and developed by Jung. Whatever one's views about the theories of Jung—and personally I am out of sympathy with them—it is undeniable that he provided an immensely erudite documentation about the prominent part symbolism has played in human thinking.[6]

The Freudian contribution had a greater influence on anthropology than on psychology, though many anthropologists were somewhat critical of the narrowness of Freudian symbolism. That narrowness has been acknowledged by Rycroft (1977):

> Psychoanalytical theory has attempted to pre-empt the concept of symbolism by asserting that the only true symbols are those which analysts encounter when interpreting dreams and neurotic symbols. By doing so, psychoanalytical theory has offended against common usage and has created well-nigh inseparable barriers between itself and other humane disciplines.
>
> p. 139

He might have added that psychoanalytic writers are also apt to engage in all kinds of highly speculative symbolic interpretations of historical personages, works of art and so on, which are often hard to take seriously. In any case, Rycroft himself expressed the view that symbolization is a general capacity of the mind, not restricted to what in psychoanalytic theory is called 'primary process thinking'. Academic psychologists appear to suffer from a reaction formation, fighting shy of anything that appears to be tainted by Freudianism, such as symbolism. Hence, they tend to confine the meaning of 'symbol' or 'symbolization' to cool and rational features of cognition. The following is fairly typical of psychological usage:

> Symbolization is defined here as the selection process, the choice of one aspect of a complex array to serve as the top of the iceberg, a light-weight mental token that can be substituted for the entire knowledge package for purposes of higher-order cognitive operations.
>
> Bates, 1979, p. 65

The result of this sharp dichotomization is the somewhat bizarre mixture one finds when looking up 'symbolization' in *Psychological Abstracts*. For instance, for the second half of 1980 one finds, on the one hand, such austere topics as symbol-substitution tasks, or chunking in recall of symbolic circuit drawings; and on the other, such quaint gems as the dream of Hippias on the eve of the battle of Marathon about losing a tooth as a case of tooth–phallus symbolism, or *The Wizard of Oz* as a drama symbolizing a girl's passage through the phallic phase!

Between these two extremes there lies a vast and, at least psychologically, largely unexplored territory. Anyone reluctant to take this seriously should consider the fact that ethnologists have observed symbolic behaviour in primates and discussed its adaptive biological function (Kortland, 1972). It is therefore surprising that even Piaget, whose fundamental orientation was biological, played down symbolic aspects of behaviour. He was rightly criticized for this by Hallpike (1979), whose chapter on *Symbolism* is one of the best in the book, being only marginally concerned with 'pre-operational thought'. Another anthropologist, Terence Turner (1973), has commented as follows on Piaget's portrayal of 'figurative' thinking as a lower form of mental activity:

> Piaget's attempt to deny all dynamic operations to figurative thought flies in the face of massive evidence for the dynamic qualities of much figurative imagery (e.g., symbolic forms such as myth, ritual and the arts). Symbolic forms in these categories can be 'dynamic' both in the sense of representing transformations of temporal processes and in the sense of producing affective, conative, and motivational effects.
>
> 1973, p. 352

It should be admitted that it is the multifaceted quality of symbolism and symbolic behaviour that makes it so elusive and hard to analyse in terms of psychological process. As far as symbolic *thinking* is concerned (abstracting from any associated emotive elements), no psychological theory exists at present to account for it. Sperber, an anthropologist mainly interested in the cognitive aspects of symbolism (some of whose ideas have already been discussed on pp. 261–2) tried to fill the gap. His proposed theory (Sperber, 1980), in a book that contains several useful discussions of the field, postulates that symbolic thought must be preceded by some rational processing. In order to be able to demonstrate this, it is of course necessary to specify the distinction between 'rational' and 'symbolic' thinking, which he attempted to do in relation to psychological theory, but in this he was building on sand. For instance, Sperber attributed to Piaget the view that ontogenetically symbolism is prior to rational thought, since Piaget had said that the child has to go first through a stage of pre-conceptual and symbolic representation. Sperber was here misled by the terminology, whose ambiguity led Piaget later to abandon the term 'symbolism', replacing it by 'the semiotic function'. Sperber's suggested processing model also owes something to Neisser (1967, 1976), but it seems to me that he perhaps attached too much weight to the few pages in which Neisser discussed a (for Neisser) somewhat peripheral issue. The major flaw in Sperber's treatment is his equation of rational thinking with syllogistic reasoning, which is far too narrow a conception. On the other hand, he said hardly anything positive about the specific characteristics of symbolic thinking, confining himself in the main to exemplifications of the kinds of 'triggers' liable to evoke it. These are themselves questionable, as some illustrations will indicate, beginning with an example of what is supposed to be rational processing:

> *There is the sound of a bell* (premise from the perceptual device).
> *When there is the sound of a bell, someone is ringing one* (premise from memory).
> *Someone is ringing a bell* (conclusion).
>
> 1980, p. 29

I shall let this pass without comment, going on to one of his triplets (a), (b), and (c), where the last is that said to be more symbolic:

> (a) Lighting a cigar with a match
> (b) Buying a cigar with a dollar bill
> (c) Lighting a cigar with a dollar bill
>
> 1980, p. 37

Without wishing to deny that (c) may be liable to trigger a richer evocation, it could just as easily be analysed as a potential syllogism on the 'bell' model:

> People who light cigars with a dollar bill are rich. This man lights his cigar with a dollar bill. Therefore this man is rich.

In sum, although Sperber's discussion is ingenious and stimulating, he has not really succeeded in pinning down the essential distinguishing features of symbolic thought. At any rate he deserves full credit for having grappled with a problem psychologists, with few exceptions (Gardner *et al.*, 1974; Gardner, 1979) have tended to ignore. One promising development is the increasing psychological interest in the nature of metaphorical thought (Ortony *et al.*, 1978; Rogers, 1978), including some experimental studies (Paivio, 1979). It is only a short step from metaphorical thought to symbolism, but in an important collection of essays on the topic (Ortony, 1979) that step was not taken; moreover, in spite of the fact that this is clearly an overlapping area of concern, only brief and passing reference was made to anthropology.

Another perhaps even more directly relevant line of work is that of Zajonc (1980), who put forward considerable evidence in support of the view that feelings are mediated by a separate system from that of cognition. This is more radical than it may sound, because it postulates that affective responses occur prior to cognitive processing. He suggested that the affective system is primary in an evolutionary sense and largely independent of the more recently developed cognitive one. Since affect is predominantly communicated by non-verbal means, Zajonc proposed that it may also be processed very differently from cognition, for instance by being encoded at the visceral or muscular levels. There is certainly ample evidence from electromyographic research that muscular activity is connected with imagination and the recall and production of emotional states. Such notions of the primacy and immediacy of affective responses, while remaining in some respects speculative, nonetheless rest on a substantial basis of empirical research. If they turn out to be broadly correct, this would vindicate the dominance of emotion implicit in Freudian theory; from the present standpoint it could shed fresh light on the manner in which symbols are capable of making an impact that is both immediate and powerful, yet largely independent of cognition as conventionally understood. The door would be opened to an experimental approach to symbolism, in which there would be scope for fruitful collaboration with anthropology, since symbolism cannot be adequately studied without relating it to its cultural context.

These two themes of collective representation and symbolism, brought sharply into focus at the interface of colour, have been singled out as exemplifying the complementarity of psychology and anthropology which is not sufficiently recognized. Apart from these crucial areas, numerous points of contact have been reviewed in these pages. Generally it may be said that psychology has much to contribute to anthropology within the broad sphere of cognition, while anthropological work not merely highlights the shortcomings of psychology in the fields of personality and social behaviour, but points towards more promising approaches such as naturalistic observation of behaviour. I am of course not suggesting that psychologists should turn themselves into anthropologists, nor imitate them slavishly; but selective borrowing might well be profitable.

There will no doubt be some readers for whom these pages will merely serve to confirm the view that anthropology, as compared with psychology, is a 'soft' discipline. This standpoint has been amusingly described autobiographically by the novelist Kurt Vonnegut, Jr (1976), who began by studying physical anthropology and archaeology but found these boring. His family pressed him to go in for science, but he was longing for poetry and was offered a way out of the dilemma:

> My adviser smiled. ''How would you like to study poetry which *pretends* to be scientific?'' he asked me. ''Is such a thing possible?'' I said. He shook

my hand. "Welcome to the field of social or cultural anthropology," he
said.

p. 176

There is an important grain of truth in this. Anthropologists, unlike
psychologists who can choose to stay ensconced in their laboratories,
cannot avoid dealing with people and have to develop something of the
sensitivity of the poet. However, poetic and scientific thinking are
perhaps not as far apart as often believed, both requiring an imaginative leap usually mediated by symbols. The rich humanity of anthropology has sometimes inspired poets, as when Auden (1966) wrote:

> Malinowski, Rivers,
> Benedict and others
> Show how common culture
>   Shapes the separate lives:
> Matrilineal races
> Kill their mothers' brothers
> In their dreams and turn their
>   Sisters into wives.

p. 152

Psychology is more prosaic, but is it more scientific? Its greatest
strength, namely, the use of the experimental method, also imposes the
severest limitation. For both practical and ethical reasons most of the
really vital aspects of human behaviour are simply not amenable to
experimental approaches, but can only be studied in natural
situations.[7] Anthropologists, by contrast, have as their central objective
the exploration of the manner in which people all over the globe cope in
their various ways, constrained by their environment, with the
vicissitudes of life; this includes not merely social behaviour and
cognition, but also what used to be called the 'passions'—love and
hate, anxieties and hopes. The psychologist who wishes to shed his or
her Western cultural blinkers and learn something about the richness
and variety of human behaviour must turn to anthropology for enlight-
enment and a broader perspective. Supposedly universal laws based on
the behaviour of college students are, except for the physiological end
of behaviour, bound to be largely illusory. Even cross-cultural psychologists, who seek to transcend such limitations, need the help of
anthropologists for their work to be fully effective.[8]

Conversely, anthropologists could perhaps take more advantage of
the special knowledge and skills of psychologists. It would be particularly salutary for them to look at their favourite notion of 'collective
representations' in a cool psychological light. In that light it stands

revealed as a kind of fiction that served a purpose in the past, but has outlived its usefulness in its present form. Collective representations as free-floating entities are a chimera all too frequently adduced in what can only be pseudo-explanations. If the notion is to be reshaped into a viable conceptual tool, it has to be more clearly articulated in its relationship to individuals. While origins are bound to be shrouded in impenetrable mist, changes that occur in the contemporary setting ought to be amenable to study once the logical status and empirical nature of collective representations have been more clearly established. In this and many other tasks, a joint approach by anthropologists and psychologists would hold out more prospect of real progress. There are sociobiologists (Lumsden and Wilson, 1981) who would go well beyond this, envisaging a unified global approach encompassing genetics, neurobiology, psychology, psychoanalysis and anthropology. The aim of such a fusion of disparate traditions would be the construction of models of 'gene-culture coevolution' which, it is claimed, could illuminate human history as well as offering a more profound understanding of the human mind. Such a grand design is unlikely to be achieved in the near future. Nevertheless it points in the same direction as that advocated in these pages, namely a transcendence of conventional academic boundaries and a return to the close connexions that once existed between psychology and anthropology. It will thus be fitting to end with the words of Rivers (1926, p. 11) who was a master of both disciplines: "How can you explain the workings of the human mind with a knowledge of the social setting . . .?"

Notes

1. For a discussion see Lévi-Strauss (1963) and D. Turner (1978).
2. At the time of writing there has been counterplay from the side of culture (Lucy and Shweder, 1979), but by the time this book appears it will certainly be out of date regarding the latest score.
3. That is, not a 'paradigm shift' in the Kuhnian sense.
4. For instance, for the *Zuni* north is yellow, west is blue, south is red and east is white (Needham, 1979, p. 13).
5. Block draws extensively on the writings of the French Marxist anthropologist Bourdieu (1977), who has gone further than many in coming to terms with psychology.
6. Jung's concept of the 'archetype' has a strong family resemblance to that of collective representations. It is interesting that Needham, notoriously averse to any psychological explanations of social facts, concluded a lengthy

discussion of unilateral figures by attributing them to an archetype! (Needham, 1980, p. 39).

7. One of the few instances where it was attempted is Milgram's (1974) study of obedience, for which he was severely criticized by many. On the other hand, it should be said that anthropologists also encounter difficult ethical problems of their own; see, for example, Rynkiewich and Spradley (1976).

8. For example, Super (1981), reviewing the shortcomings of comparative studies of behavioural development in infancy, had this to say:

> A fourth failure stems in part from the hiatus over the past 25 or 30 years in the once prominent dialogue between anthropology and psychology. For the past few decades they seem to have withdrawn from the interface, especially with regard to infancy, to tend to their own theories. Very few of the studies reviewed here achieve, or even attempt, an integration of infant care and development, on the one hand, with functional and value characteristics of the larger culture, on the other. Success in this direction requires both sound ethnographic knowledge of the culture as well as a quantitative baseline of information about infants' daily lives.
>
> pp. 246–7

References

ALLPORT, G. W. (1968). The historical background of modern social psychology. In *Handbook of Social Psychology* (G. Lindzey and E. Aronson, eds), 2nd ed., vol. 1. Addison-Wesley, Reading, Massachusetts.

ARGYLE, M. (1975). *Bodily Communication*. Methuen, London.

ASHTON, P. T. (1975). Cross-cultural Piagetian research: An experimental perspective. *Harvard Educational Review* 45, 475–506.

AUDEN, W. H. (1966). *Collected Shorter Poems, 1927–1957*. Faber, London.

BADCOCK, C. R. (1980). *The Psychoanalysis of Culture*. Blackwell, Oxford.

BAILEY, F. G. (1969). *Strategems and Spoils*. Blackwell, Oxford.

BARNES, J. A. (1971). *Three Styles in the Study of Kinship*. Tavistock Publications, London.

BARNOUW, V. (1973). *Culture and Personality*. Dorsey Press, Homewood, Illinois.

BARRY III, H. (1980). Description and uses of the Human Relations Area Files. In *Handbook of Cross-Cultural Psychology*, (H. C. Triandis and J. W. Berry, eds), vol. 2. Allyn & Bacon, Boston.

BARRY, H. and PAXSON, L. M. (1971). Infancy and early childhood: Cross Cultural Codes 2. *Ethnology* 10, 466–508.

BARRY, H., CHILD, I. L. and BACON, M. K. (1959). Relation of child training to subsistence economy. *American Anthropologist* 61, 51–63.

BARRY III, H., JOSEPHSON, L., LAUER, E. E. and MARSHALL, C. (1976). Traits inculcated in childhood: Cross-Cultural Codes 5. *Ethnology* 5, 83–114.

BARRY III, H., JOSEPHSON, L., LAUER, E. E. and MARSHALL, C. (1977). Agents and techniques for child training: Cross-Cultural Codes 6. *Ethnology* 16, 191–230.

BARTH, F. (1974). On responsibility and humanity: Calling a colleague to account. *Current Anthropology* 15, 99–102.

BARTLETT, F. C. (1923). *Psychology and Primitive Culture*. Greenwood Press, Westport, Connecticut.

BARTLETT, F. C. (1932). *Remembering*. Cambridge University Press, Cambridge.

BATES, E. (1979). *The Emergence of Symbols*. Academic Press, New York and London.

277

BATESON, G. (1972). *Steps to an Ecology of Mind.* Chandler, New York.

BATESON, G. and MEAD, M. (1942). *Balinese Character: A Photographic Analysis.* Publications of the New York Academy of Science, vol. 2, New York.

BEATTIE, J. (1964). *Other Cultures: Aims, Methods, and Achievements in Social Anthropology.* Cohen & West, London.

BEATTIE, J. (1976). Right, left, and the Banyoro. *Africa* **46**, 217–35.

BEATTIE, J. (1977). Oh, would some power the giftie gie us, to see ourselves as others see us. In *Issues in Cross-Cultural Psychology* (L. L. Adler, ed.). New York Academy of Sciences, New York.

BEATTIE, J. and MIDDLETON, J. (1969). *Spirit Mediumship and Society in Africa.* Routledge & Kegan Paul, London.

BEN-AMOS, P. (1976). Men and animals in Benin art. *Man* **11**, 243–52.

BENEDICT, R. (1935). *Patterns of Culture.* Routledge, London.

BENJAFIELD, J. and ADAMS-WEBBER, J. (1976). The golden section hypothesis. *British Journal of Psychology* **67**, 11–15.

BERLIN, B. (1978). Ethnobiological classification. In *Cognition and Categorization* (E. Rosch and B. B. Lloyd, eds). Erlbaum, New York.

BERLIN, B. and KAY, P. (1969). *Basic Color Terms: Their Universality and Evolution.* University of California Press, Berkeley, California.

BERLIN B., BREEDLOVE, D. E. and RAVEN, P. H. (1973). General principles of classification and nomenclature in folk biology. *American Anthropologist* **75**, 214–42.

BERLYNE, D. E. (1960). *Conflict, Arousal, and Curiosity.* McGraw-Hill, New York.

BERRY, J. W. (1976). *Human Ecology and Cognitive Style.* Wiley, New York.

BLACK, M. and METZGER, D. (1969). Ethnographic description and the study of law. In *Cognitive Anthropology* (S. A. Tyler, ed.). Holt, Rinehart & Winston, New York.

BLASI, A. and HOEFFEL, E. C. (1974). Adolescence and formal operations. *Human Development* **17**, 344–63.

BLOCH, M. (1977). The past and the present in the present. *Man* **12**, 278–92.

BLOCH, M. (1980). From cognition to ideology. Munro Lectures given at Edinburgh University on 17–18 November 1980.

BLURTON-JONES, N. (1975). Ethology, anthropology and childhood. In *Biological Anthropology* (R. Fox. ed.). Malaby Press, London.

BLURTON-JONES, N. and KONNER, M. J. (1973). Sex differences in the behaviour of London and Bushmen children. In *Comparative Ecology and Behaviour* (R. P. Michael and J. H. Crook, eds). Academic Press, London and New York.

BLURTON-JONES, N. and KONNER, M. J. (1976). !Kung knowledge of animal behavior. In *Kalahari Hunter-Gatherers: Studies of the !Kung San and their Neighbors* (R. B. Lee and I. De Vore, eds). Harvard University Press, Cambridge, Massachusetts.

BOAS, F. (1910). Psychological problems in anthropology. *American Journal of Psychology* **21**, 371–84.

BOAS, F. (1911/63). *The Mind of Primitive Man* (revised edition). Collier, New York.

BOAS, F. (1955). *Race, Language and Culture.* Macmillan, New York.

BOCK, P. K. (1980). *Continuities in Psychological Anthropology.* Freeman, San Francisco.

BOHANNAN, L. (1976). Shakespeare in the Bush. In *Cultural Anthropology* (J. Friedl, ed.). Harper & Row, New York.

BOISSEVAIN, J. (1974). *Friends of Friends: Networks, Manipulators, and Coalitions.* Blackwell, Oxford.

BOLTON, R. (1973). Aggression and hypoglycemia among the Quolla: a study in psychological anthropology. *Ethnology* 12, 227–57.

BOLTON, R. (1979). Differential aggressiveness and litigiousness: social support and social status hypotheses. *Aggressive Behavior* 5, 233–55.

BOLTON, R. (1981). Susto, hostility, and hypoglycemia. *Ethnology* **20**, 261–76.

BOUSSEVAIN, J. and MITCHELL, J. C. (1973). *Network analysis: Studies in human interaction.* Mouton, The Hague.

BOTT, E. (1957). *Family and Social Network.* Tavistock, London.

BOURDIEU, P. (1973). The Berber house. In *Rules and Meanings* (M. Douglas, ed.). Penguin Books, Harmondsworth.

BOURDIEU, P. (1977). *Outline of a Theory of Practice.* Cambridge University Press, Cambridge.

BOUSFIELD, J. (1979). The world seen as a colour chart. In *Classifications in Their Social Context* (R. F. Ellen and D. Reason, eds). Academic Press, London and New York.

BRONFENBRENNER, U. (1979). *The Ecology of Human Development.* Harvard University Press, Cambridge, Massachusetts.

BROWN, R. (1965). *Social Psychology.* The Free Press, New York.

BRUNER, J. S., GOODNOW, J. J. and AUSTIN, G. A. (1956). *A Study of Thinking.* Wiley, New York.

BULMER, R. (1967). Why the cassowary is not a bird. *Man* 2, 5–25.

BURTON, M. and KIRK, L. (1979). Sex differences in Masai cognition of personality and social identity. *American Anthropologist* **81**, 841–73.

BURTON, R. and WHITING, J. M. W. (1961). The absent father and cross-sex identity. *Merrill-Palmer Quarterly* 7, 85–95.

CALLAN, H. (1970). *Ethology and Society.* The Clarendon Press, Oxford.

CARSTAIRS, G. M. (1957). *The Twice-Born.* The Hogarth Press, London.

CASTANEDA, C. (1975). *Don Juan Quartet.* Simon and Schuster, New York.

CHADWICK-JONES, J. K. (1976). *Social Exchange Theory.* Academic Press, London and New York.

CHAGNON, N. A. (1968). *Yanomamö: The Fierce People.* Holt, Rinehart & Winston, New York.

CISSÉ, Y. (1973). Signes graphiques, représentations, concepts et tests relatifs à la personne chez les Malinke et les Bambara du Mali. In Colloques Internationaux, *La Notion de Personne en Afrique Noire.* Editions du Centre National de la Recherche Scientifique, Paris.

COHEN, Y. (1964). *The Transition from Childhood to Adolescence.* Aldine, Chicago.

COLBY, B. and COLE, M. (1973). Culture, memory, and narrative. In *Modes of Thought* (R. Horton and R. Finnegan, eds). Faber, London.

COLE, M. (1981). Society, mind and development and the zone of proximal development: where culture and cognition create each other (CHIP Report 106). Center for Human Information Processing, University of California, San Diego.

COLE, M. and GAY, J. (1972). Culture and memory. *American Anthropologist* **74**, 1066–84.

COLE, M. and SCRIBNER, S. (1974). *Culture and Thought.* Wiley, New York.

COLE, M., GAY, J., GLICK, J. A. and SHARP, D. W. (1971). *The Cultural Context of Learning and Thinking.* Basic Books, New York.

COOPER, D. E. (1975). Alternative logic in 'primitive thought'. *Man* **10**, 238–56.

CORBALLIS, M. C. and BEALE, T. L. (1976). *The Psychology of Left and Right.* Lawrence Erlbaum, Hillsdale, New Jersey.

COREN, S. and PORAC, C. (1977). Fifty centuries of right-handedness: The historical record. *Science* **198**, 631–2.

CRONBACH, L. J. (1975). Beyond the two disciplines of scientific psychology. *American Psychologist* **30**, 116–34.

CUTTING, J. E. and KOZLOWSKI, L. T. (1977). Recognizing friends by their walk: Gait perception without familiarity cues. *Bulletin of the Psychonomic Society* **9**, 353–6.

DANQUAH, J. B. (1944). *The Akan Doctrine of God.* Lutterworth Press, London.

DASEN, P. R. (1977). Are cognitive processes universal? A contribution to cross-cultural Piagetian psychology. In *Studies in Cross-Cultural Psychology* (N. Warren, ed.), vol. 1. Academic Press, London and New York.

DASEN, P. and HERON, A. (1980). Cross-cultural tests of Piaget's theory: Selected issues. In *Handbook of Cross-Cultural Psychology* (H. C. Triandis, A. Heron and E. Kroeger, eds), vol. 4, *Developmental Psychology.* Allyn & Bacon, Boston, Massachusetts.

DEGÉRANDO, J.-M, (1800/1969). *The Observation of Savage Peoples.* Translated by F. T. C. Moore. Routledge & Kegan Paul, London.

DEREGOWSKI, J. B. (1980). *Illusions, Patterns and Pictures.* Academic Press, London and New York.

DEVEREUX, G. (1961a). Two types of modal personality models. In *Studying personality cross-culturally* (B. Kaplan, ed.). Row Peterson, Evanston, Illinois.

DEVEREUX, G. (1961b). *Mohave Ethnopsychiatry and Suicide.* U.S. Government Printing Office, Washington, D.C.

DEVEREUX, G. (1978). *Ethnopsychoanalysis.* University of California Press, Berkeley, California.

DIAMOND, J. M. (1966). Zoological classification system of a primitive people. *Science* **151**, 1102–4.

DIETERLEN, G. (1951). *Essai sur la Religion Bambara.* Presses Universitaires de France, Paris.

DOISE, W. (1978). *Groups and Individuals.* Cambridge University Press, Cambridge.

DOISE, W. and MUGNY, G. (1981). *Le Développement Social de l'Intelligence.* Inter Éditions, Paris.

DOUGHERTY, J. W. D. (1978). Salience and relativity in classification. *American Ethnologist* **5**, 66–80.

DOUGLAS, M. (1966). *Purity and Danger.* Routledge & Kegan Paul, London.

DOUGLAS, M. (1975). *Implicit Meanings.* Routledge & Kegan Paul, London.

DU BOIS, C. (1944). *The People of Alor.* Harper Torchbook edition, 1961. University of Minnesota Press, Minnesota.

DURKHEIM, E. (1893/1964). *The Division of Labor in Society.* Free Press, New York.

DURKHEIM, E. (1895/1947). *Les Règles de la Méthode Sociologique.* Presses Universitairs de France, Paris.

DURKHEIM, E. and MAUSS, M. (1903/63). *Primitive Classification.* Cohen & West, London.

EIBL-EIBESFELD, I. (1973). *Love and Hate.* Methuen, London.

EISER, J. R. (1980). *Cognitive Social Psychology.* McGraw-Hill, London.

EKMAN, P. (ed.) (1973). *Darwin and Facial Expression.* Academic Press, New York and London.

ELLEN, R. F. (1977). Anatomical classification and the semiotics of the body. In *The Anthropology of the Body* (J. Blacking, ed.). Academic Press, London and New York.

ELLEN, R. and REASON, D. (eds) (1979). *Classification in Their Social Context.* Academic Press, London and New York.

EPSTEIN, A. L. (ed.) (1967). *The Craft of Social Anthropology.* Tavistock Publications, London.

EPSTEIN, A. L. (1969). *Matupit.* University of California Press, Berkeley, California.

EPSTEIN, A. L. (1978). *Ethos and Identity.* Tavistock Publications, London.

EPSTEIN, A. L. (1979). Tambu: The shell money of the Tolai. In *Fantasy and Symbol: Studies in Anthropological Interpretation* (R. H. Hook, ed.). Academic Press, London and New York.

EVANS-PRITCHARD, E. E. (1937). *Witchcraft, Oracles and Magic Among the Azande.* Clarendon Press, Oxford.

EVANS-PRITCHARD, E. E. (1951). *Social Anthropology.* Cohen & West, London.

EYSENCK, M. W. and EYSENCK, H. J. (1980). Mischel and the concept of personality. *British Journal of Psychology* **71**, 191–204.

FARR, R. M. (1978). On the varieties of social psychology. *Social Science Information* **17**, 503–25.

FELLOUS, M. (1976). The socialization of the child in a Bambara village (Mali). *Africa Development* **1**, 13–25.

FERNANDEZ, J. W. (1972). Fang representations under acculturation. In *Africa and the West* (P. D. Curtin, ed.). University of Wisconsin Press, Madison, Wisconsin.

FIRTH, R. (1939). *Primitive Polynesian Economy.* Routledge, London.

FIRTH, R. (1957a). *Man and Culture: An Evaluation of the Work of Bronislaw Malinowski.* Routledge & Kegan Paul, London.

FIRTH, R. (1957b). *We, the Tikopia,* 2nd ed. Allen & Unwin, London.

FIRTH, R. (1964). *Essays on Social Organization and Values.* University of London, The Athlone Press, London.

FIRTH, R. (1973). *Symbols, Public and Private.* Allen & Unwin, London.

FLAMENT, C. (1963). *Applications of Graph Theory to Group Structure.* Prentice Hall, Englewood Cliffs.

FORTES, M. (1957). Malinowski and the study of kinship. In *Man and Culture: An Evaluation of the Work of Bronislaw Malinowski* (R. Firth, ed.). Routledge & Kegan Paul, London.

FORTES, M. (1974). The first born. *Journal of Child Psychology and Psychiatry* **15**, 81–104.

FORTES, M. (1977). Custom and conscience in anthropological perspective. *International Review of Psychoanalysis* **4**, 127–54.

FOSTER, G. M. (1972). The anatomy of envy. *Current Anthropology* **13**, 165–202.

FRAKE, C. O. (1977). Playing frames can be dangerous: Some reflections on methodology in cognitive anthropology. *Quarterly Newsletter of the Institute for Comparative Human Development* **1**, 1–7.

FRAZER, J. G. (1922). *The Golden Bough* (abridged edition). Macmillan, London.

FRAZER, J. G. (1978). *The Illustrated Golden Bough.* Macmillan, London.

FREILICH. M. (ed.) (1972). *The Meaning of Culture.* Xerox College Publishing, Lexington, Massachusetts.

FREUD, S. (1919). *Totem and Taboo.* Routledge, London.

FROST, G. T. (1980). Tool behavior and the origins of laterality. *Journal of Human Evolution* **9**, 447–59.

FURTH, H. (1980). Piagetian perspectives. In *Developmental Psychology and Society* (J. Sants, ed.). Macmillan, London.

GALTON, SIR FRANCIS (1883–1928): *Inquiries into Human Faculty and Its Development.* Dent, London.

GANAY, S. DE (1949). Aspects de mythologie et de symbolique Bambara. *Journal de Psychologie Normale et Pathologique* **42**, 181–201.

GANAY, S. DE (1950). Graphies Bambara des nombres. *J. Soc. Afric.* **20**, 295–305.

GARDNER, H. (1979). Developmental psychology after Piaget: An approach in terms of symbolization. *Human Development* **22**, 73–88.

GARDNER, H., HOWARD, V. and PERKINS, D. (1974). Symbol systems. In *Media and Symbols* (D. R. Olson, ed.). University of Chicago Press, Chicago.

GAULD, A. and SHOTTER, J. (1977). *Human Action and Its Psychological Investigation.* Routledge & Kegan Paul, London, Henley and Boston.

GEERTZ, C. (1966). Religion as a cultural system. In *Anthropological Approaches to the Study of Religion* (M. Banton, ed.). Tavistock Publications, London.

GEERTZ, C. (1973). *The Interpretation of Cultures.* Basic Books, New York.

GELL, A. (1975). *Metamorphoses of the Cassowaries.* The Athlone Press, London.

GERARD, H. B. and CONOLLEY, E. S. (1972). Conformity. In *Experimental Social Psychology* (C. G. McClintock, ed.). Holt, Rinehart & Winston, New York.

GLADWIN, H. (1975). Looking for an aggregate additive model in data from a hierarchical decision process. In *Studies in Economic Anthropology* (G. Dalton, ed.). Anthropological Studies 7. American Anthropological Association, Washington, D.C.

GLUCKMAN, M. (1964). *Closed Systems and Open Minds*. Oliver & Boyd, Edinburgh and London.

GLUCKMAN, M. (1967). *The Judicial Process Among the Barotse of Northern Rhodesia*, 2nd ed. University Press, Manchester.

GLUCKMAN, M. (1968). Psychological, sociological, and anthropological explanations of witchcraft and gossip: A clarification. *Man* 3, 20–34.

GLUCKMAN, M. and EGGAN, F. (eds) (1965). *The Relevance of Models for Social Anthropology*. A.S.A. Monograph 1. Tavistock Publications, London.

GODELIER, M. (1977). *Perspectives in Marxist anthropology*. Cambridge University Press, Cambridge.

GOODENOUGH, W. (1964). Cultural anthropology and linguistics. In *Language in Culture and Society* (D. Hymes, ed.). Harper & Row, New York.

GOODENOUGH, W. (1965). Yankee kinship terminology: A problem in componential analysis. *American Anthropologist* 67, 259–87.

GOODY, E. (1972). 'Greeting', 'begging' and the presentation of respect. In *The Interpretation of Ritual* (J. S. La Fontaine, ed.). Tavistock Publications, London.

GOODY, J. (1977). *The Domestication of the Savage Mind*. Cambridge University Press, Cambridge.

GOULD, P. and WHITE, R. (1974). *Mental Maps*. Penguin, New York.

GRAVES, A. J. (1972). The attainment of conservation of mass, weight and volume in minimally educated adults. *Developmental Psychology* 7, 223.

GRIAULE, M. (1965). *Conversations with Ogotemmêli: An Introduction to Dogon Religious Ideas*. Oxford University Press, London.

HADDON, A. C. (1934). *History of Anthropology*. Watts & Co., London.

HALLOWELL, A. I. (1955). *Culture and Experience*. University of Pennsylvania Press, Philadelphia.

HALLOWELL, A. I. (1976). *Contributions to Anthropology*. University of Chicago Press, Chicago.

HALLPIKE, C. R. (1976). Is there a primitive mentality? *Man* 11, 253–70.

HALLPIKE, C. R. (1979). *The Foundations of Primitive Thought*. The Clarendon Press, Oxford.

HANSON, F. A. (1975). *Meaning in Culture*. Routledge & Kegan Paul, London.

HARRÉ, R. (1980). Man as Rhetorician. In *Models of Man* (A. J. Chapman and D. M. Jones, eds). The British Psychological Society, Leicester.

HARRINGTON, C. and WHITING, J. W. M. (1972). Socialization process and personality. In *Psychological Anthropology* (F. L. K. Hsu, ed.). Schenkman, Cambridge, Massachusetts.

HARRIS, M. (1968). *The Rise of Anthropological Theory: A History of Theories of Culture*. Routledge & Kegan Paul, London.

HARRIS, M. (1976). History and significance of the emic/etic distinction. *Annual Review of Anthropology* 5, 329–50.

HARRIS, P. and HEELAS, P. (1979). Cognitive processes and collective representations. *Archives Européennes de Sociologie* **20**, 211–41.

HEELAS, P. and LOCK, A. (1981). *Indigenous Psychologies: the Anthropology of the Self.* Academic Press, London and New York.

HEIDER, F. (1958). *The Psychology of Interpersonal Relations.* Wiley, New York.

HEINZ, H. J. and MAGUIRE, B. (n.d.). The ethnobiology of the Iko Bushmen. Botswana Society, Occasional Paper No. 1. Government Printer, Gaborone.

HELSON, R. and MITCHELL, V. (1978). Personality. In *Annual Review of Psychology* (M. R. Rosenzweig and L. W. Porter, eds). Annual Reviews Inc., Palo Alto.

HERRON, J. (ed.) (1979). *Neuropsychology of Left-Handedness.* Academic Press, New York and London.

HERZLICH, C. (1973). *Health and Illness.* Academic Press, London and New York.

HERZOG, J. D. (1973). Initiation and high school in the development of Kikuyu youths' self-concept. *Ethos* **1**, 478–89.

HOFSTADTER, R. (1972). History and the social sciences. In *The Varieties of History* (F. Stern, ed.). World Publishing Company, New York.

HOGBIN, H. I. (1946). A New Guinea childhood. *Oceania* **16**, 275–96.

HOLY, L. and STUCHLIK, M. (eds) (1981). *The Structure of Folk Models.* A.S.A. Monograph 20. Academic Press, London and New York.

HONIGMANN, J. J. (1967). *Personality in Culture.* Harper & Row, New York.

HONIGMANN, J. J. (1975). Psychological anthropology: Trends, accomplishments and future tasks. In *Psychological Anthropology* (T. R. Williams, ed.). Mouton, The Hague.

HORTON, R. (1970). African traditional thought and Western science. In *Rationality* (B. R. Wilson, ed.). Blackwell, Oxford.

HORTON, R. (1973). Lévy-Bruhl, Durkheim and the scientific revolution. In *Modes of Thought* (R. Horton and R. Finnegan, eds). Faber, London.

HORTON, R. and FINNEGAN, R. (eds) (1973). *Modes of Thought.* Faber, London.

HSU, F. L. K. (1961). *Psychological Anthropology.* Dorsey, Homewood, Illinois; Schenkman (1972), Cambridge.

HUNN, E. (1976). Toward a perceptual model of folk classification. *American Ethnologist* **3**, 508–24.

HUNN, E. (1979). The Abominations of Leviticus Revisited. In *Classifications in Their Social Context* (R. F. Ellen and D. Reason, eds). Academic Press, London and New York.

HUTCHINS, E. (1979). Reasoning in Trobriand discourse. *Q. Newsl. Lab. hum. Cognition* **1**, 13–17.

HUTCHINS, E. (1980). *Culture and Inference.* Harvard University Press, Cambridge, Massachusetts.

IMPERATO, P. J. (1977). *African Folk Medicine.* York Press, Baltimore.

IRVINE, J. T. (1974). Strategies of status manipulation in the Wolof greeting. In *Explorations in the Ethnography of Speaking* (R. Bauman and J. Sherzer, eds). Cambridge University Press, Cambridge.

JACKSON, D. N. and PAUNONEN, S. V. (1980). Personality Structure and assessment. In *Annual Review of Psychology* (M. R. Rosenzweig and L. W. Porter, eds), vol. 31. Annual Reviews, Palo Alto, California.

JAHODA, G. (1954). A note on Ashanti day names in relation to personality. *British Journal of Psychology* **45**, 192–5.

JAHODA, G. (1961). Traditional healers and other institutions concerned with mental illness in Ghana. *International Journal of Social Psychiatry* **7**, 245–68.

JAHODA, G. (1969). *The Psychology of Superstition.* Allen Lane, London.

JAHODA, G. (1970). A psychologist's perspective. In *Socialization* (P. Mayer, ed.). Tavistock Publications, London.

JAHODA, G. (1977). In pursuit of the emic–etic distinction. In *Basic Problems in Cross-Cultural Psychology* (Y. H. Poortinga, ed.). Swets & Zeitlinger, Amsterdam.

JAHODA, G. (1979). A cross-cultural perspective in social psychology. *Personality and Social Psychology Bulletin* **5**, 142–8.

JAHODA, G. (1980). Cross-cultural comparisons. In *Comparative Methods in Psychology* (M. H. Bornstein, ed.). Lawrence Erlbaum, Hillsdale, New Jersey.

JAHODA, M. (1977). *Freud and the Dilemmas of Psychology.* Hogarth Press, London.

JAHODA, M. (1980). One Model of Man or Many? In *Models of Man* (A. J. Chapman and D. M. Jones, eds). The British Psychological Society, Leicester.

JOHNSON, A. W. (1978). *Research Methods in Social Anthropology.* Edward Arnold, London.

DE JONG, P. E. (1967). The participants' view of their culture. In *Anthropologists in the Field* (P. C. W. Gutkind and D. G. Jongmans, eds). Humanities Press, New York.

JUNG, C. G. (1953). *Psychological Reflections: An Anthology of Writings.* Harper & Row, New York.

KARDINER, A. (1939). *The Individual and His Society.* Columbia University Press, New York.

KARDINER, A. (1945). *The Psychological Frontiers of Society.* Columbia University Press, New York.

KARDINER, A. (1959). Psychosocial studies. *Science* **130**, 1728.

KARDINER, A. and PREBLE, E. (1961). *They Studied Man.* Mentor, New York.

KEESING, R. M. (1972). Paradigms lost: The new ethnography and the new linguistics. *Southwestern Journal of Anthropology* **28**, 299–332.

KELLY, G. A. (1955). *The Psychology of Personal Constructs.* 2 vols. Norton, New York.

KENNEDY, J. G. (1967). Psychological and social explanations of witchcraft. *Man* **2**, 216–25.

KEYS, A., BROZEK, J., HENSCHEL, A., MICKELSEN, O. and TAYLOR, H. L. (1950). *The Biology of Human Starvation.* Vol. II. University of Minnesota Press, Minneapolis.

KIDD, D. (1905). *The Essential Kaffir.* Adam & Charles Black, London. Cited in L. E. Andor: *Aptitudes and Abilities of the Black Man in Sub-Saharan Africa, 1784–1963.* National Institute for Personnel Research, Johannesburg.

KIDD, D. (1906). *Savage Childhood: A Study of Kafir Children.* A. & C. Black, London.

KLEIN, M. (1957). *Envy and Gratitude: A Study of Unconscious Sources.* Basic Books, New York.

KLINE, P. (1977). Cross-cultural studies and Freudian theory. In *Studies in Cross-Cultural Psychology* (N. Warren, ed.), vol. 1. Academic Press, London and New York.

KLUCKHOHN, C. (1959). Common humanity, diverse cultures. In *The Human Meaning of the Social Sciences* (D. Lerner, ed.). Meridian, New York.

KORTLAND, A. (1972). *New Perspectives on Ape and Human Evolution.* Stichting voor Psychobiologie, Amsterdam.

KROEBER, A. L. (1909). Classificatory systems of relationship. *Journal of the Royal Anthropological Institute* **39**, 77–84.

LABARRE, W. (1958). The influence of Freud on anthropology. *American Imago* **15**, 275–328.

LABOUVIE-VIEF, G. (1977). Adult cognitive development: In search of alternative interpretations. *Merrill-Palmer Quarterly* **23**, 227–63.

LANCY, D. and TINDALL, B. A. (eds) (1976). *The Anthropological Study of Play.* Leisure Press, Cornwall, New York.

LANGER, E. J. (1977). The psychology of chance. *Journal for the Theory of Social Behavior* **7**, 185–208.

LAWRENCE, P. (1964). *Road Belong Cargo.* Manchester University Press, Manchester.

LEACH, E. R. (1967). An anthropologist's reflections on a social survey. In *Anthropologists in the Field* (P. C. W. Gutkind and D. G. Jongmans, eds). Humanities Press, New York.

LEACH, E. R. (1970). *Lévi-Strauss.* Fontana, London.

LEACH, E. R. (1976). *Culture and Communication.* Cambridge University Press, Cambridge.

LEMAITRE, Y. (1977). Tahitian ethnozoological classification and fuzzy logic. In *Language and Thought* (W. C. McCormack and S. A. Wurm, eds). Mouton, The Hague.

LEVINE, R. A. (1973). *Culture, Behaviour and Personality.* Hutchinson, London.

LEVINE, R. A. (1981). Psychoanalytic theory and the comparative study of human development. In *Handbook of Cross-Cultural Human Development* (R. H. and R. L. Munroe and B. B. Whiting, eds). Garland Press, New York.

LEVINE, R. A. and PRICE-WILLIAMS, D. R. (1974). Children's kinship concepts: Cognitive development and early experience among the Hausa. *Ethnology* **13**, 25–44.

LÉVI-STRAUSS, C. (1955). *Tristes Tropiques.* Plon, Paris.

LÉVI-STRAUSS, C. (1962). *La Pensée Sauvage.* Plon, Paris.

LÉVI-STRAUSS, C. (1963). *Structural Anthropology.* Basic Books, New York.

LÉVI-STRAUSS, C. (1966). *The Savage Mind.* University of Chicago Press, Chicago.

LÉVI-STRAUSS, C. (1969). *The Elementary Structures of Kinship.* Beacon Press, Boston.

LÉVI-STRAUSS, C. (1971). *L'Homme Nu*. Plon, Paris.

LÉVI-STRAUSS, C. (1978). *Myth and Meaning*. Routledge & Kegan Paul, London.

LEVY, J. (1976). A review of the evidence for a genetic component in the determination of handedness. *Behavior Genetics* 6, 429–53.

LÉVY-BRUHL, L. (1910–51). *Les Fonctions Mentales dans les Sociétés Inférieures.* Presses Universitaires de France, Paris.

LÉVY-BRUHL, L. (1922). *La Mentalité Primitive*. Alcan, Paris.

LÉVY-BRUHL, L. (1938). *L'Expérience Mystique et les Symboles chez les Primitifs.* Alcan, Paris.

LÉVY-BRUHL, L. (1949). *Les Carnets de Lucien Lévy-Bruhl*. Presses Universitaires de France, Paris.

LEWIN, K. (1947). Group decisions and social change. In *Readings in Social Psychology* (T. M. Newcomb and E. L. Hartley, eds). Holt, New York.

LEWIN, K., LIPPITT, R. and WIIITE, R. K. (1939). Patterns of aggressive behavior in experimentally created "social climates". *Journal of Social Psychology* 10, 271–99.

LEWIS, D. (1976). Observations on route finding and spatial orientation among the Aboriginal peoples of the Western Desert region of Central Australia. *Oceania* 46, 249–82.

LEWIS, I. M. (1966). Spirit possession and deprivation cults. *Man* 1, 307–29.

LEWIS, I. M. (ed.) (1977). *Symbols and Sentiments: Cross-Cultural Studies in Symbolism.* Academic Press, London and New York.

LINDZEY, G. (1961). *Projective Techniques and Cross-Cultural Research.* Appleton-Century, New York.

LLOYD, B. (1977). Culture and colour coding. In *Communication and Understanding* (G. Vessey, ed.). Harvester Press, Sussex.

LONNER, W. J. (1980). The search for psychological universals. In *Handbook of Cross-Cultural Psychology* (H. C. Triandis and W. W. Lambert, eds), vol. I. Allyn & Bacon, Boston.

LOWIE, R. H. (1937). *The History of Ethnological Theory*. Holt, Rinehart & Winston, New York.

LUCY, J. A. and SHWEDER, R. A. (1979). Whorf and his critics: Linguistic and nonlinguistic influences on color memory. *American Anthropologist* 81, 581–615.

LUKES, S. (1973). *Émile Durkheim: His Life and Work*. Allen Lane, London.

LUMSDEN, C. J. and WILSON, E. O. (1981). *Genes, Mind and Culture*. Harvard University Press, Cambridge, Massachusetts.

MAKHLOUF, C. (1979). *Changing Veils*. Croom Helm, London.

MALINOWSKI, B. (1926). *Crime and Custom in Savage Society*. Kegan Paul, London.

MALINOWSKI, B. (1927). *Sex and Repression in a Savage Society*. Routledge, London.

MALINOWSKI, B. (1931). *Culture: Encyclopaedia of the Social Sciences*. Macmillan, New York.

MALINOWSKI, B. (1944). *A Scientific Theory of Culture and Other Essays*. University of North Carolina Press, Chapel Hill.

MALINOWSKI, B. (1967). *Diary in the Strict Sense of the Term.* Harcourt Brace, New York.

MANNERS, R. A. and KAPLAN, D. (eds) (1968). *Theory in Anthropology: A Sourcebook.* Aldine, Chicago.

MAUSS, M. (1925/54). *The Gift.* Free Press, Glencoe.

MEAD, M. (1928). *Coming of Age in Samoa.* Morrow, New York.

MEAD, M. (1935). *Sex and Temperament in Three Primitive Societies.* Routledge, London; Mentor (1950), New York.

MERLEAU-PONTY, M. (1962). *Phenomenology of Perception.* Humanities Press, New York.

MIDDLETON, J. (1970a). *The Study of the Lugbara: Expectation and Paradox in Anthropological Research.* Holt, Rinehart & Winston, New York.

MIDDLETON, J. (ed.) (1970b). *From Child to Adult.* The Natural History Press, New York.

MILGRAM, S. S. (1974). *Obedience to Authority.* Harper & Row, New York.

MILL, J. S. (1879). *A System of Logic,* vol. II. 10th ed. Longmans, Green & Co., London.

MILLER, G. A., GALANTER, E. and PRIBRAM, K. (1960). *Plans and the Structure of Behavior.* Holt, Rinehart & Winston, New York.

MINTURN, L. and LAMBERT, W. W. (1964). *Mothers of Six Cultures.* Wiley, New York.

MISCHEL, W. (1979). On the interface of cognition and personality. *American Psychologist* **34**, 740–54.

MITCHELL, J. C. (ed.) (1969). *Social Networks in Urban Situations: Analyses of Personal Relationships in Central African Towns.* Manchester University Press, Manchester.

MOLES, J. A. (1977). Standardization and measurement in cultural anthropology: A neglected area. *Current Anthropology* **18**, 235–58.

MOORE, F. C. T. (1969). *See* Degérando (1800/1969).

MORGAN, L. H. (1877). *Ancient Society.* Henry Holt, New York.

MORGULIS, S. (1923). *Fasting and Undernutrition.* Dutton, New York.

MORRIS, B. (1976). Whither the savage mind? *Man* **11**, 542–57.

MOSCOVICI, S. (1961). *La Psychoanalyse: son Image et son Public.* Presses Universitaires de France, Paris.

MOSCOVICI, S. (1981). On social representations. In *Social Cognition: Perspectives on Everyday Understanding* (J. P. Forgas, ed.). Academic Press, London and New York.

MUKASA, H. (1975). *Sir Apolo Kagwa Discovers Britain* (Taban lo Liyong, ed.). Heinemann, London.

MUNROE, R. H., MUNROE, R. L. and WHITING, B. B. (eds) (1981). *Handbook of Cross-Cultural Human Development.* Garland Press, New York.

MUNROE, R. L. and MUNROE, R. H. (1975). *Cross-Cultural Human Development.* Brooks-Cole, Monterey, California.

MURDOCK, G. P. (1949). *Social Structure.* Macmillan, New York.

MURDOCK, G. P. (1975). *Outline of World Cultures.* 5th ed. Human Relations Area Files, New Haven.

MURDOCK, G. P., FORD, C. S., HUDSON, A. E., KENNEDY, R., SIMMONS, L. W. and WHITING, J. W. M. (1971). *Outline of Cultural Materials.* 4th ed. Human Relations Area Files, New Haven.

MURPHY, R. G. (1971). *The Dialectics of Social Life: Alarms and Excursions in Anthropological Theory.* Allen & Unwin, London.

MUSCHINSKE, D. (1977). The non-white as a child: G. Stanley Hall on the education of non-white peoples. *Journal of the History of the Behavioral Sciences* **13**, 328–36.

NADEL, S. F. (1942). *A Black Byzantium.* Oxford University Press, London.

NADEL, S. F. (1951). *The Foundations of Social Anthropology.* Cohen & West, London.

NADEL, S. F. (1977). Magic thinking. *Canberra Anthropology* **1**, 1–14.

NAROLL, R. (1973). Galton's problem. In *A Handbook of Method in Cultural Anthropology* (R. Naroll and R. Cohen, eds). Columbia University Press, New York.

NAROLL, R., MICHIK, G. L. and NAROLL, F. (1976). *Worldwide Theory Testing.* Human Relations Area Files, New Haven.

NASH, D. and WINTROB, R. (1972). The emergence of self-consciousness in ethnography. *Current Anthropology* **13**, 527–42.

NEEDHAM, R. (1962). *Structure and Sentiment.* University of Chicago Press, Chicago, Illinois.

NEEDHAM, R. (1972). *Belief, Language, and Experience.* Basil Blackwell, Oxford; University of Chicago Press (1972), Chicago.

NEEDHAM, R. (1973). *Right and Left.* University of Chicago Press, Chicago.

NEEDHAM, R. (1979). *Symbolic Classification.* Goodyear, Santa Monica, California.

NEEDHAM, R. (1980). *Reconnaissances.* University of Toronto Press, Toronto.

NEISSER, U. (1967). *Cognitive Psychology.* Appleton-Century-Crofts, New York.

NEISSER, U. (1975). *Cognition and Reality.* Freeman, San Francisco.

NEISSER, U. (1980). On "social knowing". *Personality and Social Psychology Bulletin* **6**, 601–5.

NERLOVE, S. B., ROBERTS, J. M., KLEIN, R. E., YARBOROUGH, C. and HABICHT, J.-P. (1974). Natural indicators of cognitive development: An observational study of rural Guatemalan children. *Ethos* **2**, 265–95.

NIKOL'SKII, V. K. (1976). "Prelogical Thought": Lévy-Bruhl's working hypothesis. *Soviet Psychology* **14**, 21–39.

NISBETT, R. and ROSS, L. (1980). *Human Inference: Strategies and Shortcomings of Social Judgement.* Prentice-Hall, Englewood Cliffs, New Jersey.

NORTHROP, F. S. C. and LIVINGSTON, H. H. (eds) (1964). *Cross-Cultural Understanding: Epistemology in Anthropology.* Harper & Row, New York.

ORTIZ, S. (1973). *Uncertainties in Peasant Farming: A Colombian Case.* The Athlone Press, University of London; Humanities Press, New York.

ORTIZ, S. (1979). Expectations and forecasts in the face of uncertainty. *Man* **14**, 64–80.

ORTONY, A. (ed.) (1979). *Metaphor and Thought.* Cambridge University Press, Cambridge.

ORTONY, A., REYNOLDS, R. E. and ARTER, J. A. (1978). Metaphor: Theoretical and empirical research. *Psychological Bulletin* **85**, 919–43.

OSGOOD, C. E. (1979). From *Yang* and *Yin* to *And* or *But* in cross-cultural perspective. *International Journal of Psychology* **14**, 1–35.

OSGOOD, C. E., MAY, W. H. and MIRON, S. (1975). *Cross-Cultural Universals of Affective Meaning.* University of Illinois Press, Urbana, Illinois.

OSHERON, D. N. and SMITH, E. E. (1981). On the adequacy of prototype theory as a theory of concepts. *Cognition* **9**, 35–58.

PAIVIO, A. (1979). Psychological processes in the understanding of metaphor. In *Metaphor and Thought* (A. Ortony, ed.). Cambridge University Press, Cambridge.

PAQUES, V. (1954). *Les Bambara.* Presses Universitaires de France, Paris.

PARSONS, A. (1964). Is the Oedipus complex universal? In *The Psychoanalytic Study of Society* (W. Muensterberger and S. Axelrad, eds), vol. 3. International University Press, New York.

PAUL, R. A. (1976). The Sherpa temple as a model of the psyche. *American Ethnologist* **3**, 131–46.

PEDERSEN, P. (1979). Non-Western psychology: The search for alternatives. In *Perspectives on Cross-Cultural Psychology* (A. J. Marsalla, R. G. Tharp and T. J. Ciborowski, eds). Academic Press, New York and London.

PELTO, P. J. (1970). *Anthropological Research: The Structure of Inquiry.* Harper & Row, New York.

PIAGET, J. (1965). *Études sociologiques.* Droz, Genève.

PIAGET, J. (1966). Necessité et signification des recherches comparatives en psychologie genetique. *International Journal of Psychology* **1**, 3–13.

PIAGET, J. (1971). *Structuralism.* Routledge & Kegan Paul, London.

PIDDINGTON, R. (1957). Malinowski's theory of needs. In *Man and Culture: An Evaluation of the Work of Bronislaw Malinowski* (R. Firth, ed.). Routledge & Kegan Paul, London.

PIKE, K. L. (1954). *Language in Relation to a Unified Theory of the Structure of Human Behavior. Part I.* Summer Institute of Linguistics, Glendale, California.

PIKE, K. L. (1966). *Language in Relation to a Unified Theory of the Structure of Human Behavior.* Mouton, The Hague.

PITT-RIVERS, J. (1977). *The Fate of Shechem.* Cambridge University Press, Cambridge.

POCOCK, D. F. (1973). *Mind, Body and Wealth: A Study of Belief and Practice in an Indian Village.* Basil Blackwell, Oxford.

PRICE-WILLIAMS, D. R. (1980). Anthropological approaches to cognition and their relevance to psychology. In *Handbook of Cross-Cultural Psychology* (H. Triandis, ed.), vol. 3. Allyn & Bacon, Boston.

QUINN, N. (1978). Do Mfantse fish sellers estimate probabilities in their heads? *American Ethnologist* **5**, 206–26.

RABAIN, J. (1979). *L'Enfant du Lignage.* Payot, Paris.

RADCLIFFE-BROWN, A. R. (1922/64). *The Andaman Islanders*. The Free Press, Glencoe, Illinois.

RADCLIFFE-BROWN, A. R. (1952). *Structure and Function in Primitive Society*. Cohen & West, London.

RANDALL, R. A. (1976). How tall is the taxonomic tree? Some evidence for dwarfism. *American Ethnologist* 3, 543–53.

RAPPAPORT, R. A. (1968). *Pigs for the Ancestors: Ritual in the Ecology of a New Guinea People*. Yale University Press, New Haven.

RATTRAY, R. S. (1923). *Ashanti*. Clarendon Press, Oxford.

RATZEL, F. (1896). *The History of Mankind*. Macmillan, London.

RAY, V. F. (1952). Techniques and problems in the study of human color perception. *Southwestern Journal of Anthropology* 8, 251–9.

READ, M. (1959). *Children of Their Fathers*. Methuen, London.

REICHEL-DOLMATOFF, G. (1976). Cosmology as ecological analysis: A view from the rain forest. *Man* 11, 307–18.

REICHEL-DOLMATOFF, G. and REICHEL-DOLMATOFF, A. (1961). *The People of Aritama: The Cultural Personality of a Colombian Mesitzo Village*. Routledge & Kegan Paul, London.

RICHARDS, A. I. (1932). *Hunger and Work in a Savage Tribe*. Routledge & Kegan Paul, London.

RICHARDS, A. I. (1939). *Land, Labour and Diet in Northern Rhodesia*. Oxford University Press, Oxford.

RICHARDS, A. I. (1956). *Chisungu*. Faber, London.

RICHARDS, A. I. (1957). The concept of culture in Malinowski's work. In *Man and Culture: An Evaluation of the Work of Bronislaw Malinowski* (R. Firth, ed.). Routledge & Kegan Paul, London.

RICHARDS, A. I. (1964). Authority patterns in traditional Buganda. In *The King's Men* (L. A. Fallers, ed.). Oxford University Press, London.

RITZER, G., KAMMEYER, K. C. W. and YETMAN, W. R. (1979). *Sociology*. Allyn & Bacon, Boston.

RIVERS, W. H. R. (1906–67). *The Todas*. Anthropological Publications, Oosterhout.

RIVERS, W. H. R. (1901). Vision. In *Physiology and Psychology, Part 1*. Reports of the Cambridge Anthropological Expedition to Torres Straits, vol. 2. Cambridge University Press, Cambridge.

RIVERS, W. H. R. (1914). *Kinship and Social Organization*. Constable, London.

RIVERS, W. H. R. (1926). *Psychology and Ethnology*. Kegan Paul, Trench, Trubner & Co., London.

ROGERS, R. (1978). *Metaphor*. University of California Press, Berkeley, California.

ROGOFF, B., SELLERS, M. J., PIRROTTA, S., FOX, N. and WHITE, S. H. (1975). Age of assignment of roles and responsibilities to children. *Human Development* 18, 353–69.

ROHEIM, G. (1943). *The Origin and Function of Culture*. Nervous and Mental Disease Monographs, no. 69. Johnson Reprint Corporation, New York.

ROHEIM, G. (1947). Psychoanalysis and anthropology. In *Psychoanalysis and the Social Sciences* (G. Roheim, ed.). International Universities Press, New York.

ROHNER, R. P. (1975). Parental acceptance–rejection and personality development: A universalistic approach to behavioral science. In *Cross-Cultural Perspectives on Learning* (R. W. Brislin, S. Bochner and W. J. Lohner, eds). Wiley, New York.

ROMNEY, K. A. and D'ANDRADE, R. G. (1964). Cognitive aspects of English kin terms. *American Anthropologist* **66**, 146–70.

ROSCH, E. (1977). Human Categorization. In *Studies in Cross-Cultural Psychology* (N. Warren, ed.), vol. 1. Academic Press, London and New York.

ROSCH, E. (1978). Principles of categorization. In *Cognition and Categorization* (E. Rosch and B. B. Lloyd, eds). Erlbaum, New York.

ROSCH, E., MERVIS, C. B., GRAY, W. D., JOHNSON, D. M. and BOYES-BRAEM, P. (1976). Basic objects in natural categories. *Cognitive Psychology* **8**, 382–439.

ROSS, E. B. (1978). Food taboos, diet, and hunting strategy: The adaptation to animals in Amazon cultural ecology. *Current Anthropology* **19**, 1–36.

ROSSI, I. (1974). Structure and history in 'The elementary structures of kinship'. In *The Unconscious in Culture* (I. Rossi, ed.). Dutton, New York.

ROY, M. (1976). The oedipus complex and the Bengali family in India. In *Psychological Anthropology* (T. R. Williams, ed.). Mouton, The Hague.

RYCROFT, C. (1977). Is Freudian symbolism a myth? In *Symbols and Sentiments* (I. Lewis, ed.). Academic Press, London and New York.

RYNKIEWICH, M. A. and SPRADLEY, J. P. (1976). *Ethics and Anthropology.* Wiley, New York.

SAHLINS, M. (1976). Colors and cultures. *Semiotica* **16**, 1–22.

SALMON, M. H. (1978). Do Azande and Nuer use a non-standard logic? *Man* **13**, 444–54.

SCHAEFER, J. M. (1977). The growth of hologeistic studies: 1889–1975. *Behaviour Science Research* **12**, 71–108.

SCHAEFER, H. R. (1980). Parental control techniques in the context of socialisation theory. Paper presented at the European colloquium on Social Development, Urbino, Italy.

SCHILDKROUT, E. (1978). Roles of children in Urban Kano. In *Sex and Age as Principles of Social Differentiation* (J. S. La Fontaine, ed.). Academic Press, London and New York.

SCHWARTZ, T. (1981). The acquisition of culture. *Ethos* **9**, 4–17.

SCHWARTZMAN, H. B. (1978). *Transformations: The Anthropology of Children's Play.* Plenum, New York.

SCHWIMMER, E. (ed.) (1978). *The Yearbook of Symbolic Anthropology* (I). Hurst, London.

SEGALL, M. H. (1979). *Cross-Cultural Psychology: Human Behavior in Global Perspective.* Brooks-Cole, Monterey, California.

SELBY, H. A. (1975). Semantics and causality in the study of deviance. In *Language, Thought, and Culture* (M. Sanches and B. G. Blout, eds). Academic Press, New York and London.

SERPELL, R. (1976). *Culture's Influence on Behavior.* Methuen, London.

SHALIT, B. (1980). The golden section relation in the evaluation of environmental factors. *British Journal of Psychology* **71**, 39–42.

SHOTTER, J. (1975). *Images of Man in Psychological Research.* Methuen, London.

SHWEDER, R. A. (1977). Likeness and likelihood in everyday thought:
Magical thinking in judgements of personality. *Current Anthropology* **18**,
637–58.

SHWEDER, R. A. (1979a). Rethinking culture and personality theory. Part I:
A critical examination of two classical postulates. *Ethos* **7**, 255–78.

SHWEDER, R. A. (1979b). Rethinking culture and personality. Part II: A
critical examination of two more classical postulates. *Ethos* **7**, 279–311.

SHWEDER, R. A. (1980). Rethinking culture and personality. Part III: From
genesis and typology to hermeneutics and dynamics. *Ethos* **8**, 60–94.

SIDIBE, M. (1929). Les sorciers mangeurs d'hommes. *Outre-Mer* **1**, 22–31.

SILVER, M. and SABINI, J. (1978). The perception of envy. *Social Psychology*
41, 105–17.

SINNOTT, J. D. (1975). Everyday thinking and Piagetian operativity in
adults. *Human Development* **18**, 430–43.

SLOBODIN, R. (1978). *W. H. R. Rivers.* Columbia University Press, New
York.

SMITH, M. B., BRUNER, J. S. and WHITE, R. W. (1956). *Opinions and
Personality.* Wiley, New York.

SOUTHWOLD, M. (1979). Religious belief. *Man* **14**, 628–44.

SPERBER, D. (1975). Pourquoi les animaux parfaits, les hybrides et les
monstres sont-ils bons à penser symboliquement? *L'Homme* **15**, 5–34.

SPERBER, D. (1980). Is symbolic thought pre-rational? In *Symbol as Sense: New
Approaches to the Analysis of Meaning* (M. L. Foster and S. H. Brandes, eds).
Academic Press, London and New York.

SPINDLER, GEORGE D. (ed.) (1970). *Being an Anthropologist.* Holt, Rinehart &
Winston, New York.

STOCKING, G. (1965). From physics to ethnology: Franz Boas' Arctic
expedition. *Journal of the History of the Behavioral Sciences* **1**, 53–66.

STURTEVANT, W. C. (1964). Studies in ethnoscience. In *Transcultural Studies
in Cognition. Special Issue of American Anthropologist* (A. K. Romney and R.
G. d'Andrade, eds), 66, Part 2.

SUGGS, R. C. (1971). Sex and personality in the Marquesas. In *Human Sexual
Behavior: Variations in the Ethnographic Spectrum* (D. S. Marshall and R. C.
Suggs, eds). Basic Books, New York.

SUPER, C. M. (1981). Behavioral development in infancy. In *Handbook of
Cross-Cultural Development* (R. H. Munroe, R. L. Munroe and B. B.
Whiting, eds). Garland, New York.

TAJFEL, H. (ed.) (1978). *Differentiation between Social Groups: Studies in the Social
Psychology of Intergroup Relations.* Academic Press, London and New York.

TAJFEL, H. (1981). *Human Groups and Social Categories.* The University Press,
Cambridge.

TAMBIAH, S. J. (1969). Animals are good to think and good to prohibit.
Ethnology **8**, 423–59.

TAMBIAH, S. J. (1973). Form and meaning of magical acts. In *Modes of Thought* (R. Horton and R. Finnegan, eds). Faber & Faber, London.

TAUXIER, L. (1927). *La Religion Bambara.* Paul Geuthner, Paris.

THOMAS, L. L., KRONEFELD, J. Z. and KRONEFELD, D. B. (1976). Asdiwal crumbles: A critique of Lévi-Straussian myth analysis. *American Ethnologist* 3, 147–73.

TIGER, L. and FOX, R. (1974). *The Imperial Animal.* Paladin, London.

TOLMAN, E. C. (1951). *Behavior and Psychological Man.* University of California Press, Berkeley, California.

TURNBULL, C. M. (1972). *The Mountain People.* Simon & Schuster, New York.

TURNER, D. H. (1974). Tradition and Transformation. Social Anthropology Studies No. 8. Australian Institute of Aboriginal Studies, Canberra.

TURNER, D. H. (1978). Ideology and elementary structures. *Anthropologica* 20, 223–48.

TURNER, D. H. (1979). Behind the myths. In *Challenging Anthropology* (D. H. Turner and G. A. Smith, eds). McGraw-Hill, Toronto.

TURNER, T. (1973). Piaget's structuralism. *American Anthropologist* 75, 351–73.

TURNER, V. W. (1957). *Schism and Continuity in an African Society.* Manchester University Press, Manchester.

TURNER, V. W. (1967). *The Forest of Symbols.* Cornell University Press, Ithaca, New York.

TURNER, V. W. (1968). *The Drums of Affliction.* Clarendon Press, Oxford.

TURNER, V. W. (1978). Encounter with Freud: The making of a comparative symbologist. In *The Making of Psychological Anthropology* (G. D. Spindler, ed.). University of California Press, Berkeley, California.

TUZIN, D. F. (1972). Yam symbolism in the Sepik: An interpretative Account. *Southwestern Journal of Anthropology* 28, 230–54.

TVERSKY, A. (1969). Intransitivity of preference. *Psychological Review* 76, 31–48.

TVERSKY, A. (1972). Elimination by aspects: A theory of choice. *Psychological Review* 79, 381–299.

TVERSKY, A. (1977). Features of similarity. *Psychological Review* 84, 327–52.

TYLER, S. A. (ed.) (1969). *Cognitive Anthropology.* Holt, Rinehart & Winston, New York.

TYLOR, E. B. (1865). *Researches into the Early History of Mankind and the Development of Civilization.* John Murray, London.

TYLOR, E. B. (1958). *The Origins of Culture.* Harper & Row, New York.

UBEROI, S. J. P. (1962). *The Politics of the Kula Ring.* Manchester University Press, Manchester.

VALLE, R. S. and KING, M. (eds) (1978). *Existential–Phenomenological Alternatives for Psychology.* Oxford University Press, New York.

VANSINA, J. (1965). *Oral Traditions.* Routledge & Kegal Paul, London.

VELSEN, J. VAN (1964). *The Politics of Kinship.* Manchester University Press, Manchester.

VERMEULEN, C. J. J. and DE RUIJTER, A. (1975). Dominant epistemological presuppositions in the use of the cross-cultural survey method. *Current Anthropology* 16, 29–52.

VONNEGUT, K., Jr (1976). *Wampeters Foma and Granfalloons.* Dell, New York.

WALLACE, A. F. C. (1961). *Culture and Personality.* Random House, New York (2nd revised edition, 1970).

WARREN, N. (1980). Universality and plasticity, ontogeny and phylogeny: The resonance between culture and cognitive development. In *Developmental Psychology and Society* (J. Sants, cd.). Macmillan, London.

WEISNER, T. S. and GALLIMORE, R. (1977). My brother's keeper: Child and sibling caretaking. *Current Anthropology* 18, 169–90.

WERNER, E. E. (1979). *Cross-Cultural Child Development.* Brooks-Cole, Monterey, California.

WERNER, H. (1957). *Comparative Psychology of Mental Development.* Revised edition. International Universities Press, New York.

WERNER, H. and KAPLAN, B. (1963). *Symbol Formation.* Wilcy, New York.

WHITING, B. B. (ed.) (1963). *Six Cultures: Studies of Child Rearing.* Wiley, New York.

WHITING, B. B. and WHITING, J. W. M. (1975). *Children of Six Cultures.* Harvard University Press, Cambridge, Massachusetts.

WHITING, J. W. M. (1959). Sorcery, sin and the superego. In *Nebraska Symposium on Motivation* (M. R. Jones, ed.). University of Nebraska Press, Lincoln, Nebraska.

WHITING, J. W. M. and CHILD, I. L. (1953). *Child Training and Personality.* Yale University Press, New Haven, Connecticut.

WHITING, J. W. M., KLUCKHOHN, R. and ANTHONY, A. (1958) The function of male initiation ceremonies at puberty. In *Readings in Social Psychology* (E. E. Maccoby, T. M. Newcomb and E. L. Hartley, eds). Holt, New York.

WHITING, J. W. M., CHILD, I. L., LAMBERT, W. W. *et al.* (1966). *Field Guide for a Study of Socialization.* Six Cultures Series, vol. 1. Wiley, New York.

WILKES, K. V. (1980). Brain states. *British Journal for the Philosophy of Science* 31, 111–29.

WILLIAMS, T. R. (ed.) (1975). *Psychological Anthropology.* Mouton, The Hague.

WILLIS, R. G. (1974). *Man and Beast.* Hart-Davies, London.

WILLIS, R. (ed.) (1975). *The Interpretation of Symbolism.* Malaby Press, London.

WITTGENSTEIN, L. (1961). *Tractatus Logico-Philosophicus.* Routledge & Kegan Paul, London.

WUNDT, W. (1916). *The Elements of Folk Psychology.* Allen & Unwin, London.

YALMAN, N. (1968). Magic. In *International Encyclopaedia of the Social Sciences* (D. L. Sills, ed.). Macmillan, New York.

YERKES, R. M. (1943). *Chimpanzees.* Yale University Press, New Haven.

YOUNG, F. W. (1965). *Initiation Ceremonies.* Bobbs-Merrill, Indianapolis.

ZAHAN, D. (1951). Études sur la cosmologie des Dogon et des Bambara du Soudan Francais. *Africa* 21, 13–20.

ZAJONC, R. B. (1980). Feeling and thinking: preferences need no inferences. *American Psychologist* 35, 151–75.

ZANDER, A. (1979). The psychology of group processes. *Annual Review of Psychology* **30**, 417–51.

ZEMPLENI-RABAIN, J. (1973). Food and the strategy involved in learning fraternal exchange among Wolof children. In *French Perspectives in African Studies* (P. Alexandre, ed.). Oxford University Press, London.

ZIMBARDO, P. G. (1969). *The Cognitive Control of Motivation.* Scott Foresman, Glenview, Illinois.

Index of Names

A

Adams-Webber, J., 265
d'Andrade, R. G., 242
Argyle, M., 155–6
Ashton, P. T., 228
Auden, W. H., 274

B

Badcock, C. R., 14
Bailey, F. J., 147, 160, 162
Bain, A., 18
Barnes, J. A., 139
Barnouw, V., 106
Barry, H., 120, 137, 139
Barth, F., 108
Bartlett, F. C., 152, 175, 245
Bastian, A., 11–13, 17, 26
Bates, E., 270
Bateson, G., 75–6, 113
Beale, T. L., 264
Beattie, J., 27–8, 52, 154, 254
Ben-Amos, P., 258
Benedict, R., 27, 82, 84
Benjafield, J., 265
Berlin, B., 245, 247–8, 267–8
Berlyne, D. E., 245
Berry, J. W., 106
Black, M., 241
Blasi, A., 238
Bloch, M., 235, 269, 275
Blurton-Jones, N., 110, 126, 133, 233
Boas, F., 25–7, 31, 81–2, 175
Bock, P. K., 106–7, 266
Bohannan, L., 152
Boissevain, J., 148–50
Bolton, R., 103–6, 108
Bornstein, M., 267
Bott, E., 162
Bourdieu, P., 258, 275
Bousfield, J., 269
Breedlove, D. E., 245

Bronfenbrenner, U., 3
Brown, R., 155–6
Bruner, J. S., 246
Bulmer, R., 260
Burton, M., 255
Burton, R., 119

C

Carstairs, G. M., 93–5, 97, 107
Castaneda, C., 210
Cattell, J. McK., 18, 27
Chadwick-Jones, J. K., 147
Chagnon, N. A., 61
Child, I. L., 117–19, 136
Cissé, Y., 190, 203, 212
Cohen, Y., 119
Colby, B., 188
Cole, M., vii, 53, 188, 223, 227
Conolley, E. S., 51
Cooper, D. E., 171
Corballis, M. C., 264
Coren, S., 256
Cronbach, L. J., 4
Cutting, J. E., 163

D

Danquah, J. B., 115
Darwin, C., 18
Dasen, P. R., 225, 227–8
Degérando, J.-M., 9–11
Deregowski, J. B., 31
Devereux, G., 45–8, 52
Diamond, J. M., 244–5
Dieterlen, G., 187, 206, 212, 251
Doise, W., 44–5, 47, 142, 229, 237
Dollard, J., 88
Dougherty, J. W. D., 247–8
Douglas, M., 30, 180, 210, 258, 260–62
DuBois, C., 85, 87

297

Subject Index